1,001 QUESTIONS & ANSWERS FOR THE GRE

Dr. Nancy L. Nolan

Paperback, electronic and CD-ROM versions published by:

Magnificent Milestones, Inc.
www.ivyleagueadmission.com

ISBN 978-1-933819-58-7

Disclaimers:

(1) This book was written as a guide; it does not claim to be the definitive word on GRE™ preparation. The opinions expressed are the personal observations of the author based on her own experiences. They are not intended to prejudice any party. Accordingly, the author and publisher do not accept any liability or responsibility for any loss or damage that have been caused, or allegedly caused, through the use of information in this book.

(2) The GRE is a registered trademark of Educational Testing Services (ETS), which sponsors the test and decides how it will be constructed, administered and used. Neither Dr. Nolan nor Magnificent Milestones, Inc. is affiliated with ETS.

(3) Admission to graduate school depends on several factors in addition to a candidate's GRE™ scores (including GPA, recommendations, interview and essays). The author and publisher cannot guarantee that any applicant will be admitted to any specific school or program if (s)he follows the information in this book.

Dedication

For students everywhere;
may the size of your dreams be exceeded only
by your tenacity to attain them.

Acknowledgements

I am deeply indebted to the students, professors, counselors and admissions officers who have shared their perceptions and frustrations about the GRE™. This book, which was written on your behalf, would not be nearly as powerful without your generous and insightful input.

I also want to thank my colleagues at www.ivyleagueadmission.com for providing a constant source of support, along with the best editorial help in the business.

1,001 Questions & Answers

For the GRE

Table of Contents

Chapter 1: Introduction to the GRE

Chapter 2: 1,001 Sample Questions for the GRE

         Verbal Sections 1 – 17

         Quantitative Sections 1 - 20

Chapter 1: Introduction to the GRE

To achieve a top score on the GRE, students should follow a three-step plan:

- Learn the concepts that are on the test
- Learn the tips, traps and strategies of the test writers
- Learn to work faster and smarter by taking timed practice tests

We address Steps 1 and 2 in our companion publication, *Guerrilla Tactics for the GRE: Secrets and Strategies the Test Writers Don't Want You to Know.* From our experience, no one should take the GRE without mastering these techniques, which can make the difference between a great score and a mediocre one.

This publication addresses Step 3, which is to build your confidence, speed, and test-taking strategies by taking mock exams under actual testing conditions. From our experience, working with sample questions isn't enough; you need to attack the questions *exactly* as they are presented on the GRE.

By design, we have organized 1,001 GRE questions in the identical format you will see on the exam:

Verbal Sections present 30 multiple choice questions in one 30-minute segment, including:

Sentence Completion questions
Analogy questions
Antonym questions
Reading Comprehension questions

Quantitative Sections present 28 questions in one 45-minute section, including:

Quantitative Comparison questions
Mathematical Word Problems
Data Interpretation questions

Let's be honest; the content of the GRE isn't particularly difficult. With unlimited time, many students could attain a top score on the exam. The biggest challenge is working at a fast enough pace to:

1. answer as many "easy" questions as possible
2. leave the hardest ones until the end
3. formulate an intelligent guessing strategy

From our experience, there is no way to accomplish these goals without working through hundreds of practice questions under actual test conditions. Ultimately, it isn't just about timing. It's about knowing your own particular strengths in each section and developing a plan to maximize them.

And that's the aspect of test preparation that few "experts" acknowledge; one size does NOT fit all. *No two students have the same strengths and weaknesses, which means that no two preparation plans will be the same.* Ultimately, it's up to YOU to identify the areas in which you need work, and to focus your time accordingly. The 1,001 questions and answers in this publication are a great start.

Use the information in whatever way makes sense to YOU. If you want to assess the level of difficulty of the math questions, use a few of the Quantitative sections as a general review of the math topics on the GRE. Check out the typical vocabulary words that show up in the reading passages and the sentence completion questions. Note the types of analogy relationships that are tested over and over again on the exam. Don't stop until you have them down cold.

Then, before the day of the test, complete several sections under timed conditions. Give yourself a few minutes at the end of each section; on the actual GRE, you will need this time to transfer your answers to your grid. Make sure that you can work hard enough, smart enough and fast enough to earn your desired score.

As you scroll through the practice sections, you may notice that we have included a disproportionate number of quantitative questions. Why? Because the GRE tests more than 15 different math concepts; they also increase the level of difficulty by presenting simple concepts as word problems, which require significant experience to master. In contrast, the verbal section tests significantly fewer concepts, which requires a smaller number of sample questions.

Finally, if you discover that you need additional help to prepare for the GRE, we are proud to offer the following publications:

1. *Guerrilla Tactics for the GRE: Secrets and Strategies the Test Writers Don't Want You to Know* presents the underlying math and grammar concepts that are tested, along with the tricky ways the test writers will try to confuse you.

2. For students who need additional practice for the quantitative section of the exam, *Math Word Problems for the GRE: When Plugging Numbers into Formulas Just Isn't Enough* offers a complete review of the thirty types of word problems you are likely to see. Learn how to answer these questions quickly and accurately on the day of the test.

3. Finally, for students who are comfortable with the concepts on the GRE and **really** want to challenge themselves before the big day, we are delighted to offer *The Toughest GRE Practice Test We've Ever Seen*. Use this publication – and complete the mock exam - AFTER you have completed your preparation program. See how your performance compares to those of other highly competitive students. For an exam this important, why leave your preparation to chance?

Chapter 2: 1,001 Sample Questions for the GRE

From our experience, the best way to build your confidence and speed before the GRE is to take mock exams *under actual testing conditions*. Accordingly, that is how we have arranged the 1,001 GRE questions and answers:

The **17 Verbal Sections each** present 30 multiple choice questions in one 30-minute segment, including:

Sentence Completion questions
Analogy questions
Antonym questions
Reading Comprehension questions

The **20 Quantitative Sections each** present 28 questions in one 45-minute section, including:

Quantitative Comparison questions
Mathematical Word Problems
Data Interpretation questions

At the end of each section, we present a comprehensive answer key (including explanations) for those questions.

Use these practice questions to:

a.   analyze your strengths
b.   overcome your deficiencies
c.   master the tricks and traps of each section of the exam
d.   get the score you deserve

Verbal Section 1: 30 questions   30 Minutes

Directions: For each question in this section, select the best answer from the choices given and fill the corresponding circle on the answer sheet.

1. When she realized the _____ of her mistake, Sandra became humble and apologetic.

    a.   insouciance
    b.   gravure
    c.   reticence
    d.   enormity
    e.   prudence

2. Jenny had a tendency to be _____ with her friends by loaning them money and buying them expensive gifts.

    a.   parsimonious
    b.   cogent
    c.   munificent
    d.   capricious
    e.   mendicant

3. Jane's _____ attitude at work was particularly impressive, considering her recent painful injury.

    a.   nascent
    b.   assiduous
    c.   indolent
    d.   ethereal
    e.   timorous

4. When the FBI investigated the fraud at Enron, they made a startling discovery; some of the formulas to over-inflate earnings required such _____ strategies that only the most _____ agents could decipher them.

    a.   onerous...nefarious
    b.   extraneous.... decorous
    c.   intricate...adroit
    d.   amorphous...calumniate
    e.   anachronistic...extrapolate

5. Only an authority in mathematics could _____ the _____ subject matter that the Nobel Prize winner discussed.

    a.   attenuate....esoteric
    b.   portent....intricate
    c.   condone....ambiguous
    d.   reproduce....heretical
    e.   debunk....fabricated

6. Although the communes of the 1960 were devoted to positive values, such as sharing and simplicity, their residents gained a reputation for being rebellious and _____.

    a.   banal
    b.   pedantic
    c.   caustic
    d.   hedonistic
    e.   rudimentary

Long after the fighting and violence had ceased, the civil war that followed the disintegration of the U.S.S.R. left its people in a state of social, political and economic uncertainty. As a young man in Tbilisi, Georgia, Vladimir Ingo was intrigued by the challenges that would accompany the transition from a communist regime to a free market economy. Although there would undoubtedly be problems relating to unemployment, corruption and a lack of infrastructure, the influx of foreign and U.S. investments would also create exciting opportunities for those who were prepared to seize them. Georgia's development into a thriving free market economy, in which the public and private sectors would enjoy unprecedented growth and prosperity, offered a once-in-a-lifetime chance for young people to guide the area's financial and social re-development.

9

Of the former Soviet nations, Georgia faced unique challenges in its transition to a free economy. Although it attracted significant foreign investments, its residents were unprepared to manage these resources. This scenario created a strong demand for American-educated financial executives to lead and manage companies in the private sector that would provide solutions in the public's best interest.

14

Unfortunately, as Ingo predicted, the underlying challenges defied simple solutions. In 2001, the United States provided a loan guarantee to a leading bank in the Republic of Georgia to provide residential mortgage lending through the Overseas Private Investment Corporation (OPIC). On a theoretical basis, this meant that residents, for the first time, would be able to enjoy the financial and psychological benefits of home ownership. Additionally, tax reforms were implemented in 2003 to establish favorable conditions for local and foreign investors. Yet progress remained hindered by several practicalities, including widespread unemployment and a limited access to credit. Even now, about half of the 5 million residents of Georgia survive on less than $30 a month. In such an impoverished environment, in which people struggle to buy food, the idea of buying a home or qualifying for credit is beyond comprehension.

24

To succeed in a transitional economy, most individuals, small businesses and micro-entrepreneurs need funding, education and ongoing economic support. Under Ingo's direction, the United States Agency for International Development (USAID) completed a business plan for a non-profit organization (NGO) that would provide micro-finance, credit/services and loans to small businesses and Georgian entrepreneurs. The NGO will assess the overall infrastructure of the Georgian financial system, provide targeted technical assistance and customized financial training to micro-finance entities. Ultimately, it will expand access to capital for micro, small, and medium-sized enterprises in Georgia, which will foster innovation and increase the number of high-paying jobs in the underserved Akhalkalaki region. In the long run, these small businesses will play a key role in expanding the Georgian economy.

34

The USAID plan also addresses the implications of corruption, which has hindered Georgia's economic development and undermined the trust of many supporting international organizations. Despite the efforts of the World Bank and the International Finance Corporation (IFC), along with social advocate George Soros, most Georgians have simply lost faith in the government's ability to enforce its own laws and regulations. Years after the fall of communism, many refuse to pay taxes. Under Ingo's guidance and direction, the USAID NGO will support a new anti-corruption campaign that emphasizes education and implementation. To instill confidence in the younger generation, the campaign will implement a program at schools and universities and offer credits to students who volunteer at the NGO. With government support and leadership, including an ongoing awareness program, Georgia can finally eradicate the cancer of corruption and fulfill its social, political and economic potential.

45

7. The main idea of this passage is:

    a.   to discuss the effects of corruption in Georgia
    b.   to praise Vladimir Ingo's managerial skills
    c.   to discuss the challenges Georgia faces to transition to a free market economy
    d.   to discuss American opportunities to invest in Georgia
    e.   to restore the faith of Georgian citizens in their government

8. According to the author, which of the following factors does NOT influence home ownership in Georgia:

    a.   the availability of credit
    b.   level of foreign investment in the region
    c.   low wages
    d.   high unemployment
    e.   unstable property values

9. In Line 32, the word *underserved* most nearly means

    a.   uneducated
    b.   undeveloped
    c.   old
    d.   inner city
    e.   widespread

10. According to the author, what is the primary purpose of the NGO?

    a.   to eradicate corruption in Georgia
    b.   to provide subsidies to impoverished citizens
    c.   to inspire consumer confidence
    d.   to finance and support small business development
    e.   to create jobs

11. According to the passage, corruption has impacted the people of Georgia in several negative ways. Which of the following was NOT mentioned as a ramification of corruption?

    a.   Loss of confidence in law enforcement
    b.   Refusal to pay taxes
    c.   Public protests and demonstrations
    d.   Undermined the trust of international organizations
    e.   Slowed economic development

12. The author of the passage infers that Ingo

    a.   owns a small business in Georgia
    b.   was behind the OPIC initiative
    c.   is committed to re-building the Georgian economy
    d.   is a corrupt political official
    e.   has underestimated the problems in Georgia

13. The author's tone can best be described as

    a.   grave
    b.   neutral
    c.   disappointed
    d.   puzzled
    e.   optimistic

Directions: *For each question in this section, select the answer choice that means the exact OPPOSITE of the bold-faced word.*

14. **DELIBERATE**:

    a.   Capricious
    b.   Commodious
    c.   Copious
    d.   Covetous
    e.   Redundant

15. **DISINGENUOUS**:

    a.   Articulate
    b.   Candid
    c.   Dubious
    d.   Effervescent
    e.   Erudite

16. **COGENT**:

    a.   Commodious
    b.   Prosaic
    c.   Heinous
    d.   Timorous
    e.   Cryptic

17. **CAPITULATE**:

    a.   Arcane
    b.   Sardonic
    c.   Torturous
    d.   Recalcitrant
    e.   Wanton

18. **BEHEMOTH:**

    a.   Baneful
    b.   Callous
    c.   Infinitesimal
    d.   Pecuniary
    e.   Sanguine

19. **ARCANE:**

    a.   Anachronism
    b.   Commonplace
    c.   Esoteric
    d.   Discreet
    e.   Disparate

20. **EBULLIENT**:

    a.   Cantankerous
    b.   Jovial
    c.   Nettle
    d.   Provident
    e.   Melancholy

21. **LACONIC**:

    a.   Economical
    b.   Succinct
    c.   Verbose
    d.   Jocular
    e.   Paltry

22. **INDOLENT:**

    a. Austere
    b. Cohesive
    c. Ingenious
    d. Diligent
    e. Lethargic

23. **NASCENT:**

    a. Cognizant
    b. Delineate
    c. Embryonic
    d. Emerging
    e. Obsolete

Directions: Each of the following questions includes a pair of words or phrases that are separated by a colon. Likewise, each of the five answer choices also includes a pair of word or phases that are presented in a similar manner. Select the answer choice in which the <u>relationship</u> between the two words is most similar to that of the original pair.

24. **FAST: EXPEDITIOUS::**

    a. Delightful: morose
    b. Boring: meandering
    c. Intrepid: brave
    d. Slow: pecuniary
    e. Orator: speech

25. **DERIVATIVE: ORIGINAL::**

    a. Apprehensive: relieved
    b. Paranoid: delusional
    c. Impeccable: detail
    d. Odious: defile
    e. Distaff: distend

26. **LARCENY: CRIME::**

    a. Attorney: advocate
    b. Building: prison
    c. Logical: thought
    d. Obtuse: difficulty
    e. Blouse : garment

27. **PACE: RUN::**

    a. Activity: club house
    b. Athlete: marathon
    c. Spaceship: alien
    d. Rain: hurricane
    e. Tears: crying

28. **PSYCHOLOGY: SOCIAL SCIENCE::**

 a. Curriculum: humanities
 b. Nurses: staff
 c. Bandages: cotton
 d. Transportation: automobile
 e. Funeral: grief

29. **ENERGETIC: LETHARGY::**

 a. Disappointment: frown
 b. Worried: aggravation
 c. Elevator: ascension
 d. Magazine: read
 e. Healthy :illness

30. **HYPHEN: JOIN::**

 a. Knife : cut
 b. Sentence: explain
 c. Ocean: boat
 d. Newspaper: edit
 e. Mirror: frame

Verbal 1: Answer Key for Verbal 1

Sentence Completion

1. In this sentence, the correct word would be a synonym for magnitude, gravity, significance, or enormity. Hence, answer choice D, enormity, is correct.

2. In this case, we are looking for a word that means generous or benevolent. The correct choice is answer C, munificent.

3. Here, we are seeking a positive word that relates to good performance in the workplace. The correct answer choice is B, assiduous, which means hard working.

4. The sentence provides plenty of key words that indicate that the first missing word is a negative one that describes the fraudulent strategies to overstate earnings at Enron. We can also conclude that the second missing word describes the type of agent who could understand (and decipher) these strategies. The *correct* answer, choice C, is perfectly understandable; none of the other combinations makes a bit of sense.

5. In this question, the only key words are authority in mathematics and Nobel Prize winner. Further, there are no words that indicate a contrast, which leads us to believe that both words will go in the same direction. At first blush, the topic of the sentence seems to indicate that the words *must* be positive. After all, this is a Nobel Prize winner we are talking about.

Look again. There is nothing in this sentence that indicates tone, which means that **any** set of answer choices in which the words go in the same direction is fair game. Students who immediately assume that the first word HAS to be positive would eliminate answer choice E, which is the correct answer. Once they did, they would find themselves with answer choices that made little or no sense.

6. The correct answer is a synonym for rebellious, which is choice D, hedonistic

Reading Comprehension

7. Answer choice C is correct. The passage describes the challenges that Georgia will face to make a successful transition to a free market economy. Choices A, D and E are too narrow in scope to be the main

idea. Choice B is incorrect, because the transition has not yet succeeded; hence, it is too soon to evaluate Ingo's leadership skills with 100% clarity.

8. The correct answer is E. All of the other factors are mentioned in the paragraph about home ownership.

9. The correct answer is B. Thus far, the area has not attracted business interest or investment.

10. Answer choice D is correct. Although all of the other factors are mentioned in the passage, they are not the *main* function of the NGO. Its underlying goal is to provide micro-financing for small businesses and entrepreneurs, which will create jobs and reduce unemployment. The subsidies are not intended for impoverished individuals.

11. The correct answer is C. All of the other answer choices were mentioned in the final paragraph of the passage.

12. The correct answer is C. The passage discusses Ingo's familiarity with Georgia's challenges and his commitment to conquering them.

13. The correct answer is E. The final sentence confirms the author's sense of optimism about the plan to re-build Georgia.

Antonyms

14. Deliberate means intentional or planned, while capricious means changeable or erratic. Choice A is correct.

15. Disingenuous means dishonest, while candid means honest. Choice B is correct.

16. Cogent means logical and convincing, while cryptic means hidden or puzzling. Choice E is correct.

17. Capitulate means to surrender, while recalcitrant means stubborn. Choice D is correct.

18. Behemoth means huge, while infinitesimal means small. Choice C is correct.

19. Arcane means secret or mysterious, while commonplace means common or obvious. Choice B is correct.

20. Ebullient means happy or cheerful, while melancholy means sad or depressed. Choice E is correct

21. Laconic means terse or concise, while verbose means wordy. Choice C is correct.

22. Indolent means lazy or idol, while diligent means hard working. Choice D is correct.

23. Nascent means budding or emerging, while obsolete means outdated. Choice E is correct.

Analogy

24. The words are synonyms. Choice C is correct.

25. The words are antonyms. Choice A is correct.

26. The first word is a type of the second. Choice E is correct.

27. The second word is a stronger version of the first. Choice D is correct.

28. The first word is a subset of the second. Choice B is correct.

29. People who meet the first criteria word do not possess the second criteria. Choice E is correct.

30. You use X to accomplish Y. Choice A is correct.

Verbal Section 2: 30 questions   30 Minutes

Directions: *For each question in this section, select the best answer from the choices given and fill the corresponding circle on the answer sheet.*

1. Despite the disapproval from the crowd, the speaker argued _____ on behalf of his cause.

    a.   hypocritically
    b.   ingenuously
    c.   facetiously
    d.   vehemently
    e.   irreverently

2. Only a _____ could have anticipated the unusual combination of life-changing events that occurred that fateful day.

    a.   engineer
    b.   humanitarian
    c.   clairvoyant
    d.   philanthropist
    e.   statistician

3. Claire attributed her strong sense of _____ to her parents, who encouraged her to give back to the community.

    a.   spirituality
    b.   perspective
    c.   complacency
    d.   decadence
    e.   generosity

4. Dylan was a _____ writer whose works include twenty novels, four textbooks and _____ newspaper and magazine articles.

    a.   prosperous - sage
    b.   natural - spirited
    c.   technical - sardonic
    d.   verbose – opinionated
    e.   prolific – numerous

5. In her ninth month of pregnancy, Carol ate large quantities of food to _____ her appetite.

    a.   dissipate
    b.   mitigate
    c.   satisfy
    d.   solicit
    e.   masticate

6. Although she led a(n) _____ life, Sara had a(n) _____ understanding of the world.

    a.   urbane - minimal
    b.   repetitive - tantalizing
    c.   sheltered - unblemished
    d.   isolated - simple
    e.   prodigious – courageous

The most prominent error in conversation is not saying too little that amounts to much, but too much that amounts to little. Talkativeness is a characteristic more common of the ignorant than of the wise. Shenstone says, "The common fluency of speech in many men and women is due to a scarcity of matter and a scarcity of words; for whoever is master of a language and has a mind full of ideas, will be apt, in speaking, to hesitate upon the choice of both; but common speakers have only one set of ideas and one set of words to clothe them in— and these are always ready at the mouth. Just so people can come faster out of a church when it is almost empty, than when a crowd is at the door!" But although, according to the old proverb, "a still tongue denotes a wise head," the faculty of speech should not be neglected, merely because it may be misused.

9

Conversation is not a gift bestowed only upon those whom genius favors; on the contrary, many men eminent for their fluency of style in writing have been noted for habitual taciturnity in their intercourse with society. Hazlitt remarked, that "authors should be read, not heard!" Charles II of England, not only the wittiest of monarchs, but one of the liveliest of men, is said to have been so charmed in reading the humor of Butler's "Hudibras," that he disguised himself as a private gentleman and was introduced to the author, whom, to his astonishment, he found to be one of the dullest of companions. On the other hand, some of the humblest men with whom one falls into company, possessed of but little variety, and less extent of information, are highly entertaining talkers. The particular topic of remark does not form so essential a part of an interesting conversation, as the words and manner of those who engage in it. Robert Burns, sitting down on one occasion to write a poem, said: "Which way the subject theme may gang, let time or chance determine; perhaps it may turn out a song or probably a sermon."

21

In the same manner, the subject of a conversation need not be made a matter of study or special preparation. Men may talk of things momentous or trivial, and in either strain be attractive and agreeable. But quitting the consideration of the thought, to refer to the mode of its expression, it must be remarked and insisted that to "murder the king's English" is hardly less a crime than to design against one of the king's subjects. If committed from ignorance, the fault is at least deplorable; but if from carelessness, it is inexcusable. The greatest of sciences is that of language; the greatest of human arts is that of using words. No "cunning hand" of the artificer can contrive a work of mechanism that is to be compared, for a moment, with those wonderful masterpieces of ingenuity, which may be wrought by him who can skillfully mould a beautiful thought into a form that shall preserve, yet radiate its beauty.

31

A mosaic of words may be fairer than inlaid precious stones. The scholar who comes forth from his study a master of the English language is a workman who has at his command hardly less than a hundred thousand finely-tempered instruments, with which he may fashion the most cunning device. This is a trade which all should learn, for it is one that every individual is called to practice. The greatest support of virtue in a community is intelligence; intelligence is the outgrowth of knowledge; and the almoner of all knowledge is language. The possession, therefore, of the resources, and a command over the appliances of language, is of the utmost importance to every individual. Words are current coins of the realm, and they who do not have them in their treasury, suffer a more pitiable poverty than others who have not a penny of baser specie in their pocket; and the multitude of those who have an unfailing supply, but which is of the wrong stamp, are possessed only of counterfeit cash, that will not pass in circles of respectability.

42

7. What is the main point of the passage?

    a.   Language is a universal tool that unites us all
    b.   The most intelligent among us are linguists
    c.   Language is a precious gift that should be cultivated and used with care
    d.   Conversational flow should not be restricted by the participants
    e.   Writing requires time and effort to master

8. Which of the following most accurately expresses Shenstone's sentiments?

    a.   Those who speak the best know the most
    b.   Those with the least to say tend to speak the most
    c.   Words allow the common man to speak with mastery
    d.   Speaking in church is boorish and ill-advised
    e.   Words are common, but language is an art

9. In Line 9, what does "*faculty*" mean?

    a.   Teacher
    b.   Hyperbole
    c.   Example
    d.   Staff
    e.   Power

10. In Line 11, what does "*taciturnity*" mean?

    a.   Flowery
    b.   Reluctance
    c.   Boastful
    d.   Circumspect
    e.   Humility

11. According to the author, which of the following best describes the reaction of Charles II of England to Butler?

    a.   He found Butler charming and witty
    b.   He found both the man and his work to be woefully overrated
    c.   He enjoyed Butler's work but found him dull in person
    d.   They became close companions upon their first meeting
    e.   They shared a love of intelligent discourse

12. According to the author, what is inexcusable?

    a.   Disrespecting the King of England
    b.   Making careless grammatical mistakes
    c.   Speaking too much
    d.   A lack of education
    e.   Using a cunning hand

13. According to the author, what is the relationship between language and words?

    a.   Language is a virtue of intelligence, while words are an outgrowth of knowledge
    b.   Words are a virtue of intelligence, while language is the almoner of knowledge
    c.   Language is the greatest of sciences and using words is the greatest human art
    d.   Language is the greatest art, which relies upon the science of words
    e.   Language supports the virtue of a community through the mosaic of words

14. In Line 34, what does "*instruments*" mean?

    a.   Words
    b.   Letters
    c.   Books
    d.   Thoughts
    e.   Tools

15. In Line 36, what does "*almoner*" mean"?

    a.   Virtue
    b.   Goodness
    c.   Source
    d.   Antipathy
    e.   Benevolence

16. According to the author, which of the following is the best example of "counterfeit cash"?

    a. Illiteracy
    b. Apathy
    c. Slang
    d. Education
    e. Verbosity

Directions: For each question in this section, select the answer choice that means the exact OPPOSITE of the bold-faced word.

17. **PAUCITY**:

    a. Contingency
    b. Dearth
    c. Probable
    d. Plethora
    e. Congenial

18. **PLIANT**:

    a. Inflexible
    b. Supple
    c. Docile
    d. Irascible
    e. Diligent

19. **DIFFIDENT**:

    a. Reticent
    b. Self-effacing
    c. Commonplace
    d. Audacious
    e. Cautious

20. **QUELL**:

    a. Adhere
    b. Solicit
    c. Incite
    d. Mollify
    e. Repress

21. **JOCULAR**:

    a. Inimical
    b. Jovial
    c. Sophomoric
    d. Potent
    e. Serious

22. **PUNCTILIOUS**:

    a. Careless
    b. Meticulous
    c. Courteous
    d. Mendacious
    e. Indigenous

23. **SCINTILLATING**:

    a. Esoteric
    b. Lackluster
    c. Medieval
    d. Turgid
    e. Divine

24. **DERIDE**:

    a. Augment
    b. Equivocate
    c. Scorn
    d. Endorse
    e. Hinder

Directions: Each of the following questions includes a pair of words or phrases that are separated by a colon. Likewise, each of the five answer choices also includes a pair of word or phases that are presented in a similar manner. Select the answer choice in which the relationship between the two words is most similar to that of the original pair.

25. **TRUTH: HONESTY::**

    a. Putrid: odor
    b. Character: family
    c. Zealot: fervid
    d. Generosity: kindness
    e. Abatement: fissure

26. **AGRONOMY: SOIL::**

    a. Aviation: clouds
    b. University: books
    c. Recipe: chicken
    d. Character: discipline
    e. Entomology: insects

27. **HYPOCRITICAL: DISINGENUOUS::**

    a. Enigmatic: concise
    b. Ingenious: clever
    c. Distant: excessive
    d. Equitable: endogamous
    e. Banal: original

28. **DEBT: BANKRUPTCY::**

    a.   Alcohol: inebriation
    b.   Rain: meteorology
    c.   Ice cream: dairy
    d.   Clothing: underwear
    e.   Money: spending

29. **VEIL: LACE::**

    a.   Automobile: seat
    b.   Character: mindset
    c.   Mirror: glass
    d.   Calcium: vitamin
    e.   Roof: house

30. **DEATH: LIFE::**

    a.   Time: second
    b.   Finite: infinity
    c.   Conclusion: novel
    d.   Seam: dress
    e.   Island: ocean

Answer Key for Verbal Section 2

Sentence Completion

1. The correct word means strongly, which is choice D, vehemently.

2. The correct word means psychic, which is choice C, clairvoyant.

3. The correct word means selflessness, which is choice E, generosity.

4. The first word means active, while the second means many; the best choice is E, prolific – numerous.

5. The word means to satisfy, which is choice C.

6. The two words are opposites; the best choices is A, urbane – minimal.

Reading Comprehension

7. The passage explains the importance of language in society, including the need to master it in order to speak and write effectively. The best answer is choice C – the others are incorrect in focus and scope.

8. According to Shenstone, those with the least to say tend to speak the most. Choice B is correct.

9. In context, the word "faculty" means power. Choice E is correct.

10. Taciturnity means reluctant or disinclined to talk. Choice B is correct.

11. In paragraph two, Lines 13 -15, the author reveals that Charles enjoyed Butler's work but found him dull in person. Choice C is correct.

12. According to Line 26, carelessness in grammar is inexcusable. Choice B is correct.

13. The passage directly states (in Lines 26 – 27) that language is the greatest of sciences and using words is the greatest human arts. Choice C is correct.

14. In the passage, the word "instruments" refers to the words a person uses to make is point. Choice A is correct.

15. In the passage, the word "almoner" means the source or distributor of knowledge. Choice C is correct.

16. According to the passage, "counterfeit coins" are words that are either incorrect or ill-suited to the situation. Choice C, slang, is the best answer.

Antonyms

17. Paucity means lack or rarity, while plethora means overabundance. Choice D is correct.

18. Pliant means flexible, which is the opposite of inflexible. Choice A is correct.

19. Diffident means shy and timid, while audacious means bold and brave. Choice D is correct.

20. Quell means to subdue or suppress, while incite means to provide or stimulate. Choice C is correct.

21. Jocular means funny or humorous, which is the opposite of serious. Choice E is correct.

22. Punctilious means scrupulous or thorough, which is the opposite of careless. Choice A is correct.

23. Scintillating means lively or sparkling, while lackadaisical means dull. Choice B is correct.

24. Deride means to ridicule or mock, while endorse means to approve. Choice D is correct.

Analogy

25. The first word provides evidence of the second. Choice D is correct.

26. The first word is the study of the second word. Choice E is correct.

27. The words are synonyms. Choice B is correct.

28. The first word causes the second. Choice A is correct.

29. The first item is made from the second. Choice C is correct.

30. The first word is the ending of the second word. Choice C is correct.

Directions: For each question in this section, select the best answer from the choices given and fill the corresponding circle on the answer sheet.

1. Although Rick is a wealthy man, he is notorious for his _____ ways.

    a. parsimonious
    b. influential
    c. pragmatic
    d. savvy
    e. indolent

2. Michael tended to be argumentative in class; moreover, his condescending tone tended to _____ his classmates.

    a. amplify
    b. reciprocate
    c. intoxicate
    d. placate
    e. alienate

3. Despite Julie's ebullience in the classroom, she was often _____ in social situations.

    a. melancholy
    b. condescending
    c. scintillating
    d. innovative
    e. philosophical

4. The _____ passengers wondered if the pilot could handle the _____ turbulence.

    a. weary - teeming
    b. apprehensive - unexpected
    c. angry - copious
    d. frantic - flagrant
    e. belligerent – daunting

5. When the rumors of impropriety began to circulate, only the Senator's most _____ friends continued to defend him.

    a. felonious
    b. judicious
    c. steadfast
    d. gracious
    e. effusive

6. When Cara was diagnosed with mononucleosis, she was _____ by her fearful classmates.

    a. critiqued
    b. celebrated
    c. aggrandized
    d. ostracized
    e. exhausted

In theory, governments provide a significant source of a people's collective political identity as well as the main arena in which individuals can organize for political action. Yet, in actuality, the type of government is a key indicator of how effective that political action will be. In the United States, individuals who are frustrated by the presidential system often suggest that Americans would be better served if the U.S. adopted a parliamentary system of government. Although both systems are democratic, the differences between them would create major changes in American politics if the U.S. completely switched over to a parliamentary system. Assuming, for example, that the U.S. adopted a unicameral parliamentary political system with a Proportional Representation (PR) electoral system, its citizens would immediately enjoy greater government efficiency, accountability, an increase in voter turnout and less waste of taxpayer money.

10

The fusion of powers in a parliamentary system creates a supreme legislative, executive, and judicial authority that can develop policies in a straightforward manner, without the checks and balances of a presidential system. In the U.S., where power is fragmented by the separation of powers, Congress is not obligated to pass legislation that the President proposes. Likewise, every bill passed by Congress must be reviewed by the President, who can either veto it or sign it into law. This process, which can be further complicated by the judicial branch, creates significant barriers that can slow down or halt the passage of law.

17

In contrast, the parliamentary system in Great Britain has fused its executive and legislative branches into the cabinet, the controlling and directing body of parliament, which operates by majority rule. To implement policy, the majority party expresses its power through the cabinet to bring about its desired legislation. In effect, if the cabinet enjoys party solidarity, it does not need to wonder if its policy will be stalled in the legislature or other branches of government. As long as the majority of cabinet members support the proposed legislation, parliament can implement policy quickly and effectively.

24

Candidates in a parliamentary system are also more likely to be held accountable for the promises they make when they run for office than candidates in a presidential system. After all, once the majority seizes power in the parliament, they enjoy the complete control of the cabinet. Voters, consequently, know exactly who to blame for their current situation: the party or parties in power. In contrast, voters in a presidential system are seldom sure who to blame because the fragmented system creates so many independent sources of power that an unhappy policy cannot be blamed on any one of them. As a result, voters who cannot accurately reward or blame their elected officials may vote less on policy-related criteria and more on a candidate's personality.

32

In many countries, the cabinet must report regularly to parliament about how it is managing the affairs of the state, which provides an extra level of accountability that is missing in a presidential system. In Great Britain, the Prime Minister must appear before parliament each week to answer blunt and direct interrogations from the opposition. The U.S. presidential system, however, does not have an equivalent forum in which the executive branch must account for its actions on a regular basis. Sadly, history suggests that when public officials cannot be held accountable, it becomes easier for them to spend public money or initiate policy contrary to their election promises.

40

Changing the U.S. electorate system from a Single Member District Plurality system (SMDP) to a Proportional Representation (PR) would most likely increase voter turnout, because it would eliminate the idea that any individual vote is wasted. In a PR system, people vote for parties, whose percentage of seats in the legislature is equivalent to the percentage of the electoral vote the party receives. To illustrate, picture the United State as one large state consisting of only one district and only 100 available seats in parliament. Each party running for a seat would create a list of their top 100 members, who would be their potential candidates. However, the number of actual candidates that the party would eventually send to parliament would depend on the percentage of votes that the party received. In this scenario, if a party received 20 percent of the votes in the election, it would secure 20 seats in parliament, which would go to the top 20 candidates on its list. Likewise, if a party received 50 percent of the votes, it would secure 50 seats in parliament, which would go to the top 50 candidates on its list.

52

In contrast, a SMDP system divides the state or country into several districts that have separate elections for their representatives. The resulting legislature includes the candidates who won a plurality of the vote in their respective districts. If the population of a district heavily favors a candidate from one particular party, the people from an opposing or minority party may feel that their vote is wasted, since their candidate can't possibly win the election. Far too often, people get discouraged by the SMDP system and eventually stop voting, which reduces the overall turnout. In a PR system, however, people are more willing to participate because they know that their vote will contribute to a percentage of seats obtained in the legislature, even if their party does not receive the majority of the votes.

61

By eliminating specific district representatives, the PR system would also reduce taxpayer spending on projects that only benefit one district. In the SMDP system, representatives may try to divert state money to pet projects that reward their own districts for their vote. Instead, the PR system features candidate lists that are organized state-wide, whereby candidates envision the nation as a single district whose efficient and effective representation is in their party's best interest. Consequently, the PR system creates a political environment that encourages a spirit of mutuality, rather than selfishness.

68

Although the current system of presidential government in the United States is effective, it could benefit from several of the components in the parliamentary and PR systems. In theory, the parliamentary system offers improved accountability and efficiency, and limits the waste of taxpayer money on pet projects. However, the current U.S. election process is a cherished and deeply entrenched part of American culture that dates back to the Constitution. Despite its inherent flaws, most U.S. citizens are satisfied with the presidential system and are not sufficiently motivated to change. In the absence of a political crisis, it is highly unlikely that Americans will champion the parliamentary system as a viable alternative.

76

7. What is the main point of the passage?

   a. The PR electorate system of government is superior to the presidential system.
   b. With minor concessions, the U.S. can improve its electorate process by adopting certain points of the PR electorate system,
   c. An SMDP electorate system is superior to the PR system.
   d. Although the parliamentary system of government offers several benefits to citizens, the U.S. is unlikely to adopt it in the near future.
   e. The U.S. electorate process offers its citizens a unique set of checks and balances that should not be compromised.

8. In Line 2, what does "*arena*" mean?

   a. chambers
   b. stage
   c. meeting place
   d. stadium
   e. forum

9. According to the passage, U.S. citizens would enjoy many benefits if they adopted a PR electoral system of government. Which of the following is NOT one of those benefits?

   a. Less waste of taxpayer money
   b. Greater accountability
   c. Greater representation for women and minorities
   d. Increased voter turnout
   e. Greater government efficiency

10. According to the author, to what can the slow pace of the legislative process in the U.S. be attributed?

   a. The solidarity of the Cabinet
   b. the fusion of powers created by a supreme legislative, executive and judicial authority
   c. the President's right to veto any bill passed by Congress
   d. the staggered election years for Senators and Congressman, which can affect the support for any given bill
   e. the tendency of Congressmen to vote along party lines, which creates an adversarial political environment

11. In Great Britain, how are policies passed?

   a. by special approval of the Prime Minister
   b. exclusively by the legislative branch
   c. by majority rule in all three branches of government
   d. by majority rule in the cabinet
   e. by a public election

12. According to the author, why do voters in the U.S. vote according to a candidate's personality?

    a.   they support the special interests of that candidate
    b.   they are more intuitive than citizens in other countries
    c.   they are influenced by political advertisements, which emphasize the candidate's personality
    d.   they do not feel that they can hold the candidates accountable for policy success or failure
    e.   they trust their candidates more than citizens in other countries

13. According to the passage, why are British officials less likely to spend public money?

    a.   They are given limited spending authority compared to U.S. officials
    b.   The Prime Minister makes all budgetary decisions
    c.   They are more frugal by nature
    d.   They are given a specific budget each year which cannot be adjusted for any reason
    e.   They must account for their actions on a regular basis

14. Which of the following statements is NOT true about the PR system?

    a.   Each district has a separate election for its representatives
    b.   It eliminates the idea that a single vote is wasted
    c.   People vote for parties, rather than candidates
    d.   It usually increases voter turnout
    e.   The percentage of seats a party receives in the legislature is equivalent to the percentage of the electoral vote the party receives

15. In Line 63, what does "*pet*" mean?

    a.   bi-partisan
    b.   pork barrel spending
    c.   special interest
    d.   corrupt
    e.   covert

16. According to the author, under what circumstances would the U.S, change its current system of government?

    a.   The emergence of a viable third political party
    b.   An amendment to the Constitution
    c.   A political crisis
    d.   To eliminate the national debt
    e.   The successful impeachment of the President

Directions: For each question in this section, select the answer choice that means the exact OPPOSITE of the bold-faced word.

17. **EXTRICATE**:

    a.   Entangle
    b.   Extract
    c.   Explain
    d.   Expand
    e.   Contract

18. **DEMUR**:

    a. Object
    b. Decorous
    c. Diffident
    d. Bold
    e. Acquiesce

19. **PRODIGIOUS**:

    a. Extraordinary
    b. Average
    c. Copious
    d. Reckless
    e. Cautious

20. **ADULATE:**

    a. Decry
    b. Lionize
    c. Contaminate
    d. Attest
    e. Solicit

21. **PUGNACIOUS**:

    a. Erratic
    b. Argumentative
    c. Truculent
    d. Serene
    e. Normal

22. **DEARTH**:

    a. Agrarian
    b. Famine
    c. Superfluity
    d. Prosaic
    e. Fractious

23. **HAUGHTY**:

    a. Paltry
    b. Intrepid
    c. Immutable
    d. Self-aggrandizing
    e. Unpretentious

24. **PARSIMONIOUS**:

    a. Conciliatory
    b. Prudent
    c. Miserly
    d. Munificent
    e. Antagonistic

Directions: *Each of the following questions includes a pair of words or phrases that are separated by a colon. Likewise, each of the five answer choices also includes a pair of word or phases that are presented in a similar manner. Select the answer choice in which the* <u>relationship</u> *between the two words is most similar to that of the original pair.*

25. **EARN: SPEND::**

    a. Advocate: litigate
    b. Crawl: walk
    c. Borrow: buy
    d. Spell: speak
    e. Laugh: cry

26. **SEAMSTRESS: THREAD::**

    a. Director: theatre
    b. Crossing guard: uniform
    c. Salesman: suit
    d. Plumber: auger
    e. Athlete: contract

27. **SCIENTIST: LABORATORY::**

    a. Navigator: ship
    b. Captain: military
    c. Attorney: judge
    d. Nurse: medicine
    e. Singer: piano

28. **SEVER: KNIFE::**

    a. Stir: coffee
    b. Straw: drink
    c. Draw: write
    d. Sing: song
    e. Carry: bag

29. **PREVARICATE: EVADE::**

    a. Cryptic: cogent
    b. Sardonic: compassionate
    c. Irascible: mellow
    d. Fortuitous: noisome
    e. Inchoate: amorphous

30. **DILETTANTE: EXPERT::**

    a. Unctuous: fulsome
    b. Languid: torpid
    c. Dauntless: timorous
    d. Placate: confuse
    e. Dolor: plaintive

Answer Key for Verbal Section 3

Sentence Completion

1. The word although indicates a contrast. Another clue in the sentence is the word notorious, which means famous in a negative way. Therefore, we can conclude that the missing word means the opposite of generous. The correct answer choice would be a synonym for cheap or tight-fisted, which is A, parsimonious.

2. The semi-colon in this sentence, along with the word moreover, indicates that the second clause will amplify the first. Another clue is the word condescending, which describes the negative attitude to which Michael's classmates are responding. Our missing word, therefore, must be a synonym for alienate, which is answer choice E.

3. In this sentence, we are looking for a word that means the opposite of ebullient (lively and excited). Acceptable words would be any terms that convey shyness or social awkwardness. The correct answer choice is A, melancholy.

4. The first word means worried, while the first means sudden; the closest answer choice is B, apprehensive – unexpected.

5. The word means the same as loyal, which is choice C, steadfast.

6. The word means avoided or shunned, which is choice D, ostracized.

Reading Comprehension

7. Choice D is correct. The other choices are either too broad or narrow in scope.

8. Choice E is correct. In this context, *arena* is a forum, or opportunity to exchange ideas.

9. Choice C is correct. All of the other answer choices are mentioned in the passage.

10. Choice C is correct. The answer is presented in Lines 14 – 16.

11. Choice D is correct. The answer is presented in Lines 18 – 23.

12. Choice D is correct. The answer is presented in Lines 28 - 31.

13. Choice E is correct. The answer is presented in Lines 33 – 36.

14. Choice A is correct. The other answer choices are presented in the sixth paragraph, Lines 41 – 51.

15. Choice C is correct. In this context, a *pet issue* is a special interest.

16. Choice C is correct. The answer is presented in the final sentence of the passage.

Antonyms

17. Extricate means to free or rescue, while entangle means to trap. Choice A is correct.

18. Demur means to protest, while acquiesce means to agree or give in. Choice E is correct.

19. Prodigious means exceptional, while average means normal. Choice B is correct.

20. Adulate means to praise, while decry means to criticize. Choice A is correct.

21. Pugnacious means argumentative, while serene means peaceful. Choice D is correct.

22. Dearth means a lack of something, while superfluity means an excess. Choice C is correct.

23. Haughty means arrogant and self-aggrandizing, while unpretentious means modest. Choice E is

correct.

24. Parsimonious means miserly, while munificent means generous. Choice D is correct.

Analogy

25. You must do X before you can Y. Choice B is correct.

26. A person in profession X uses Y. Choice D is correct.

27. A person in profession X works in location Y. Choice A is correct.

28. To accomplish X, you must use Y. Choice A is correct.

29. The words are synonyms. Choice E is correct.

30. The words are antonyms. Choice C is correct.

Verbal Section 4: 30 questions   30 Minutes

Directions: For each question in this section, select the best answer from the choices given and fill the corresponding circle on the answer sheet.

1. The Senator's desire to impress her constituents, not her commitment to Hurricane Katrina victims, was the impetus for her _____ disaster recovery referendum.

       a.   autocratic
       b.   assiduous
       c.   dogmatic
       d.   provident
       e.   effusive

2. Although she was proud of her many accomplishments, Rachel remained _____ when she was offered praise.

       a.   turgid
       b.   mercurial
       c.   mendicant
       d.   impudent
       e.   demure

3. Unlike other students, who took a familiar approach to the problem, Janet's solution was _____ and clever.

       a.   hackneyed
       b.   ingenuous
       c.   ambiguous
       d.   original
       e.   immutable

4. Beth remained _____ for many months after her mother's funeral.

       a.   fluvial
       b.   inimical
       c.   inculcate
       d.   promontory
       e.   plaintive

5. Greta's _____ wardrobe belies her _____ nature.

       a.   paltry - lucid
       b.   garish - valorous
       c.   sophisticated - simple
       d.   practical -multifaceted
       e.   juvenile – lowly

6. Although critics praised the movie, most viewers were offended by its _____ violence, which did not advance the plot.

       a.   fortuitous
       b.   hedonistic
       c.   malodorous
       d.   mawkish
       e.   gratuitous

Civilization in its onward march has produced only three important non-alcoholic beverages--the extract of the tea plant, the extract of the cocoa bean, and the extract of the coffee bean. Of these three, coffee is universal in its appeal. In fact, for millions of people, coffee is no longer a luxury or an indulgence; it is a corollary of human energy and human efficiency. People love coffee because of its two-fold effect--the pleasurable sensation and the increased efficiency that it produces.

6

On a socioeconomic basis, coffee is a surprisingly democratic beverage. Not only is it the drink of fashionable society, but it is also a favorite beverage of the men and women who do the world's work, whether they toil with brain or brawn. It has been acclaimed "the most grateful lubricant known to the human machine," and "the most delightful taste in all nature." Yet, ironically, no "food drink" has ever encountered so much opposition as coffee. Given to the world by the church and dignified by the medical profession, nevertheless, it has also suffered from religious superstition and medical prejudice. During the thousand years of its development, coffee has experienced fierce political opposition, nonsensical fiscal restrictions, unjust taxes, irksome duties; but, surviving all of these, it has triumphantly moved on to a foremost place in the catalog of popular beverages.

15

But coffee is something more than a beverage. It is one of the world's greatest adjuvant foods whose unique flavor and aroma give it unique palatability and comforting effects. Men and women drink coffee because it adds to their sense of well-being. It not only smells good and tastes good to all mankind, heathen or civilized, but all respond to its wonderful stimulating properties. The chief factors in coffee goodness are the caffeine content and the caffeol. Caffeine supplies the principal stimulant, which increases the capacity for muscular and mental work without a harmful reaction. In contrast, the caffeol supplies the indescribable Oriental fragrance that entices us through the nostrils, forming one of the principal elements that make up the lure of coffee. There are several other constituents, including certain innocuous so-called caffetannic acids, which, in combination with the caffeol, give the beverage its rare gustatory appeal.

25

The year 1919 awarded coffee one of its brightest honors. An American general said that coffee shared with bread and bacon the distinction of being one of the three nutritive essentials that helped win the World War for the Allies. So this symbol of human brotherhood has played a not inconspicuous part in "making the world safe for democracy." Yet, like all good things in life, the drinking of coffee may be abused. Indeed, those having an idiosyncratic susceptibility to alkaloids should be temperate in the use of tea, coffee, or cocoa. In every high-tensioned country there is likely to be a small number of people who, because of certain individual characteristics, cannot drink coffee. To suit these people who are caffeine-sensitive, coffee makers have developed a curious collection of so-called coffee substitutes, which are "neither fish nor flesh, nor good red herring." Most of them have been shown by official government analyses to be sadly deficient in food value--their only alleged virtue. One contemporary attacker of the national beverage bewails the fact that no palatable hot drink has been found to take the place of coffee. The reason is not hard to find. There can be no substitute for coffee. Dr. Harvey W. Wiley has ably summed up the matter by saying, "A substitute should be able to perform the functions of its principal. A substitute to a war must be able to fight. Sadly, a coffee substitute will never be the nectar of the Gods that I lovingly call coffee."

40

7. What is the main point of the passage?

    a. To explain the botanical origin of coffee
    b. To explain why the church and the medical profession oppose excessive consumption of coffee
    c. To explain the practical role of caffeine and caffeol
    d. To explain the pitfall of caffeine-sensitivity
    e. To explain why coffee is the most popular beverage in the world

8. In Line 3, what does "*corollary*" mean?

    a. Inkling
    b. Essence
    c. Opponent
    d. Factor
    e. Source

9. According to the author, coffee has experienced all of the following EXCEPT:

    a. Political opposition
    b. Fiscal restrictions
    c. Unjust taxes
    d. Legal prejudice
    e. Religious superstition

10. In Line 16, what does "*adjuvant*" mean?

    a. Supportive
    b. Universal
    c. Affordable
    d. Aromatic
    e. International

11. According to the author, what is the role of caffeine in coffee?

    a. It gives coffee its gustatory appeal
    b. It makes coffee a medical nuisance
    c. It increases the drinker's mental and physical capacity
    d. It is one of the principal elements that make up the lure of coffee
    e. It can easily be replaced by a synthetic compound in coffee substitutes

12. According to Dr. Harvey W. Wiley, which of the following words or expressions best describes coffee substitutes?

    a. Clever and sophisticated
    b. Woefully inadequate
    c. A necessary evil
    d. Somewhat undesirable
    e. Medically superior

13. From this passage, we can infer that the author.......

    a. Works for a coffee manufacturer
    b. Acknowledges the political opposition to coffee
    c. Is sensitive to high doses of alkaloids such as caffeine
    d. Is enthusiastic about coffee
    e. Believes that caffeine-sensitivity is just a myth

14. In which of the following was this passage most likely published?

    a. A history book about the World Wars
    b. A cookbook
    c. An article in a food magazine
    d. A medical journal
    e. A psychology textbook

Directions: *For each question in this section, select the answer choice that means the exact OPPOSITE of the bold-faced word.*

15. **ANTIPATHY**:

   a.   Hostility
   b.   Prosperity
   c.   Pomposity
   d.   Benevolence
   e.   Philanthropy

16. **BREVITY:**

   a.   Cowardice
   b.   Elocution
   c.   Rhetoric
   d.   Valor
   e.   Verbosity

17. **MAGNANIMOUS**:

   a.   Noble
   b.   Petty
   c.   Austere
   d.   Dull
   e.   Yoke

18. **AMORPHOUS**:

   a.   Distinct
   b.   Nebulous
   c.   Absolution
   d.   Fervid
   e.   Incredulous

19. **INCONGRUOUS**:

   a.   Inappropriate
   b.   Mendacious
   c.   Indignant
   d.   Fervent
   e.   Steady

20. **PRODIGAL**:

   a.   Sardonic
   b.   Profligate
   c.   Cautious
   d.   Dissolute
   e.   Infinitesimal

21. **PALLID**:

   a.   Ashen
   b.   Dark
   c.   Sinister
   d.   Penury
   e.   Wealthy

22. **CHIMERA**:

    a.   Anachronism
    b.   Benevolence
    c.   Fantasy
    d.   Reality
    e.   Amoeba

23. **SUBLIME**:

    a.   Ludicrous
    b.   Magnificent
    c.   Majestic
    d.   Dilatory
    e.   Atypical

Directions: *Each of the following questions includes a pair of words or phrases that are separated by a colon. Likewise, each of the five answer choices also includes a pair of word or phases that are presented in a similar manner. Select the answer choice in which the* <u>relationship</u> *between the two words is most similar to that of the original pair.*

24. **SCHIZOPHRENIA: MENTAL ILLNESS::**

    a.   Marathon: contest
    b.   Baldness: hereditary
    c.   Avenue: city
    d.   Pinto: bean
    e.   Carousel: roller coaster

25. **SPRINKLE: RAIN::**

    a.   Tan: burn
    b.   Storm: sunshine
    c.   Luggage: bag
    d.   Title: descriptor
    e.   Familiarity: discomfort

26. **IGNORANCE: WISDOM::**

    a.   Anger: dissention
    b.   Paranoia: emotional
    c.   Seizures: health
    d.   Assets: taxation
    e.   Unfaithful: concubine

27. **COLLANDER: DRAIN::**

    a.   Contract: attorney
    b.   Letter: communication
    c.   Computer: office
    d.   Canyon: excavation
    e.   Door: leave

28. **PAPER: TREES::**

    a. Flowers: bees
    b. Soap: fat
    c. Grain: rice
    d. Summer: harvest
    e. Book: knowledge

29. **ERUDITE: BOOKISH::**

    a. Tyrannical: prehistoric
    b. Gullible: sonorous
    c. Encumber: circuitous
    d. Astute: truism
    e. Ephemeral: transient

30. **HOMOGENEOUS: ECLECTIC::**

    a. Collaborative: cumbersome
    b. Forage: sojourn
    c. Remission: pusillanimous
    d. Diminutive: miniature
    e. Dissonance: harmony

Answer Key for Verbal Section 4

Sentence Completion

1. The correct answer is a word that means generous, which is answer choice E, *effusive*.

2. The correct answer is a word that means humble or unassuming. Choice E (demure) is the best answer.

3. The correct answer is a word that means original or innovative. Hence, choice D (*original*) is correct.

4. The correct answer means sad, which is choice E, plaintive.

5. The two words are opposites; the correct answer is choice C, sophisticated – simple.

6. The correct answer is a negative word for excessive, which is choice E, gratuitous.

Reading Comprehension

7. Choice E is correct. The main point of the passage is to explain the worldwide appeal of coffee.

8. Choice E. In context, corollary means source.

9. Choice D is correct. All of the other answer choices are mentioned in Lines 12 – 14.

10. Choice A is correct. In context, adjuvant means helpful or supportive.

11. Choice C is correct. The answer is stated in Lines 20 – 21.

12. Choice B is correct. Dr. Wiley feels that coffee substitutes are woefully inadequate.

13. Choice D is correct. The author is overwhelmingly enthusiastic about coffee's appeal.

14. Choice C is correct. The passage contains basic information and is light in tone; it was written for a general audience.

Antonym

15. Antipathy means hostility or hatred, which is the opposite of benevolence. Choice D is correct.

16. Brevity means concise, while verbosity means long-winded. Choice E is correct.

17. Magnanimous means big, while petty means small and trifling. Choice B is correct.

18. Amorphous means vague and nebulous, which is the opposite of distinct. Choice A is correct.

19. Incongruous means inconsistent or inappropriate which is the opposite of steady. Choice E is correct.

20. Prodigal means wasteful or reckless, which is the opposite of cautious. Choice C is correct.

21. Pallid means pale or while, which is the opposite of dark or rosy. Choice B is correct.

22. A chimera is a fantasy or daydream, which is the opposite of reality. Choice D is correct.

23. Sublime is inspirational or magnificent, which is the opposite of ludicrous. Choice A is correct.

Antonym

24. The first is a type of the second. Choice D is correct.

25. The first is a less intense version of the second. Choice A is correct.

26. Those who have X do not have Y. Choice C is correct.

27. You use X to accomplish Y. Choice E is correct.

28. X is made from Y. Choice B is correct.

29. The words are synonyms. Choice D is correct.

30. The words are antonyms. Choice E is correct.

Verbal Section 5: 30 questions   30 minutes

Directions: For each question in this section, select the best answer from the choices given and fill the corresponding circle on the answer sheet.

1. Their _____ meetings in the middle of the night made their spouses justifiably _____.

    a.   persistent - exhausted
    b.   professional - hostile
    c.   insignificant - bewildered
    d.   clandestine - suspicious
    e.   innocuous – dubious

2. A _____ student is far more likely to be admitted to a top college than one who is _____.

    a.   flamboyant – self-deprecating
    b.   fortuitous - stalwart
    c.   successful - deliberate
    d.   diligent - mediocre
    e.   zealous – duplicitous

3. Jeffrey demonstrated great _____ when he left the security of his homeland in search of a better life.

    a.   discretion
    b.   wanderlust
    c.   courage
    d.   volatility
    e.   repression

4. Bill's rare combination of skills _____ his _____ salary.

    a.   sparked - disappointing
    b.   minimized - ample
    c.   induced - judicious
    d.   belied - competitive
    e.   justified – astronomical

5. After years of living on her own, Jennifer is 100% _____.

    a.   disheartened
    b.   captivating
    c.   self-reliant
    d.   callous
    e.   obstinate

6. Diane's _____ at her engagement party was _____ by the realization that she could not marry her boyfriend until after college.

    a.   apprehension - inspired
    b.   jubilation - enhanced
    c.   elation - tempered
    d.   distress - erased
    e.   turmoil – moderated

On a theoretical basis, fruits and vegetables are considered to be kindling foods, which supply certain mineral elements that are not present in sufficient proportions in the coal foods, such as meats, starches, and fats. Furthermore, the product of fruit and vegetable digestion and burning in the body helps to neutralize the waste products from meats, starches, and fats. Thirdly, fruits and vegetables have a overwhelmingly beneficial effect upon the blood, the kidneys, and the skin. In fact, their reputation for "purifying the blood" and "clearing the complexion" is really well deserved. The keenness of our liking for fruit at all times, and our special longing for greens and sour foods in the spring, after their scarcity in our diet all winter, is a true sign of their wholesomeness.

9

Not the least of their advantages is that fruits and vegetables contain a large proportion of water; and this, though diminishing their fuel value, supplies the body with a naturally filtered and often distilled supply of this necessary element of life. One of the best ways to avoid that burning summer thirst, which leads you to flood your unfortunate stomach with melted icebergs, in the form of ice water, ice cold lemonade, or soda water, is to take an abundance of fresh fruits and green vegetables.

15

Many vegetables contain small amounts of starch, but few of them enough to count upon as fuel, except potatoes, which must rightfully be classified with the coal foods. Most fruits contain a certain amount of sugar-- how much can usually be estimated from their taste, and how little can be gathered from the statement that even the sweetest of fruits, like ripe pears or ripe peaches, contain only about eight per cent sugar. They are all chiefly useful as flavors for the less interesting staple foods, particularly the starches. In fact, our instinctive use of them to help down bread and butter, or rice, or puddings of various sorts, is a natural and proper one. Like vegetables, fruits also contain various salts which are useful in neutralizing certain acid substances formed in the body.

24

Soldiers in war, or sailors upon long voyages, who are fed a diet consisting chiefly of salted or preserved meat, with bread or hard biscuit and sugar, but without either fruits or fresh vegetables, are likely to develop a disease called scurvy. Little more than a century ago, hundreds of deaths occurred every year in the British and French navies from this disease, and the crews of many a long exploring voyage--like Captain Cook's—or of searchers for the North Pole, have been completely disabled or even destroyed entirely by scurvy. It was discovered that by adding to the diet fruit, or fresh vegetables like cabbage or potatoes, scurvy could be entirely prevented, or cured.

32

But how much real fuel value do fruits and vegetables have? In order to get the nourishment contained in a pound loaf of bread, or a pound of roast beef, you would have to eat: twelve large apples or pears, four and one-half quarts of strawberries; a dozen bananas, seven pounds of onions; two dozen large cucumbers; ten pounds of cabbage; or one-half bushel of celery. Notwithstanding their slight fuel value, there are few more valuable and wholesome elements in the diet than an abundant supply of fresh fruits and green vegetables. If at all possible, all people should have a garden, if only the tiniest patch, and grow them for their own use, both because of their wholesomeness and freshness when so grown, and because of the valuable exercise in the open air, and the enjoyment and interest afforded by their care.

41

7. What is the main point of the passage?

    a.   To explain the fuel value of fruits and vegetables
    b.   To discuss the nutritional value and health benefits of fruits and vegetables
    c.   To compare the nutritional value of kindling foods to coal foods
    d.   To explain the cause and prevention of scurvy
    e.   To explain the nutritional deficiencies of fruits and vegetables

8. In Line 3, what does "*neutralize*" mean?

    a.   Incite
    b.   Deodorize
    c.   Defuse
    d.   Accelerate
    e.   Putrefy

9. According to the author, all of the following are coal foods EXCEPT:

    a. Potatoes
    b. Meats
    c. Starches
    d. Kale
    e. Fats

10. According to the author, which of the following is NOT a health benefit of fruits and vegetables?

    a. They improve human vision
    b. They improve the complexion
    c. They purify the blood
    d. They supply water to the body
    e. They supply mineral elements

11. According to the author, what is the chief use of fruits?

    a. They sweeten food without adding a significant amount of sugar
    b. They provide an inexpensive source of protein, compared to meats, starches, and fats
    c. They neutralize acids in the body
    d. They enhance the complexion because they are low in fat
    e. They flavor less interesting foods, such as starches

12. According to the author, all of the following will help to prevent scurvy EXCEPT:

    a. Potatoes
    b. Cabbage
    c. Tallow
    d. Pears
    e. Celery

13. From the passage, we can infer that the author…..

    a. Believes that fruits and vegetables provide too little food value to justify their cost
    b. Believes that kindling foods are inferior to coal foods
    c. Is enthusiastic about the importance of fruits and vegetables in the human diet
    d. Believes that pesticide use destroys the benefits of fruits and vegetables
    e. Believes that a vegan diet is far superior to one that includes meats, starches, and fats

Directions: *For each question in this section, select the answer choice that means the exact OPPOSITE of the bold-faced word.*

14. **UPBRAID:**

    a. Reproach
    b. Elude
    c. Indicate
    d. Refine
    e. Acclaim

15. HALLOW:

 a. Deify
 b. Desecrate
 c. Desert
 d. Dilate
 e. Chide

16. PITHY:

 a. Elaborate
 b. Terse
 c. Taint
 d. Accumulate
 e. Bravery

17. ENIGMATIC:

 a. Cryptic
 b. Paramount
 c. Fiendish
 d. Straightforward
 e. Garish

18. DISSONANT:

 a. Cacophonous
 b. Harmonious
 c. Superfluous
 d. Chaste
 e. Homogenous

19. GORGE:

 a. Ravine
 b. Pastoral
 c. Consolidate
 d. Decay
 e. Nibble

20. EMINENT:

 a. Renowned
 b. Prominent
 c. Anonymous
 d. Impending
 e. Distant

21. INIMICAL:

 a. Favorable
 b. Hostile
 c. Cumbersome
 d. Habitual
 e. Impotent

22. VISCOUS:

a. Thick
b. Glutinous
c. Fluctuate
d. Fluid
e. Benevolent

23. SOPORIFIC:

a. Mature
b. Monotonous
c. Stimulating
d. Irreverent
e. Puerile

Directions: Each of the following questions includes a pair of words or phrases that are separated by a colon. Likewise, each of the five answer choices also includes a pair of word or phases that are presented in a similar manner. Select the answer choice in which the relationship between the two words is most similar to that of the original pair.

24. MUTED: SUBDUED::

a. Ginger: auburn
b. Mountain: molehill
c. Character: personable
d. Immoral: destitute
e. Spiritual: nascent

25. LICENTIOUS: MORAL::

a. Exigent: dupe
b. Explicit: directive
c. Consensus: dogmatic
d. Anachronism: analogous
e. Attenuate: exacerbate

26. CRIME: INCARCERATION:

a. Inspection: efficiency
b. Manipulation: subterfuge
c. Variety: heterogeneity
d. Overeating: obesity
e. Sacrament: piety

27. CENSURE: BOLSTER::

a. Enumerate: itemize
b. Linchpin: peon
c. Efficacy: anomaly
d. Bombastic: audacious
e. Perfidious: opprobrium

28. **FORENSICS: CRIME::**

    a. Instrumentation: analyses
    b. Geology: seismology
    c. Cosmetology: beauty
    d. Weather: meteorology
    e. Geography: seasons

29. **AUTHOR: MANSCRIPT::**

    a. Actor: role
    b. Administrator: office
    c. Soldier: weapon
    d. Software engineer: code
    e. Astronaut: rocket

30. **FINE: EXTRAORDINARY::**

    a. Malinger: illness
    b. Simile: metaphor
    c. Gregarious: misanthrope
    d. Impervious: rare
    e. Losing: defeat

Answer Key for Verbal Section 5

Sentence Completion

1. The first word means secret, while the second means suspicious; the best answer is choice D, clandestine – suspicious.

2. The first word means hardworking, while the second word means lazy; the best answer is choice D, diligent – mediocre.

3. The correct word means courage, which is choice C.

4. The two words support each other; the best answer is choice E, justified – astronomical.

5. The word means independent, which is choice C, self-reliant.

6. The first word is positive, while the second is negative; the correct choice is C, elation – tempered.

Reading Comprehension

7. Choice B is correct. The objective of the passage is to discuss the nutritional value and health benefits of fruits and vegetables.

8. Choice C is correct. In context, neutralize mean to defuse or render harmless.

9. Choice D is correct. All of the other choices are listed in the passage as coal foods.

10. Choice A is correct. All of the other answer choices are mentioned in the passage.

11. Choice E is correct. The answer is presented on Line 20.

12. Choice C is correct. All of the other answer choices are mentioned it the passage.

13. Choice C is correct. The author is enthusiastic about the importance of fruits and vegetables in the human diet.

Antonym

14. Upbraid means to scold or reproach, while acclaim means to admire or honor. Choice E is correct.

15. Hallow means to bless something or make it sacred, which is the opposite of desecrate. Choice B is correct.

16. Pithy means terse or concise, which is the opposite of elaborate. Choice A is correct.

17. Enigmatic means mysterious or puzzling, which is the opposite of straightforward. Choice D is correct.

18. Dissonant means harsh or jarring, which is the opposite of harmonious. Choice B is correct.

19. Gorge means to overeat, which is the opposite of nibble. Choice E is correct.

20. Eminent means well-known, which is the opposite of anonymous. Choice C is correct.

21. Inimical means hostile or contrary, which is the opposite of favorable. Choice A is correct.

22. Viscous means thick or resistance to flow, which is the opposite of fluid or liquid. Choice D is correct.

23. Soporific means sleep-inducing, which is the opposite of stimulating. Choice C is correct.

Analogy

24. The words are synonyms. Choice A is correct.

25. The words are antonyms. Choice E is correct.

26. The fist word causes the second. Choice D is correct.

27. The words are antonyms. Choice B is correct.

28. X is the study of Y. Choice C is correct.

29. X creates Y. Choice D is correct.

30. The first word is a less intense version of the second word. Choice E is correct.

Verbal Section 6: 30 minutes   30 questions

Directions: For each question in this section, select the best answer from the choices given and fill the corresponding circle on the answer sheet.

1. Because medicine is a _____ profession, many students enroll in pre-medical courses with dollar signs in their eyes.

    a.   precarious
    b.   eminent
    c.   lucrative
    d.   prestigious
    e.   rigorous

2. To _____ the irate man whose flight was cancelled, the gate agent offered a complimentary dinner and hotel room.

    a.   excoriate
    b.   mediate
    c.   acknowledge
    d.   placate
    e.   solicit

3. Like her sister, who was extremely cautious, Jane was a _____ young woman.

    a.   munificent
    b.   prudent
    c.   discrete
    d.   indolent
    e.   dauntless

4. Due to shyness, Sara declined many social invitations in favor of more _____ pursuits.

    a.   spiritual
    b.   industrious
    c.   productive
    d.   lucrative
    e.   solitary

5. When the husband and wife failed to reach a compromise, a separation became _____.

    a.   depressing
    b.   unthinkable
    c.   inevitable
    d.   unprecedented
    e.   indefinite

6. The bystander was _____ for her attempt to revive the injured man, despite a lack of medical training,

    a.   investigated
    b.   commended
    c.   chastised
    d.   deplored
    e.   prosecuted

The eleventh century, during which feudal power rose to its height, was also the period when a reaction set in among the townspeople against the nobility. The spirit of Rome revived with that of the bourgeois and infused a feeling of opposition to the system which followed the conquest of the Teutons. "But," says M. Henri Martin, "what reappeared was not the Roman municipality of the Empire, stained by servitude, although surrounded with glittering pomp and gorgeous arts, but it was something coarse and almost semi-barbarous in form, though strong and generous at its core, and which, as far as the difference of the times would allow, rather reminds us of the small republics which existed previous to the Roman Empire."

8

Two strong impulses, originating from two totally dissimilar centers of action, irresistibly propelled this great social revolution, with its various and endless aspects, affecting all of central Europe, and being more or less felt in the west, the north, and the south. On one side, the Greek and Latin partiality for ancient corporations, modified by a democratic element, and an innate feeling of opposition characteristic of barbaric tribes; and on the other, the free spirit and equality of the old Celtic tribes rising suddenly against the military hierarchy, which was the offspring of conquest. Europe was roused by the double current of ideas which simultaneously urged her on to a new state of civilization, and more particularly, to a new organization of city life.

16

Italy was naturally destined to be the country where the new trials of social regeneration were to be made, but she presented the greatest variety of customs, laws, and governments, including the Emperor, Pope, bishops, and feudal princes. In Tuscany and Liguria, the march towards liberty was continued almost without effort; whilst in Lombardy, on the contrary, the feudal resistance was most powerful. Everywhere, however, cities became more or less completely enfranchised, though some more rapidly than others. In Sicily, feudalism swayed over the countries, but in the greater part of the peninsula, the democratic spirit of the cities influenced the enfranchisement of the rural population. The feudal caste was in fact dissolved; the barons were transformed into patricians of the noble towns which gave their republican magistrates the old title of consuls.

25

The Teutonic Emperor in vain sought to seize and turn to his own interest the sovereignty of the people, who had shaken off the yokes of his vassals: the signal of war was immediately given by the newly enfranchised masses and the imperial eagle was obliged to fly before the banners of the besieged cities. Happy indeed might the cities of Italy have been had they not forgotten, in their prosperity, that union alone could give them the possibility of maintaining that liberty which they so freely risked in continual quarrels amongst one another.

31

7. What is the main point of the passage?

    a.   Despite the opposition, Italians refused to relinquish their freedom
    b.   The Italian social revolution was guided by two strong, but mutually opposing, forces
    c.   Without unity, the Italian cities were unable to maintain their liberty
    d.   The eleventh century was a period of great wealth and refinement in Italy
    e.   The democratic spirit in Italian cities eventually conquered the feudalistic tendencies in rural areas

8. According to the author, what followed the conquest of the Teutons?

    a.   Opposition to the system
    b.   The fall of the bourgeois
    c.   The rise of the nobility
    d.   Cultural refinement
    e.   A widespread commitment to education and literacy

9. According to M. Henri Martin, the entity that appeared in Italy after the fall of the Roman Empire was characterized by all of the following EXCEPT:

    a.   Coarseness
    b.   Generosity
    c.   Semi-barbaric
    d.   Stained by servitude
    e.   Strength

10. According to the author, which two impulses propelled the European social revolution?

    a.   Celtic conquests versus Greek and Latin democracy
    b.   Celtic barbarism versus Greek and Latin corporations
    c.   Celtic military versus Greek and Latin barbarism
    d.   Celtic conquest of Greek and Latin democracy
    e.   Celtic spirit of freedom and equality versus Greek and Latin opposition

11. In Line 17, what does "*regeneration*" mean?

    a.   Dedication
    b.   Revision
    c.   Renewal
    d.   Exploration
    e.   Blending

12. According to the author, Italian society in the eleventh century included all of the following EXCEPT:

    a.   Feudal princes
    b.   Sicilian priests
    c.   Bishops
    d.   Emperor
    e.   Pope

13. According to the author, in what place was feudal resistance most powerful?

    a.   Tuscany
    b.   Rome
    c.   Liguria
    d.   Lombardy
    e.   Sicily

14. In Line 21, what does "*enfranchised*" mean?

    a.   Free
    b.   Wealthy
    c.   Educated
    d.   Political
    e.   Patrician

15. In Line 27, to what does the word "*yokes*" refer?

    a.   Garments
    b.   Ideology
    c.   Weapons
    d.   Values
    e.   Oppression

16. What is the author's tone in the passage?

    a.   Superior
    b.   Ironic
    c.   Neutral
    d.   Aghast
    e.   Conciliatory

17. **ITINERANT**:

    a.   Convivial
    b.   Infamous
    c.   Peripatetic
    d.   Stationary
    e.   Protective

18. **CIRCUITOUS:**

    a.   Tortuous
    b.   Oblique
    c.   Direct
    d.   Aerial
    e.   Heterogeneous

19. **UTILITARIAN:**

    a.   Effective
    b.   Impractical
    c.   Mendacious
    d.   Loquacious
    e.   Bold

20. **PARADOX**:

    a.   Ironic
    b.   Honorable
    c.   Sanguinary
    d.   Harbinger
    e.   Consistent

21. **INTERLOPER**:

    a.   Insider
    b.   Interpreter
    c.   Gatekeeper
    d.   Monarch
    e.   Renegade

22. **DISPATCH**:

    a.   Aggrandize
    b.   Transmit
    c.   Slaughter
    d.   Preserve
    e.   Defer

23. **GRAPPLE**:

    a. Seize
    b. Release
    c. Breach
    d. Obstruct
    e. Devise

24. **IMPINGE**:

    a. Encroach
    b. Vilify
    c. Ignore
    d. Postpone
    e. Withdraw

Directions: *Each of the following questions includes a pair of words or phrases that are separated by a colon. Likewise, each of the five answer choices also includes a pair of word or phases that are presented in a similar manner. Select the answer choice in which the* <u>relationship</u> *between the two words is most similar to that of the original pair.*

25. **FENCE: BARRIER::**

    a. Bone: limb
    b. Tree: branch
    c. Beam: support
    d. Garment: thread
    e. Hand: grasp

26. **INACTIVITY: ATROPHY::**

    a. Growth: aging
    b. Melting: warmth
    c. Exercise: melancholy
    d. Debt: insolvency
    e. Dedication: fortitude

27. **DEXTERITY: SCULPTOR::**

    a. Persuasiveness: salesman
    b. Justice: prosecutor
    c. Fertilizer: farmer
    d. Animals: veterinarian
    e. Cowardice: fearful

28. **LAMPOON: CARICATURE::**

    a. Monograph: fiction
    b. Fictitious: conjured
    c. Musical: theatre
    d. Saloon: karaoke
    e. Protagonist: antihero

29. **CONTAMINATED: PURE::**

    a.   Unlikely: know
    b.   Soluble: float
    c.   Incredible: prove
    d.   Moving: stationary
    e.   Articulate: amoral

30. **TAXATION: WEALTH::**

    a.   Truth: corruption
    b.   Dieting: weight
    c.   Insanity: medication
    d.   Misrepresentation: lawsuit
    e.   Speed: duration

Answer Key for Verbal 6

Sentence Completion

1. The word *because* indicates both support and explanation. Hence, we know that the second part of the sentence will follow the same direction as the first part. The second clue is *dollar signs*, which tells us that the missing word is a synonym for lucrative or well paying. (choice C).

2. In this sentence, the missing word is a verb that means to satisfy, appease or compensate. The correct answer is D, or *placate*.

3. The correct answer is a synonym of cautious, which is prudent, answer choice B.

4. The correct word means quiet or alone, which is choice E, solitary.

5. The correct word means unavoidable, which is choice C, inevitable.

6. The correct word means praised, which is choice B, commended.

Reading Comprehension

7. Choice C is correct. The main point of the passage is stated in the final line. If the Italian cities had unified rather than quarreled, they might have maintained their liberty.

8. Choice A is correct. The answer is on Line 3.

9. Choice D is correct. The answers are mentioned in Lines 4 – 6.

10. Choice E is correct. The answer is presented in Lines 11 – 14.

11. Choice C is correct. In this context, regeneration means renewal.

12. Choice B is correct. All of the other answer choices are mentioned in Lines 18 – 19.

13. Choice D is correct. The answer is presented in Line 20.

14. Choice A is correct. In this context, enfranchised means free.

15. Choice E is correct. In this context, the word yokes means oppression.

16. Choice C is correct. The author presents the information in a neutral tone.

Antonym

17. Itinerant means wandering, which is the opposite of stationary. Choice D is correct.

18. Circuitous means roundabout, which is the opposite of direct. Choice C is correct.

19. Utilitarian means useful and functional, which is the opposite of impractical. Choice B is correct.

20. A paradox is a irony or an apparent inconsistency, which is the opposite of consistent. Choice E is correct.

21. An interloper is an intruder, which is the opposite of an insider. Choice A is correct.

22. To dispatch is to transmit or give away, which is the opposite of retain or preserve. Choice D is correct.

23. Grapple means to grab or seize, which is the opposite of release. Choice B is correct.

24. To impinge means to impose or intrude, which is the opposite of withdraw. Choice E is correct.

Analogy

25. The second word explains the function of the first word. Choice C is correct.

26. The second word is a consequence of the first word. Choice D is correct.

27. Skill X is used in Y profession. Choice A is correct.

28. The words are synonyms. Choice B is correct.

29. Something that is X cannot be Y. Choice D is correct.

30. The first word reduces the second. Choice B is correct.

Verbal Section 7:   30 minutes   30 questions

Directions: For each question in this section, select the best answer from the choices given and fill the corresponding circle on the answer sheet.

1. When she took the stand, the crime victim _____ the self-serving claims of the defendant.

    a.   incensed
    b.   repudiated
    c.   acknowledged
    d.   bolstered
    e.   nettled

2. The mood at the airport became _____ when the news of the crash was announced.

    a.   pliant
    b.   laconic
    c.   plethoric
    d.   timorous
    e.   dolorous

3. Stephen King novels are known for their _____ plotlines, in which the reader never knows what will come next.

    a.   convoluted
    b.   derivative
    c.   intrepid
    d.   felonious
    e.   suspenseful

4. After hearing so many _____ reviews for the horror movie, Rachel was _____ by its banal plot.

    a.   positive – elated
    b.   negative – scintillated
    c.   lackluster – enthralled
    d.   captivating - disappointed
    e.   valorous – dejected

5. Janice _____ endorsed her husband's plans to buy a house, despite her worries about their finances.

    a.   obligingly
    b.   warily
    c.   valiantly
    d.   enthusiastically
    e.   cautiously

6. Although the candidate promised to lower taxes, his audience was _____ of his sincerity.

    a.   skeptical
    b.   convinced
    c.   belligerent
    d.   tenacious
    e.   amenable

In and of itself, competition can be a healthy ingredient in the workplace, which produces better quality products or services at the lowest possible price. It can also stimulate the search for new technologies or better ways to satisfy customers. Pushed to extremes, however, competition can often reach an intensity that results in unethical practices and detrimental consequences.

5

Such intense competition, along with the desire to maximize profits and personal wealth, lead the formerly successful Enron Corporation down an unethical and illegal path. In the early days, Enron experienced significant growth and gained substantial credibility as a natural gas company. Later on, however, most of its successful operations were replaced by the illusion of successful initiatives. Over time, executives were no longer able to generate large profits, and, in fact, gambled away a substantial part of the company's financial resources. As a result, Enron's top executives began to actively borrow funds from Wall Street investors to make up the difference. The company's financial deficits, however, were effectively hidden from the investment bankers, as well as the remainder of the financial community.

14

As a result of many unwise and unethical domestic and foreign investments, extravagant corporate expenditures by the enterprise's top executives and a series of scandals involving irregular mark-to-market accounting procedures, Enron filed the largest bankruptcy in the American history on December 2, 2001.

18

Most people don't realize that Enron, like many other American corporations, possessed its very own Code of Ethics, in which the company tried to position itself as an international employer, a creator of innovative energy solutions, as well as a global corporate citizen. It assured all of its employees that these great responsibilities were not taken lightly by the corporation's executive management, which was committed to conducting itself in a respectful manner. The Code of Ethics continued to explain that Enron felt very strongly about its core values; it demanded that its employees treat each other as they would like to be treated themselves. Further, the Code of Ethics emphasized the importance of honoring all promises to clients and corporate prospects. Finally, it listed open communication and excellence at the top of its list of core values. Most impressively, all employees, including executive managers, were held to the same standards in respect to the company's vision and values. As required by most firms, Enron also mandated a signed compliance form that verified that each employee would adhere to the stipulated corporate standards.

30

Upon the approval of the company's Board of Directors, Enron's Chairman, Kenneth Lay presented the Code of Ethics in July 2000. Ironically, on May 25th, 2006, Mr. Lay was convicted of one count of conspiracy, three counts of securities fraud, three counts of bank fraud and two wire fraud counts. In addition, Mr. Lay was found guilty of signing misleading audit representation letters and making false statements and presentations to securities analysts and rating agencies.

36

Subsequently, Jeffrey K. Skilling, Enron's former Chief Executive Officer since February 2001, was also found guilty of nineteen (out of twenty-eight) felony charges filed against him during the financial collapse of the corporation. Just to name a few, the courts found Skilling guilty of one count of conspiracy, one count of insider trading, five counts of making false statements and presentations to securities analysts and twelve counts of securities fraud.

42

Lastly, Enron's former Chief Financial Officer, Andrew S. Fastow, played a key role in hiding the corporation's massive losses through the mark-to-market and creative accounting practices. On October 31, 2002, Fastow was found guilty of seventy-eight counts of conspiracy, money laundering and fraud. In exchange for his testimony against other Enron top executives, Andrew Fastow agreed to serve a ten-year prison term. Kenneth Lay and Jeffrey Skilling faced up to 185 years in prison for their fraudulent activities and conspiracy at Enron. Lay, however, died of a heart attack before his sentence could be imposed.

49

There are many lessons to remember from the story of Enron's rise, prominence, and financial collapse. Although some people feel it is an account of justified achievement, growth, innovation, and creativity, most agree it is an unfortunate (but true) testimony of human greed, ambition, competitive deceit, and arrogance. Enron's story shows that the company's Code of Ethics didn't really mean anything because it was not applied equally to everyone in the corporation. There must be a genuine and strong commitment from top management to reinforce and support the principles and values that are set forth in a corporate Code of Ethics. Further, funds should be made available in each corporate budget to conduct ethics training (and possibly hire ethics officers) to communicate, implement, and integrate the ethical behavior into the firm's culture.

58

7. According to the author, all of the following are positive effects of competition EXCEPT:

    a. more educated workforce
    b. better ways to satisfy customers
    c. better quality products
    d. lowest possible price
    e. improves the search for new technologies

8. In Line 12, what does "*deficit*" mean?

    a. expenditure
    b. subterfuge
    c. impairment
    d. deficiency
    e. disadvantage

9. According to the author of the passage, which of the following is NOT a reason for Enron's bankruptcy?

    a. Irregular accounting procedures
    b. Unethical foreign investments
    c. Extravagant executive expenses
    d. Tax evasion
    e. Bank fraud

10. In Line 34, what does "*audit*" mean?

    a. government
    b. examination
    c. repercussion
    d. regulatory
    e. seizure

11. According to the author, which of the following best conveys the value of a corporation's Code of Ethics?

    a. It assures Wall Street investors of a firm's mission and goals
    b. It attracts the right type of employee at all levels of the organization
    c. It is only valuable if top managers support and reinforce its principles
    d. It is an essential public relations tool
    e. It has no intrinsic value

12. What is the tone of the passage?

    a. apathetic
    b. vainglorious
    c. dejected
    d. incredulous
    e. objective

13. Which of the following is the best title for the passage?

    a. The Criminal Consequences of Enron
    b. How Top Enron Managers Betrayed Their Corporate Code of Ethics
    c. How Enron Fell from Grace
    d. Fraud at Enron: The New Corporate Culture
    e. Enron: The Aftermath

14. **VERACITY**:

    a. Anachronism
    b. Authenticity
    c. Deception
    d. Emolument
    e. Dulcet

15. **BEATITUDE**:

    a. Misery
    b. Bliss
    c. Drivel
    d. Cleft
    e. Pastoral

16. **BESTRIDE**:

    a. Apologize
    b. Dismount
    c. Patronize
    d. Praise
    e. Petrify

17. **AVER**:

    a. Profess
    b. Swerve
    c. Romanticize
    d. Augment
    e. Refute

18. **AGGRANDIZE**:

    a. Elaborate
    b. Diminish
    c. Conceal
    d. Reconcile
    e. Irritate

19. **MUTINOUS:**

    a. Disconnected
    b. Seditious
    c. Revolutionary
    d. Subservient
    e. Clever

20. **RISIBLE**:

   a. Impressive
   b. Laughable
   c. Mediocre
   d. Nostalgic
   e. Savage

21. **RELENTLESS**:

   a. Deplorable
   b. Harsh
   c. Gentle
   d. Unyielding
   e. Permissive

22. **RESCIND:**

   a. Atrophy
   b. Rebuke
   c. Peruse
   d. Validate
   e. Conspire

23. **RIBALD**:

   a. Refined
   b. Extraordinary
   c. Scintillating
   d. Resilient
   e. Flippant

24. **DEADLOCK:**

   a. Derivation
   b. Anachronism
   c. Credence
   d. Progress
   e. Embryonic

Directions: *Each of the following questions includes a pair of words or phrases that are separated by a colon. Likewise, each of the five answer choices also includes a pair of word or phases that are presented in a similar manner. Select the answer choice in which the* <u>relationship</u> *between the two words is most similar to that of the original pair.*

25. **ROOF: SHINGLES::**

   a. Patch: cloth
   b. Skin: cells
   c. Bedspread: canopy
   d. Tree; seeds
   e. Lobster: shell

26. **CLASSROOM: SCHOOL::**

   a.   Bed: room
   b.   Cubicle: secretary
   c.   Desk: office
   d.   Closet: janitorial
   e.   Cell: prison

27. **ARID: HUMIDITY::**

   a.   Safe: danger
   b.   Invisible: perception
   c.   Homogeneous: character
   d.   Miserly: affluence
   e.   Sterile: mercurial

28. **ANODYNE: INSIPID::**

   a.   Charismatic: wan
   b.   Derivative: innovative
   c.   Centrifuge: separation
   d.   Exhilarating: heady
   e.   Nuclei: electron

29. **SKEIN: YARN::**

   a.   Package: peanuts
   b.   Hub cap : wheel
   c.   Ball: string
   d.   Revolution: tire
   e.   Thread: needle

30. **NEPTUNE: PLANET::**

   a.   Pencil: ruler
   b.   Mop: broom
   c.   Armoire: furniture
   d.   Hair: appendage
   e.   Dog: canine

Answer Key for Verbal Section 7

Sentence Completion

1. We are looking for a word that indicates that the witness disputed the defendant's self-serving statements. The correct answer is B, repudiated.

2. The correct word is choice E, dolorous, which means extremely sad.

3. The correct word means uncertain or scary. The correct answer is E, suspenseful.

4.. The word *banal* indicates that the second word will be negative, while the word *after* suggests that the first word will be positive. The correct answer choice is D, captivating – disappointed.

5. The word *despite* indicates that the missing word will be a synonym for positive. The correct answer is D, enthusiastically.

6. The word *although* denotes contrast, which means we are looking for a word that means unlikely to keep a promise. The correct answer is A, skeptical.

Reading Comprehension

7. Choice A is correct. All of the other choices are mentioned in the first paragraph of Passage A.

8. Choice D is correct. In this context, *deficit* means deficiency.

9. Choice D is correct. All of the other choices are mentioned in the passage.

10. Choice B is correct. In this *context*, audit means examination.

11. Choice C is correct. The author explains his position in Lines 53 – 55.

12. Choice E is correct. The author is objective in tone.

13. Choice B is correct. The other choices are either too broad or too narrow in scope.

Antonym

14. Veracity means truth, which is the opposite of deception. Choice C is correct.

15. Beatitude is a state of bliss, which is the opposite of misery. Choice A is correct.

16. Bestride means to mount a horse, which is the opposite of dismount. Choice B is correct.

17. Aver means to claim or profess, which is the opposite of refute. Choice E is correct.

18. Aggrandize means to enhance or elaborate, which is the opposite of diminish. Choice B is correct.

19. Mutinous means rebellious or unruly, which is the opposite of subservient. Choice D is correct.

20. Risible means laughable or funny, which is the opposite of impressive. Choice A is correct.

21. Relentless means ruthless and unyielding, which is the opposite of gentle. Choice C is correct.

22. Rescind means to overturn or repeal something, which is the opposite of validate. Choice D is correct.

23. Ribald means rude or vulgar, which is the opposite of refined. Choice A is correct.

24. Deadlock means an impasse or stalemate, which is the opposite of progress. Choice D is correct.

Analogy

25. The first word is made up of the second word. Choice B is correct.

26. The second word is composed of the first word. Choice E is correct.

27. Something that is X lacks Y. Choice A is correct.

28. The words are synonyms. Choice D is correct.

29. X is a long, unbroken, rolled-up quantity of Y. Choice C is correct.

30. The first word is an example of the second word. Choice C is correct.

Verbal Section 8:   30 minutes   30 questions

Directions: For each question in this section, select the best answer from the choices given and fill the corresponding circle on the answer sheet.

1. Sheila's _____ to alcohol _____ her chances for a promotion at work.

    a.   addiction - mediated
    b.   predisposition- alleviated
    c.   resistance – obscured
    d.   aversion – aggrandized
    e.   proclivity – sabotaged

2. Ovarian cancer is a(n) _____ disease, because it cannot be diagnosed until an advanced stage, when the chance of survival is _____.

    a.   insidious - minimal
    b.   pervasive - infinitesimal
    c.   virulent - optimistic
    d.   tenacious - slim
    e.   aggressive – progressive

3. The designer employed a(n) _____ style, which combined different colors, styles and periods.

    a.   eccentric
    b.   luxuriant
    c.   eclectic
    d.   whimsical
    e.   flippant

4. Carol was a _____ reader who _____ all genres of books.

    a.   respectful - condensed
    b.   voracious - deplored
    c.   reluctant - eschewed
    d.   latent - suggested
    e.   pugnacious – epitomized

5. The _____ house was too _____ for even the largest family.

    a.   luxuriant - unique
    b.   miniscule - panoramic
    c.   opulent - spacious
    d.   penurious - perfunctory
    e.   flagrant – laconic

6. The relationship between the warring spouses was _____ at best.

    a.   contentious
    b.   dauntless
    c.   calumniate
    d.   subdued
    e.   culpable

At WorldCom, there was a colossal gap between the company's Code of Ethics and the actual behaviors observed at the firm. In fact, WorldCom's story is an example of an enterprise in which the Code of Ethics was a purely theoretical document that had nothing to do with the actual conduct of its top executives. Management's behavior towards the company's employees, clients, prospects, auditors, investors, bankers, and financial community was the antithesis of the outstanding principles that they touted in their public relations materials. No doubt, this repulsive behavior revealed the organization's true priorities, and served as a warning for other business enterprises in their fields of operation.

8

In his article entitled "Lessons from WorldCom," Mark McCormack explains that WorldCom's story represents a trend that has existed in the United States over the last twenty-five years. Far too often, Western corporations rely on short-term versus long-range results in order to influence the Wall Street community. Today's investors unrealistically expect business enterprises to consistently generate large profits quarter after quarter. WorldCom simply exploited this rigid measurement system to its fullest capacity.

14

According to McCormack, it is unlikely that Wall Street investors will change their obsession with short-term numbers anytime soon. However, this does not mean that WorldCom should adhere to its questionable management tactics regarding investor expectations. By creating and spinning off quasi-owned subsidiaries, companies create opportunities for dishonest and creative accounting, which will eventually be traced back to the parent company. Even legitimate subsidiaries should be established sparingly. Far too often, enterprises that devote significant interest to their side businesses can create possible conflicts of interest.

21

Businesses also need to be able to trust their bottom-line numbers. Top executives should not encourage the company accountants to "pretty up" the numbers to deliver an artificial result. Further, executives need to be able to discuss the company's numbers with the public in an open and honest manner. Some executive officers believe that a bit of data manipulation is needed to be competitive in today's market. However, as McCormack explains, "Today, people are more than willing to assume that where there is smoke, there is fire." A firm must show that it values character, which can only be accomplished by encouraging open communication, giving the employees more responsibility, and working towards the company goals without relying too heavily on favors. Companies who value performance will reveal their true profits, unlike Enron, which suffered severe consequences for putting a deceptive spin on their actual performance.

31

In 2002, Congress and the Securities Exchange Commission created the Sarbanes-Oxley Act to "force corporate executives to be proactive and accountable regarding the communication of their firm's financial position." This regulation was created to restore investors' faith in the integrity of corporate America and public markets. Kelly Financial Resources confirms that effective business communication is critical to educate the public about the problems surrounding their company. The scandals at Enron, WorldCom, and Tyco have encouraged the executives of other corporations to provide fair information about their organizations to Wall Street, which has improved their bottom-line. Ultimately, better communication yields happier, more engaged employees, which increases productivity and profits.

40

Strong and positive ethics have also been identified as one of the most important qualities in Bill Gates and Steve Jobs, who are two of the most ethical and exemplary business leaders in corporate America. Without exception, ethics and integrity govern how these executives conduct all aspects of their day-to-day business. By bringing a sense of fairness, respect and credibility to their interactions, Gates and Jobs set the tone for their organizations' cultures. Further, their strong positive ethics and open business communications help to build their corporations' brand names, which draw new customers and create sustained, long-term profits.

47

Competition and profit maximization have an adverse impact on ethics and communication in business, but being ethical does not have to mean losing profits. Generating wealth is necessary to make a good and positive impact on the community, but communicating ethically is also in the best interest of corporations and their stakeholders. Furthermore, such integrity can not be imposed by the law; it is a mindset that business leaders choose to adopt when making and communicating their everyday business decisions.

7. In the passage, what trend has Mark McCormack observed over the past twenty-five years?

    a. Companies rely on short-term results to deliver higher profits
    b. Companies move operations offshore to avoid taxation
    c. Companies use subsidiaries for unethical purposes
    d. Companies use creative accounting practices
    e. Corporate executives earn ridiculously high salaries

8. In Line 23, what does *"pretty"* mean?

    a. minimize
    b. highlight
    c. exaggerate
    d. falsify
    e. sanitize

9. What is the implication of Mark McCormack's quote on Line 26: *"Today, people are more than willing to assume that where there is smoke, there is fire."*

    a. Thanks to WorldCom, investors think all corporate executives are corrupt.
    b. As long as a company has good numbers, investors will remain loyal.
    c. The minute the SEC announces a company is under investigation, investors flee.
    d. If investors see a corporation's true financial numbers, they will assume the worst and take their money elsewhere.
    e. Investors only trust financial statements that are verified by an independent third party.

10. According to the passage, implementation of the Sarbanes-Oxley Act will accomplish all of the following EXCEPT:

    a. Improve the quality and quantity of information provided to Wall Street
    b. Encourage the use of outside accounting firms
    c. Improve employee happiness
    d. Improve productivity
    e. Restore investors' faith in corporate America

11. According to the author, which of the following corporate directives would Kelly Financial Resources be most likely to support?

    a. Formal training in ethics for all corporate CEOs
    b. Lower salaries and fewer perks for CEOs
    c. Stronger penalties for the illegal use of subsidiaries
    d. Annual IRS audits for all Fortune 1000 companies
    e. A communication campaign to educate the public about a company's problems

12. Which of the following does the author attribute to Bill Gates?

    a. Strong ethics and integrity
    b. Open communication
    c. Commitment to cross-cultural training
    d. A and B
    e. A, B and C

13. According to the author, what is the impact of competition on business?

    a. Positive impact on profits
    b. Negative impact on ethics and communication
    c. Positive impact on employee morale
    d. Negative impact on investment community
    e. Savvy leadership

14. What is the overall objective of the passage?

    a.   To find viable ways to prevent similar scandals to the one at WorldCom.
    b.   To discuss WorldCom's Code of Ethics.
    c.   To explain why all corporations are essentially corrupt.
    d.   To warn the investment community.
    e.   To explain the ramifications of the WorldCom scandal on the company's executives.

Directions: *For each question in this section, select the answer choice that means the exact OPPOSITE of the bold-faced word.*

15. **EXTRANEOUS:**

    a.   Ordinary
    b.   Superfluous
    c.   Pertinent
    d.   Miserly
    e.   Repetitive

16. **CATACLYSMIC:**

    a.   Soothing
    b.   Calamitous
    c.   Meandering
    d.   Deceitful
    e.   Lucrative

17. **PIQUANT**:

    a.   Curiosity
    b.   Frustration
    c.   Ignominy
    d.   Spicy
    e.   Mild

18. **ELUCIDATE**:

    a.   Acknowledge
    b.   Explicate
    c.   Evade
    d.   Muddle
    e.   Clarify

19. **VERTIGO**:

    a.   Health
    b.   Steadiness
    c.   Envy
    d.   Avarice
    e.   Potency

20. **ARCHETYPE**:

    a. Epitome
    b. Monarch
    c. Plebian
    d. Femme fatale
    e. Copycat

21. **FOMENT**:

    a. Defuse
    b. Stimulate
    c. Inject
    d. Clarify
    e. Ruin

22. **PALPITATE**:

    a. Augment
    b. Whine
    c. Dispute
    d. Stop
    e. Synchronize

23. **INSUPERABLE**:

    a. Impossible
    b. Affordable
    c. Easy
    d. Inexpensive
    e. Judgmental

24. **CONCESSION**:

    a. Forthright
    b. Immutable
    c. Vindication
    d. Cliché
    e. Hearsay

Directions: *Each of the following questions includes a pair of words or phrases that are separated by a colon. Likewise, each of the five answer choices also includes a pair of word or phases that are presented in a similar manner. Select the answer choice in which the* <u>relationship</u> *between the two words is most similar to that of the original pair.*

25. **OBLIVIOUS: MINDFUL::**

    a. Shrewd: devious
    b. Meticulous: pedantic
    c. Obese: corpulent
    d. Subtle: evident
    e. Chronic: inveterate

26. **ECCENTRIC: MAVERICK::**

   a. Visible: perceptible
   b. Auditory: decibel
   c. Morbid: jubilant
   d. Rapt: penultimate
   e. Permanent: sporadic

27. **UNCOUTH: SOPHISTICATION::**

   a. Limber: dexterity
   b. Vague: indecisiveness
   c. Forthright: candor
   d. Affluent: capital
   e. Moribund: maturity

28. **PREVARICATE: DISSEMBLE::**

   a. Amalgamate: negotiate
   b. Correspondence: documentation
   c. Proactive: remedial
   d. Fortitude: infirmity
   e. Tractable: polite

29. **SNEAKY: CONCEAL::**

   a. Healthy: meticulous
   b. Amorous: love
   c. Organized: professional
   d. Myopic: permissive
   e. Ardent: patronize

30. **TENNIS: RACKET::**

   a. Football: stadium
   b. Soccer: head
   c. Baseball: glove
   d. Guitarist: string
   e. Surgeon: scalpel

Answer Key for Verbal Section 8

Sentence Completion

1. The words are opposites; the best answer is choice E, proclivity – sabotaged.

2. The first word is negative, while the second means slim; the correct choice is A, insidious – minimal.

3. The correct word means *includes many styles*, or choice C, eclectic.

4. We are looking for two words that go in the same direction. Ironically, in this case, they are not positive words. The correct answer choice is C, because a *reluctant* reader *eschews* all types of books.

5. The strongest clue is *for even the largest family*, which indicates that the second word is a synonym for large. The correct answer choice is C, opulent – spacious.

6. The correct answer is a synonym for warring, which is A, contentious.

Reading Comprehension

7. Choice A is correct. The answer is in Lines 10 – 12.

8. Choice D is correct. In this context, *pretty up* means to falsify (to deliver an artificial result).

9. Choice D is correct. McCormack was referring to the investor response to poor financial numbers.

10. Choice B is correct. All of the other choices are mentioned in Lines 32 – 39.

11. Choice E is correct. The answer is mentioned in Lines 35 – 36.

12. Choice D is correct. The answer is in Lines 41 – 46. Cross-cultural training is not mentioned.

13. Choice B is correct. The answer is in Line 48.

14. Choice A is correct. The goal of the passage was to suggest ways to prevent similar scandals in the future.

Antonym

15. Extraneous means irrelevant or superfluous, which is the opposite of pertinent. Choice C is correct.

16. Cataclysmic means tragic or disastrous, which is the opposite of soothing. Choice A is correct.

17. Piquant means hot or spicy, which is the opposite of mild. Choice E is correct.

18. Elucidate means to clarify or explain, which is the opposite of muddle. Choice D is correct.

19. Vertigo means dizziness or lightheadedness, which is the opposite of steadiness. Choice B is correct.

20. An archetype is an original or classic, which is the opposite of a copycat. Choice E is correct.

21. Foment means to increase or stimulate, which is the opposite of defuse. Choice A is correct.

22. Palpitate means to throb or beat, which is the opposite of stop or cease. Choice D is correct.

23. Insuperable means impossible, which is the opposite of easy. Choice C is correct.

24. A concession is a compromise or surrender, which is the opposite of immutable. Choice B is correct.

Analogy

25. The words are antonyms. Choice D is correct.

26. The words are synonyms. Choice A is correct.

27. Those who are X do not possess Y. Choice D is correct.

28. The words are synonyms. Choice E is correct.

29. Someone who is X does Y. Choice B is correct.

30. To play X, you must hit the ball with Y. Choice B is correct.

Verbal Section 9: 30 minutes   30 questions

Directions: For each question in this section, select the best answer from the choices given and fill the corresponding circle on the answer sheet.

1. For patients with arthritis, few kitchen chores are as _____ as scrubbing greasy pans.

    a.   perennial
    b.   riveting
    c.   pungent
    d.   onerous
    e.   itinerant

2. To succeed as a researcher, a student must display a love of reading, a knack for organization and a _____ attention to detail.

    a.   rudimentary
    b.   meticulous
    c.   implicit
    d.   bewildering
    e.   habitual

3. The flower girl looked _____ in her flowing red dress and matching headband.

    a.   enchanting
    b.   aromatic
    c.   fragile
    d.   magical
    e.   unblemished

4. Wendy's blind date, who arrived an hour late with no explanation, was the _____ of the sophisticated gentleman she expected.

    a.   cessation
    b.   antithesis
    c.   personification
    d.   relative
    e.   regression

5. It was only at age 50, when Steven began to take music lessons, that his _____ talent as an artist began to _____.

    a.   considerable - mitigate
    b.   meager - wane
    c.   latent - emerge
    d.   misguided - falter
    e.   innate – abrogate

6. Rather than _____ to her mother's wishes, Gayle had the _____ to pursue her own path.

    a.   nullify - beneficence
    b.   object - audacity
    c.   adhere - courage
    d.   concede - propensity
    e.   panegyrize – execration

Directions: The passage below is followed by questions based on its content. Answer the questions, based on what is stated or implied in the passage and any introductory material that may be provided.

In recent years, people have demonstrated an insatiable appetite for technology that enables them to remain in touch on the go. As a result, individual consumers, along with countless public, private, and government organizations, have purchased a plethora of mobile and hand-held devices that offer sophisticated software applications, Internet and e-mail access, instant messaging, voice calls, and networking features that are accessible in a portable package. The biggest reason, however, for such explosive growth in mobile technologies is the potential cost savings for the organizations that use them. Advanced mobile and wireless devices allow firms to communicate independently of their physical locations. In addition, by 2010, wireless technology is forecasted to outperform wired networks due to its preferable cost, reliability, and functionality. Despite these benefits, however, mobile devices pose ever-changing security challenges for a corporation's top management to ensure the integrity, privacy, and security of their corporate data.

11

Mobile devices provide remote access to a company's data, which provides tremendous flexibility to their users. This flexibility, however, leaves the company's networks and data vulnerable to security breaches and viruses. Furthermore, many companies are struggling to find ways to protect the increasing amount of sensitive information that is stored in laptops, PDAs, BlackBerries, cell phones, USB drives, and other portable devices, which can be easily stolen, lost, or carried away due to their small size. And, sadly, once a mobile device is lost, the subsequent costs extend far beyond the physical replacement of the unit. In many cases, the greatest threat is the loss of sensitive or proprietary data that has been stored on the device.

19

Due to their portability, laptops, PDA's, smart phones, and USB memory sticks are far more difficult to secure than traditional workstation computers. Every day, employees at private, public, and government organizations transfer sensitive information from secured networks to mobile devices and remove them from the company premises. Although some companies prohibit CD burners at their workstation computers, laptops, PDAs, and USB drives are as commonplace as house keys. Even more troubling, when cheap USB memory devices are missing, employees may not even report it.

26

Unfortunately, the loss of these devices is all too common. Last year, about 750,000 laptops were stolen; about 97% of stolen PC's are never recovered. Every month, thousands of mobile phones are also stolen. If they are smart phones, they could contain private information like computer files and email messages, which could spark an unwanted leak of sensitive company information. According to a survey performed by the Yankee Group in 2005, 37% of respondents attributed the disclosure of company information to USB drives.

32

In a survey last year, the Technology Security Institute of the Federal Bureau of Investigation reported that 75% of respondents experienced laptop and mobile device theft, which was more than any other type of attack or misuse, including denial of service attacks, telecommunications fraud, unauthorized access of information, viruses, system penetration, sabotage, website defacement, and misuse of a public web application.

37

According to a survey performed by the Weiss Institute, 81% of information security professionals reported that their companies had experienced the loss of one or more laptops containing sensitive information. The study also reported that hand-held devices and laptops posed the greatest risk of data loss, followed by USB memory sticks. Sensitive information could include customer data, employee records, vendor information, intellectual property (such as product or research data, corporate plans, and strategies), and even the secret personal correspondence of key employees, which might make them vulnerable to blackmail.

44

Currently, there are numerous products and services to recover missing or stolen devices. Companies like SmartProtec provide software that can trace stolen property and return it to its rightful owner. Mr. Shively, an inventory manager for a company that processes medical records, recently installed SmartProtec software on more than 900 computers that are used by employees who travel between hospitals to scan patient records. If a computer is stolen, Mr. Shively simply has to call a hotline; the next time that laptop is connected to the internet, it will automatically send a message to the servers at SmartProtec headquarters that identifies its location. Immediately afterwards, the same information is forwarded to the police, who can retrieve the stolen laptop.

52

SmartProtec provides a similar service for cell phones, which allows users to register their devices. This simple step makes it dangerous for thieves to possess or re-sell stolen items. SmartProtec works with the police and other authorities to recover stolen devices, and offers rewards to the individuals who find them. The serial numbers of all devices are stored in a SmartProtec database, so there is no need for the owner to write it on a piece of paper and worry about losing it. The moment the device is lost or stolen, the owner must immediately change its status from "In Possession" to "Lost" or "Stolen." When police recover a stolen item, or someone finds a lost device, SmartProtec allows them to contact the owner through the serial number, without disclosing any personal information. Moreover, SmartProtec collaborates with FedEx to deliver the recovered device directly to the owner's doorstep.

62

Executives must keep these security services in their proper perspective. Although SmartProtec can trace stolen property and return it safely to its rightful owner, no amount of technology can substitute completely for the actions of people. Ultimately, security is only as good as each company's individual policies.

66

7. According to the author, what is the main reason for the fast growth of mobile technologies?

    a.   Computer networking
    b.   Voice mail applications
    c.   Potential cost savings
    d.   Internet access and email
    e.   Instant messaging

8. By 2010, what technological change do industry experts expect?

    a.   Corporations will no longer allow employees to store sensitive data on mobile devices
    b.   SmartProtec will capture more than eighty-percent of the wireless security market
    c.   The theft of mobile devices will spark a corresponding rise in identity theft
    d.   Due to problems associated with theft, USB memory devices will be prohibited at most major corporations
    e.   Wireless technology will outperform wired networks

9. According to the passage, what percentage of stolen computers is recovered?

    a.   3%
    b.   37%
    c.   75%
    d.   81%
    e.   97%

10. The passage mentions all of the following mobile devices EXCEPT:

    a.   Smart phones
    b.   USB drives
    c.   BlackBerries
    d.   Memory sticks
    e.   Portable microchips

11. In Line 41, what does "*sensitive*" mean?

    a.   Easily hurt
    b.   Classified
    c.   Clandestine
    d.   Delicate
    e.   Reactionary

12. Which organization conducted a survey to determine how sensitive company information was erroneously disclosed?

    a.   Yankee Group
    b.   Federal Bureau of Investigation
    c.   Weiss Institute
    d.   SmartProtec
    e.   Technology Security Institute

13. In the survey conducted by the Weiss Institute, which of the following is NOT mentioned as a type of record kept on corporate computers?

   a. Vendor information
   b. Corporate strategies
   c. Secret personal correspondence
   d. Health and medical records
   e. Employee records

14. In which scenario would the SmartProtec system NOT be helpful?

   a. The thief takes the laptop outside the United States
   b. The owner forgets the hotline number
   c. The thief does not attempt to log onto the Internet
   d. The laptop is dropped
   e. The laptop is sold to a pawn shop

15. In Line 59, what does *"serial"* mean?

   a. identifying
   b. in order
   c. repetitive
   d. rank
   e. production

16. Which of the following best conveys the author's attitude about the security of mobile devices?

   a. There is no realistic way to secure them.
   b. The risks are minimal compared to the benefits these devices offer.
   c. Portable storage devices should be banned at most companies to prevent security risks.
   d. Their security depends on each company's policies.
   e. A system like SmartProtec provides adequate protection for most users' needs.

Directions: For each question in this section, select the answer choice that means the exact OPPOSITE of the bold-faced word.

17. **MAGNANIMOUS**:

   a. Upright
   b. Zealous
   c. Selfish
   d. Overexposed
   e. Dishonest

18. **SUPERSEDE**:

   a. Proceed
   b. Recede
   c. Negate
   d. Counteract
   e. Regress

19. **DIMINUTIVE**:

   a. Humongous
   b. Miniscule
   c. Rude
   d. Statuesque
   e. Clumsy

20. **CREDULITY**:

   a. Exuberance
   b. Secretive
   c. Innocence
   d. Wariness
   e. Youthful

21. **VACILLATE**:

   a. Restrain
   b. Waiver
   c. Abscond
   d. Waver
   e. Decide

22. **SAGE**:

   a. Mystic
   b. Simpleton
   c. Scholar
   d. Bland
   e. Confused

23. **UNERRING**:

   a. Definitive
   b. Fashionable
   c. Faulty
   d. Repetitive
   e. Polished

24. **COMPLIANT:**

   a. Biddable
   b. Unyielding
   c. Redundant
   d. Innovative
   e. Disingenuous

Directions: Each of the following questions includes a pair of words or phrases that are separated by a colon. Likewise, each of the five answer choices also includes a pair of word or phases that are presented in a similar manner. Select the answer choice in which the relationship between the two words is most similar to that of the original pair.

25. **VOCIFERATE: LISTEN::**

    a. Disregard: disdain
    b. Negotiate: confer
    c. Traverse: cross
    d. Escalate: depreciate
    e. Mediate: referee

26. **VOLATILITY: PRECARIOUS::**

    a. Theoretical: oblique
    b. Monotheistic: doctrine
    c. Justice: litigation
    d. Malevolent: surrender
    e. Chicanery: trick

27. **FANATICISM: TOLERANCE::**

    a. Rapacity: gluttony
    b. Resistance: antibodies
    c. Nettle: exasperate
    d. Malingering: indolent
    e. Meager: derisory

28. **TRADUCE: COMMEND::**

    a. Miraculous: ordinary
    b. Asperse: slander
    c. Simplicity: austere
    d. Wealthy: accumulate
    e. Spiritual: meditate

29. **QUERULOUS: COMPLAIN::**

    a. Lazy: pontificate
    b. Fastidious: clean
    c. Petulant: sleep
    d. Salubrious: endure
    e. Meticulous: negotiate

30. **MALADROIT: LUMBERING::**

    a. Considerate: rude
    b. Conscious: sentient
    c. Travail: deny
    d. Resolution: vacillate
    e. Meandering: clandestine

Answer Key for Verbal Section 9

Sentence Completion

1. The correct word means difficult, which is choice D, onerous.

2. The correct word means careful, which is choice B, meticulous.

3. The correct word means beautiful, which is choice A, enchanting.

4. The correct word means opposite, which is choice B, antithesis.

5. The first word means natural or hidden, while the second means appeared. The correct choice is C latent-emerge.

6. The first word means honor or obey, while the second means courage. The correct choice is C, adhere-courage.

Reading Comprehension

7. Choice C is correct. The answer is in Line 6.

8. Choice E is correct. The answer is in Line 8.

9. Choice A is correct. On Line 28, the author reports that 97% of stolen computers are NOT recovered.

10. Choice E is correct. All of the other devices are mentioned in the passage.

11. Choice B is correct. In this context, *sensitive* means classified.

12. Choice A is correct. The answer is in Line 30.

13. Choice D is correct. The other choices are mentioned in Lines 41 - 43.

14. Choice C is correct. According to Lines 49 - 50, the laptop can only be traced if the thief logs onto the Internet, at which time its location can be determined from its IP number. If the thief does not log onto the Internet, the unit cannot be traced.

15. Choice A is correct. The *serial* number corresponds with the ownership certificate, which identifies the registered user of the laptop.

16. Choice D is correct. The author states this conclusion in the final sentence of the passage.

Antonym

17. Magnanimous means generous or noble, which is the opposite of selfish. Choice C is correct.

18. Supersede means to surpass or go forward, which is the opposite of regress. Choice E is correct.

19. Diminutive means small or tiny, which is the opposite of humongous. Choice A is correct.

20. Credulity means innocent or trusting, which is the opposite of wariness. Choice D is correct.

21. Vacillate means to waver or hesitate, which is the opposite of decide. Choice E is correct.

22. Sage means scholarly or intellectual, which is the opposite of a simpleton. Choice B is correct.

23. Unerring means correct or certain, which is the opposite of faulty. Choice C is correct.

24. Compliant means obedient or submissive, which is the opposite of unyielding. Choice B is correct.

Analogy

25. The words are antonyms. Choice D is correct.

26. The words are synonyms. Choice E is correct.

27. The words are antonyms. Choice A is correct.

28. The words are antonyms. Choice A is correct.

29. One who is X tends to do Y. Choice B is correct.

30. The words are synonyms. Choice B is correct.

Verbal Section 10:   30 minutes   30 questions

Directions: For each question in this section, select the best answer from the choices given and fill the corresponding circle on the answer sheet.

1. To convince a jury, attorneys must present compelling _____ to support their arguments.

    a.   conjectures
    b.   evidence
    c.   theories
    d.   speculations
    e.   documents

2. Given John's _____ nature, we are not surprised that he changes jobs so frequently.

    a.   ideological
    b.   vehement
    c.   ingenious
    d.   implacable
    e.   capricious

3. To choose the optimal cancer treatment, patients must evaluate the potential risks and _____ in a clear and rational manner.

    a.   benefits
    b.   speculation
    c.   symptoms
    d.   prognosis
    e.   economy

4. The prolonged recovery from Hurricane Katrina revealed a _____ of political, social, and financial problems in the ravaged areas.

    a.   concoction
    b.   desert
    c.   plethora
    d.   resentment
    e.   gridlock

5. Despite the intensity of the political campaign, the candidate inspired little _____ in his constituents.

    a.   apathy
    b.   affluence
    c.   provocation
    d.   exuberance
    e.   reticence

6. A dedicated student would never display such a _____ attitude toward her studies.

    a.   blatant
    b.   recalcitrant
    c.   munificent
    d.   haughty
    e.   cavalier

Passage 1

During the sixteenth century, the most celebrated sheep in France were those of Berri and Limousin; and of all butchers' meat, veal was reckoned the best. In fact, calves intended for the tables of the upper classes were fed in a special manner: they were allowed for six months, or even for a year, nothing but milk, which made their flesh most tender and delicate. Contrary to the present taste, kid was more appreciated than lamb, which caused the rôtisseurs frequently to attach the tail of a kid to a lamb, so as to deceive the customer and sell him a less expensive meat at the higher price. This was the origin of the axiom which described a cheat as "a dealer in goat by halves."

8

In other places, butchers were far from acquiring the same importance which they did in France and Belgium, where much more meat was consumed than in Spain, Italy, or even in Germany. Nevertheless, in almost all countries there were certain regulations, sometimes eccentric, but almost always rigidly enforced, to ensure a supply of meat of the best quality and in a healthy state. In England, for instance, butchers were only allowed to kill bulls after they had been baited with dogs, no doubt with the view of making the flesh more tender. At Mans, it was laid down in the trade regulations that "no butcher shall be so bold as to sell meat unless it shall have been previously seen alive by two or three persons, who will testify to it on oath; and, anyhow, they shall not sell it until the persons shall have declared it wholesome."

17

To the many regulations affecting the interests of the public must be added that forbidding butchers to sell meat on days when abstinence from animal food was ordered by the Church. These regulations applied less to the vendors than to the consumers, who, by disobeying them, were liable to fine or imprisonment, or to severe corporal punishment by the whip or in the pillory. We find that Clément Marot was imprisoned and nearly burned alive for having eaten pork during Lent. In 1534, Guillaume des Moulins, the Count of Brie, asked permission for his mother, who was then eighty years of age, to cease fasting; the Bishop of Paris only granted dispensation on the condition that the old lady should take her meals in secret and out of sight of every one, and should still fast on Fridays.

26

The severity of the punishment for these transgressions increased during times of religious dissensions. Erasmus says, "He who has eaten pork instead of fish is taken to the torture like a parricide." An edict of Henry II, 1549, forbade the sale of meat during Lent to persons who should not be furnished with a doctor's certificate. Charles IX forbade the sale of meat to the Huguenots; and it was ordered that the privilege of selling meat during the time of abstinence should belong exclusively to the hospitals. Orders were given to those who retailed meat to take the address of every purchaser, although he had presented a medical certificate, so that the necessity for his eating meat might be verified. Subsequently, the medical certificate had to be endorsed by the priest, specifying what quantity of meat was required. Even in these cases, the use of butchers' meat alone was granted, pork, poultry, and game being strictly forbidden.

36

7. What is the main point of the passage?

    a.   To explain the best ways to tenderize meat
    b.   To explain the reasoning for attaching a kid to a lamb
    c.   To explain the religious implications of meat consumption in sixteenth century Europe
    d.   To discuss the regulations regarding meat consumption in Europe during the sixteenth century
    e.   To explain the extreme tyranny of Charles IX regarding the consumption of food

8. According to the author, in France, what was the best way to ensure that a calf's meat was tender?

    a.   They were baited by dogs before they were killed
    b.   They were declared wholesome by two people before they were killed
    c.   The meat was cooked slowly with moisture
    d.   They were fed nothing but milk for at least six months before slaughter
    e.   The meat was consumed within 24 hours of the calf's slaughter

9. In Line 6, what does "*axiom*" mean?

    a. Maxim
    b. Law
    c. Irony
    d. Allegation
    e. Corollary

10. Customers who ate illegal meat were punished in all of the following ways EXCEPT:

    a. Fines
    b. Starvation
    c. Whipping
    d. Imprisonment
    e. Pillory

11. In Line 28, what does "*parricide*" mean?

    a. Death via food poisoning
    b. Death by starvation
    c. Murder of a relative
    d. Religious execution
    e. Animal sacrifice

12. What is the most likely source of the passage?

    a. A food journal
    b. A history book
    c. A cookbook
    d. A religious sermon
    e. A print ad for the beef industry

Passage 2

The coffee tree, scientifically known as Coffea arabica, is native to Abyssinia and Ethiopia, but grows well in Java, Sumatra, and other islands of the Dutch East Indies; in India, Arabia, equatorial Africa, the islands of the Pacific, in Mexico, Central and South America, and the West Indies. The plant belongs to the large sub-kingdom of plants known scientifically as the Angiosperms, which means that the plant reproduces by seeds which are enclosed in a box-like compartment, known as the ovary, at the base of the flower. The word Angiosperm is derived from two Greek words, sperma, a seed, and aggeion, a box or ovary.

7

This large sub-kingdom is subdivided into two classes. The basis for this division is the number of leaves in the little plant which develops from the seed. The coffee plant, as it develops from the seed, has two little leaves, and therefore belongs to the class Dicotyledoneæ. This word dicotyledoneæ is made up of the two Greek words, di(s), two, and kotyledon, cavity or socket. It is not necessary to see the young plant that develops from the seed in order to know that it had two seed leaves; because the mature plant always shows certain characteristics that accompany this condition of the seed.

14

In every plant having two seed leaves, the mature leaves are netted-veined, which is a condition easily recognized even by the layman; also the parts of the flowers are in circles containing two or five parts, but never in threes or sixes. The stems of plants of this class always increase in thickness by means of a layer of cells known as a cambium, which is a tissue that continues to divide throughout its whole existence. The fact that this cambium divides as long as it lives, gives rise to a peculiar appearance in woody stems by which we can, on looking at the stem of a tree of this type when it has been sawed across, tell the age of the tree.

21

In the spring the cambium produces large open cells through which large quantities of sap can run; in the fall it produces very thick-walled cells, as there is not so much sap to be carried. Because these thin-walled open cells of one spring are next to the thick-walled cells of the last autumn, it is very easy to distinguish one year's growth from the next; the marks so produced are called annual rings.

26

The flower of the coffee plant is separated into sub-classes according to whether the flower's corolla is all in one piece, or is divided into a number of parts. The coffee flower is arranged with its corolla all in one piece, forming a tube-shaped arrangement, and accordingly the coffee plant belongs to the sub-class Sympetalæ, or Metachlamydeæ, which means that its petals are united.

31

Within the Dicotyledoneæ classification, plants are separated into orders according to their varied characteristics. The coffee plant belongs to an order known as Rubiales. These orders are again divided into families. Coffee is placed in the family Rubiaceæ, or Madder Family, in which we find herbs, shrubs or trees, represented by a few American plants, such as bluets, or Quaker ladies, small blue spring flowers, common to open meadows in northern United States; and partridge berries (Mitchella repens).

37

The Madder Family has more foreign representatives than native genera, among which are Coffea, Cinchona, and Ipecacuanha (Uragoga), all of which are of economic importance. The members of this family are noted for their action on the nervous system. Coffea, as is well known, contains an active principle known as caffeine which acts as a stimulant to the nervous system and in small quantities is very beneficial. Cinchona supplies us with quinine, while Ipecacuanha produces ipecac, which is an emetic and purgative.

43

All botanists do not yet agree in their classification of the species and varieties of the Coffea genus. M.E. de Wildman, curator of the Royal Botanical Gardens at Brussels, in his Les Plantes Tropicales de Grande Culture, says the systematic division of this interesting genus is far from finished; in fact, it has only yet begun.

47

13. What is the main point of the passage?

    a.   To explain the economic value of the Madder Family
    b.   To explain the botanical classification of the coffee plant
    c.   To explain the origin of Dicotyledoneæ
    d.   To explain the significance of annual rings
    e.   To differentiate between Dicotyledoneæs and Rubiales

14. Coffee grows naturally in all of the following locations EXCEPT:

    a.   Africa
    b.   Slovakia
    c.   India
    d.   Mexico
    e.   West Indies

15. According to the author, where is the aggeion?

    a.   Within the seed
    b.   On a netted-veined leaf
    c.   At the base of the flower
    d.   Within the woody stem
    e.   In a one-piece tube

16. What is the purpose of the cambium?

    a.   It holds the ovary
    b.   It stimulates the nervous system
    c.   It allows us to classify plants by their number of leaves
    d.   It allows us to determine the age of a tree
    e.   It supplies the seeds for reproduction

17. In Line 27, what is a *"corolla"*?

    a. Stem
    b. Leaf
    c. Petal
    d. Root
    e. Seed

18. All of the following are Rubiaceæ EXCEPT:

    a. Cacao
    b. Bluets
    c. Partridge berries
    d. Shrubs
    e. Herbs

Directions: *For each question in this section, select the answer choice that means the exact OPPOSITE of the bold-faced word.*

19. **ACME**:

    a. Nadir
    b. Zenith
    c. Chaotic
    d. Paramount
    e. Placid

20. **UNSCATHED**:

    a. Bawdy
    b. Virginal
    c. Sophisticated
    d. Injured
    e. Honorable

21. **CONCLAVE:**

    a. Assembly
    b. Solitary
    c. Convex
    d. Caucus
    e. Infirmity

22. **ABASE**:

    a. Snivel
    b. Humiliate
    c. Extol
    d. Circumvent
    e. Annoy

23. **CONCORD**:

    a.   Stationary
    b.   Heroic
    c.   Docile
    d.   Conflict
    e.   Potent

24. **CENSURE**:

    a.   Reduce
    b.   Praise
    c.   Litigate
    d.   Repudiate
    e.   Discourteous

Directions: *Each of the following questions includes a pair of words or phrases that are separated by a colon. Likewise, each of the five answer choices also includes a pair of word or phases that are presented in a similar manner. Select the answer choice in which the* relationship *between the two words is most similar to that of the original pair.*

25. **CURIOUS: INVESTIGATE::**

    a.   Confused: befuddle
    b.   Indecisive: annoy
    c.   Maladroit: stumble
    d.   Savvy: negotiate
    e.   Zealous: optimize

26. **VENERATE: MOCK::**

    a.   Blame: deny
    b.   Habitual: unusual
    c.   Condescend: brevity
    d.   Demeaning: strategic
    e.   Visceral: primeval

27. **ARREST: DETAIN::**

    a.   Convict: defend
    b.   Imply: ignore
    c.   Meander: sprint
    d.   Supply: refill
    e.   Walk: move

28. **PRUNE: SHEARS::**

    a.   Pasta: boil
    b.   Rice: hull
    c.   Peaches: harvest
    d.   Drive: vehicle
    e.   Augment: scoop

29. **MEDDLE: DISREGARD::**

    a. Purity: adulterate
    b. Membrane: atom
    c. Spontaneous: unexpected
    d. Cantankerous: tetchy
    e. Void: abyss

30. **PROSELYTIZE: INDUCE::**

    a. Flail: whirl
    b. Surrender: resist
    c. Suggest: insist
    d. Succumb: ignore
    e. Romanticize: consider

Answer Key for Verbal Section 10

Sentence Completion

1. The correct word means documentation, which is choice B, evidence.

2. The correct word means fickle, which is choice E, capricious.

3. The correct word means benefits, which is choice A.

4. The correct answer means many, which is choice C, plethora.

5. The correct word means excitement, which is choice D, exuberance.

6. The correct answer means the opposite of dedicated, which is choice E, cavalier.

Reading Comprehension

7. Choice D is correct. The main point of the passage is to discuss the regulations regarding meat consumption in Europe during the sixteenth century.   The other answer choices are wrong in scope.

8. Choice D is correct. The answer is presented in Lines 3 – 4.

9. Choice A is correct. In this context, axiom means a maxim, saying, or proverb.

10. Choice B is correct. The other answer choices are all presented in Lines 20 - 21.

11. Choice C is correct. Parricide means the murder of a relative.

12. Choice B is correct. The passage is an excerpt from a history book.

13. The main point of the passage is to explain the botanical classification of the coffee plant. Choice B is correct.

14. Lines 1 -3 mention all of the places that are listed except Slovakia. Choice B is correct.

15. Lines 5 -6 state that the aggeion is at the base of the flower. Choice C is correct.

16. According to Lines 18 – 20, the cambium produces the cells that create the annual ring, which allow us to age the tree. Choice D is correct.

17. A corolla is a petal. Choice C is correct.

18. According to Lines 34 – 36, all are Rubiaceæ except cacao. Choice A is correct.

Antonym

19. Acme means peak or top, which is the opposite of nadir. Choice A is correct.

20. Unscathed means unharmed or intact, which is the opposite of injured. Choice D is correct.

21. A conclave is a meeting or assembly, which is the opposite of solitary. Choice B is correct.

22. Abase means to degrade or belittle, which is the opposite of praise or extol. Choice C is correct.

23. Concord means agreement or unity, which is the opposite of conflict. Choice D is correct.

24. Censure means fault or criticize, which is the opposite of praise. Choice B is correct.

Analogy

25. People who are X tend to do Y. Choice C is correct.

26. The words are antonyms. Choice B is correct.

27. The second word is an implication of the first word. Choice E is correct.

28. To do X, you use Y. Choice D is correct.

29. The words are antonyms. Choice A is correct.

30. The words are synonyms. Choice A is correct.

Verbal Section 11:   30 minutes   30 questions

Directions: *For each question in this section, select the best answer from the choices given and fill the corresponding circle on the answer sheet.*

1. Compared to the _____ of New York City, life in Kansas is downright _____.

    a.   fast pace - banal
    b.   crime rate - agrarian
    c.   sophistication – mundane
    d.   vibrancy - archaic
    e.   wealth – reverent

2. Although her parents were diehard liberals, Jayne's political views tend to be quite _____.

    a.   apathetic
    b.   indifferent
    c.   tentative
    d.   conservative
    e.   independent

3. The defense attorney argued _____ that his client be shown _____.

    a.   logically - clemency
    b.   cleverly - justice
    c.   methodically - innocent
    d.   passionately - leniency
    e.   persuasively – mitigation

4. Rather than _____ the mediation, the parties _____ their adversarial positions.

    a.   participate in - mollified
    b.   dispute - disclosed
    c.   abandon– cited
    d.   challenge - castigated
    e.   support – adhered to

5. Although the insecticide was extremely effective, its _____ fumes were distasteful to consumers.

    a.   flagrant
    b.   noxious
    c.   illogical
    d.   medicinal
    e.   antioxidant

6.   Despite his pressure to withdraw U.S troops from Iraq, President Bush remained _____ in his commitment to the war.

    a.   vainglorious
    b.   arrogant
    c.   authoritarian
    d.   immutable
    e.   tractable

Directions: *The passages below are followed by questions based on their content. Answer the questions, based on what is <u>stated</u> or <u>implied</u> in the passage and any introductory material that may be provided.*

Passage 1

Jealousy is an accidental passion, for which the faculty indeed is unborn. In its nobler form and in its nobler motives it arises from love, and in its lower form it arises from the deepest and darkest Pit of Satan. Jealousy arises either from weakness, which from a sense of its own want of lovable qualities is not convinced of being sure of its cause, or from distrust, which thinks the beloved person capable of infidelity. Sometimes all these motives may act together.

6

The noblest jealousy, if the term noble is appropriate, is a sort of ambition or pride of the loving person who feels it is an insult that another one should assume it is possible to supplant his love, or it is the highest degree of devotion which sees a declaration of its object in the foreign invasion, as it were, of his own altar. Jealousy is always a sign that a little more wisdom might adorn the individual without harm.

11

The lowest species of jealousy is a sort of avarice of envy which, without being capable of love, at least wishes to possess the object of its jealousy alone by the one party assuming a sort of property right over the other. This jealousy, which might be called the Satanic, is generally to be found with old withered "husbands," who the devil has prompted to marry young women and who forthwith dream night and day of cuckold's horns. These Argus-eyed keepers are no longer capable of any feeling that could be called love, they are rather as a rule heartless house-tyrants, and are in constant dread that someone may admire or appreciate his unfortunate slave.

18

The general conclusion will be that jealousy is more the result of wrong conditions which cause uncongenial unions, and which through moral corruption artificially create distrust than a necessary accompaniment of love. Jealousy is a passion with which those who are most afflicted who are the least worthy of love. An innocent maiden who enters marriage will not dream of getting jealous; but all her innocence cannot secure her against the jealousy of her husband if he has been a libertine. Those are wont to be the most jealous who have the consciousness that they themselves are most deserving of jealousy. Most men in consequence of their present education and corruption have so poor an opinion not only of the male, but even of the female sex, that they believe every woman at every moment capable of what they themselves have looked for among all and have found among the most unfortunate, the prostitutes. No libertine can believe in the purity of woman; it is contrary to nature. A libertine therefore cannot believe in the loyalty of a faithful wife.

29

There may be occasions where jealousy is justifiable. If a woman's confidence has been shaken in her husband, or a husband's confidence has been shaken in his wife by certain signs or conduct, which have no other meaning but that of infidelity, then there is just cause for jealousy. There must, however, be certain proof as evidence of the wife's or husband's immoral conduct. Imaginations or any foolish absurdities should have no consideration whatever, and let everyone have confidence until his or her faith has been shaken by the revelation of absolute facts.

36

No couple should allow their associations to develop into an engagement and marriage if either one has any inclination to jealousy. It shows invariably a want of sufficient confidence, and that want of confidence, instead of being diminished after marriage, is liable to increase, until by the aid of the imagination and wrong interpretation the home is made a hell and divorce a necessity. Let it be remembered, there can be no true love without perfect and absolute confidence, jealousy is always the sign of weakness or madness. Avoid a jealous disposition, for it is an open acknowledgment of a lack of faith.

43

7. What is the main point of the passage?

   a. Jealousy is a sign of weakness or madness
   b. Jealousy is justifiable when infidelity has occurred
   c. Jealousy is a misguided form of personal pride
   d. Jealous people believe that others are jealous as well
   e. Jealous people are incapable of honest communication

8. In Line 8, what does "*supplant*" mean?

   a. Mollify
   b. Repudiate
   c. Diminish
   d. Prove
   e. Supersede

9. In Lines 15 - 16, to whom does the author refer as "Argus-eyed keepers?

  a. People who suffer from unrequited love
  b. Old husbands who do not trust their younger wives around other men
  c. Unfaithful spouses who flaunt their extramarital affairs
  d. Unfaithful spouses who presume their spouses are also cheating
  e. Spouses who lack confidence in their romantic appeal

10. In Line 23, what does "*libertine*" mean?

  a. Withholding affection
  b. Sociopath
  c. Self-involved
  d. Morally depraved
  e. Morally superior

11. The author states all of the following about jealousy EXCEPT:

  a. Those who are most jealous are least worthy of love
  b. Those who are most jealous believe that they are also deserving of jealousy
  c. Most men who seek the company of prostitutes believe that women will also seek the same type of immoral companionship
  d. Jealous is a necessary accompaniment of love
  e. Moral corruption artificially creates distrust

12. What is the likely source of the passage?

  a. A religious sermon
  b. A newspaper article about marriage
  c. A documentary about sexually transmitted diseases
  d. A psychology textbook
  e. An argument in a college debate

Passage 2

Arbuckle Brothers are direct importers of green coffee on a large scale, and are known also as heavy buyers "on the street." The roasting capacity of their Brooklyn plant is from 8,000 to 9,000 bags per day. The cylinder equipment of twenty-four Burns roasters is supplemented by four "Jumbo" roasters of Arbuckle build, each capable of roasting thirty-five bags at one time. The Ariosa package business grew from the smallest beginnings to more than 800,000 packages per day. Although individual brands have not held their lead of late years, the volume of the package-coffee business is greater than ever. Many jobbers now pack brands of their own, besides handling the Arbuckle brands.

8

To ship more than one hundred cars of coffee and sugar in a single day calls for shipping facilities that could be had only by organizing a railroad and waterfront terminal, known as Jay Street Terminal, equipped with freight station, locomotives, tugboats, steam lighters, car floats, and barges. City deliveries of coffee and sugar call for a fleet of thirty-five large motor trucks that are housed in the firm's own garage and repaired in their own shops.

14

Within the company's Brooklyn plant, a printing shop vibrates with the whirr of epic printing presses turning out thousands of coffee-wrappers and circulars; in fact, the first three-color printing press was expressly designed and built for Arbuckle Brothers. Then, there is a sunny first-aid hospital on top of the Pearl Street warehouse where a physician is ready to relieve sudden illness and accidental injuries. On the eleventh floor there is a huge dining room where the Brooklyn clerical forces get their noonday lunches. This feeding of the inner man (and woman) is matched by the power-house where twenty-six large steam boilers must be fed their quota of coal. In the winter months, when warmth must come for the workers as well as power for the wheels, the coal consumption runs up as high as four hundred tons per day.

23

The barrel factory, with a daily capacity of 6,800 sugar barrels, is located about a mile away, where barrel staves and heads are received from the firm's own stave mill in Virginia, made from logs cut on their own timber lands in Virginia and North Carolina. A more self-contained plant would be hard to imagine. During the busy sugar season, the firm dumps from eight to ten thousand bags of raw sugar per day, and these bags are washed and dried daily as they are emptied. A huge rotary drier of the firm's own design does the work of about three miles of clothes lines.

30

Even after the coffees have been sold and paid for, there still remains an important task, and that is to redeem the signature coupons which the consumers cut from the packages and return for premiums. Lest some regard this as an insignificant phase of the business, it may be stated that in a single year the premium department has received over one hundred and eight million coupons calling for more than four million premiums, including handkerchiefs, lace curtains, shears, and Torrey razors. Finger rings are perennial favorites, and so insistent is the demand for the rings offered as premiums, that Arbuckle Brothers are regarded as the largest distributors of finger rings in the world. One of their premium rings is a wedding ring; and if all the rings of this pattern serve their intended purpose, it is estimated that the firm has assisted at more than eight hundred thousand weddings.

40

Turning from the utilities at the plant to the trades and professions represented, other than the trained sugar and coffee workers, the facility also employs various engineers, chauffeurs, teamsters, machinists, coppersmiths, carpenters, masons, painters, plumbers, riggers, typesetters and pressmen, and last but not least, the chef and table waiters. One of the most remarkable things about the growth of this business enterprise is that it is not the result of buying out, or consolidating with, competitors; but has resulted from a steady wholesome growth along conservative business lines. Consolidations are often desirable and effective; but when a great business has been built without any such consolidations, the conclusion is inevitable that somewhere in the establishment there must have been a corresponding amount of wisdom, foresight, energy, and honorable business dealing. Those were the things for which John Arbuckle stood firm, and for which he will always be remembered.

51

13. What is the main point of the passage?

    a.   To explain the economic impact of the Arbuckle Brothers facility on the city of Brooklyn
    b.   To explain why John Arbuckle became the "king of coffee"
    c.   To explain the size and scope of the Arbuckle Brothers coffee facility in Brooklyn
    d.   To explain the complexity of producing and selling a natural commodity such as coffee
    e.   To explain why Arbuckle Brothers is the largest employer in Brooklyn

14. According to the author, all of the following functions are performed at the Brooklyn facility EXCEPT:

    a.   Feeding the workers
    b.   Washing the raw coffee beans
    c.   Providing First Aid
    d.   Printing wrappers and circulars
    e.   Redeeming premium coupons

15. In Line 15, what does "epic" mean?

    a.   Illustrious
    b.   Proprietary
    c.   Antiquated
    d.   Massive
    e.   Efficient

16. In Line 25, what does "stave" mean?

    a.   Base
    b.   Lid
    c.   Spigot
    d.   Liner
    e.   Opening

17. According to the author, what is the most popular premium?

    a. Handkerchiefs
    b. Curtains
    c. Rings
    d. Razors
    e. Shears

18. According to the author, what is John Arbuckle's legacy?

    a. He was the largest and most reliable employer in Brooklyn
    b. He grew his business steadily and honorably, without consolidating with competitors
    c. By keeping most functions in-house, he kept the price of his products low and the quality high
    d. He developed and built his own roasters, which gave him an edge in a competitive market
    e. By offering premiums, he built a level of customer loyalty that no competitor could match

Directions: *For each question in this section, select the answer choice that means the exact OPPOSITE of the bold-faced word.*

19. **PREVAIL**:

    a. Trap
    b. Withdraw
    c. Reject
    d. Deny
    e. Fail

20. **SMOLDER**:

    a. Protrude
    b. Smother
    c. Joy
    d. Withdraw
    e. Unite

21. **UNOBTRUSIVE:**

    a. Discreet
    b. Striking
    c. Cowardly
    d. Triumphant
    e. Succulent

22. **GENESIS**:

    a. Conception
    b. Hope
    c. Covenant
    d. Death
    e. Oasis

23. **STIPULATION**:

   a. Prerequisite
   b. Legislation
   c. Unconditional
   d. Declaration
   e. Notification

24. **ANTITHESIS**:

   a. Parallel
   b. Opposite
   c. Conclusion
   d. Partner
   e. Codicil

Directions: *Each of the following questions includes a pair of words or phrases that are separated by a colon. Likewise, each of the five answer choices also includes a pair of word or phases that are presented in a similar manner. Select the answer choice in which the* <u>relationship</u> *between the two words is most similar to that of the original pair.*

25. **LUCID: CONVOLUTED::**

   a. Marginal: subsidiary
   b. Ascetic: materialistic
   c. Buoyant: jaunty
   d. Bohemian: vagabond
   e. Terse: morose

26. **SCANTY: EXIGUOUS::**

   a. Speech: extemporaneous
   b. Mellow: relaxing
   c. Tyranny: liberty
   d. Unravel: solve
   e. Pious: sanctimonious

27. **SHAMAN: MYSTIC::**

   a. Nurse: medical
   b. Attorney: shyster
   c. Physician: doctor
   d. Artist: muse
   e. Healer: holistic

28. **STALWART: ROBUST::**

   a. Ameliorate: maintain
   b. Affluent: middling
   c. Eloquent: reserved
   d. Coarse: churlish
   e. Haughty: diffident

29. **ATTENUATE: INTENSIFY::**

   a. Walk: run
   b. Increase: expand
   c. Worrisome: problematic
   d. Curette: wedge
   e. Athletic: sedentary

30. **SANTA: SLEIGH::**

   a. Ghost: nightmare
   b. Admiral: ship
   c. Bunny: Easter
   d. Pilot: airport
   e. Songs: carols

Answer Key for Verbal Section 11

Sentence Completion

1. The first word means fast or sophisticated, while the second word means the opposite; the correct combination is choice C, sophistication- mundane.

2. The correct answer is the opposite of liberal, or D, conservative.

3. Both words are positive; the correct choice is D, passionately- leniency.

4. The words will be similar to each other; the correct choice is E, support- adhered to.

5. The correct answer means strong or unpleasant, which is choice B, noxious.

6. The word despite indicates contrast, which means that the correct answer means steadfast or resolute; the best choice is D, immutable.

Reading Comprehension

7. Choice A is correct. The answer is stated directly in Line 41.

8. Choice E is correct. In context, supplant means supersede.

9. Choice B is correct. The answer is stated in Lines 14 – 17.

10. Choice D is correct. In this context, libertine means morally depraved or dissolute.

11. Choice D is correct. All of the other answer choices are presented in Lines 19 – 28.

12. Choice D is correct. The passage is an excerpt from a psychology textbook. The tone and subject matter of the passage do not match the other four answer choices.

13. Choice C is correct. The other answers are either too broad or narrow in scope.

14. Choice B is correct. All of the other answer choices are presented in the passage.

15. Choice D is correct. In context, epic means large or massive.

16. Choice A is correct. In context, the word stave means base or bottom.

17. Choice C is correct. The answer is stated in Lines 35 – 39.

18. Choice B is correct. The answer is stated directly in Lines 44 – 49.

Antonym

19. Prevail means to succeed, which is the opposite of fail. Choice E is correct.

20. Smolder means to seethe with rage, which is the opposite of joy. Choice C is correct.

21. Unobtrusive means bland or inconspicuous, which is the opposite of striking. Choice B is correct.

22. Genesis means origin or beginning, which is the opposite of death. Choice D is correct.

23. A stipulation is a condition or requirement, which is the opposite of unconditional. Choice C is correct.

24. Antithesis means opposite or reverse, which is the opposite of parallel. Choice A is correct.

Analogy

25. The words are antonyms. Choice B is correct.

26. The words are antonyms. Choice C is correct.

27. The words are synonyms for the same profession. Choice C is correct.

28. The words are synonyms. Choice D is correct.

29. The words are antonyms. Choice E is correct.

30. X travels via Y. Choice B is correct.

Directions: For each question in this section, select the best answer from the choices given and fill the corresponding circle on the answer sheet.

1. Despite his claims of innocence, Sam's alibi for the night of the crime was _____ at best.

    a.   recalcitrant
    b.   tentative
    c.   logical
    d.   plausible
    e.   infinitesimal

2. Bill's anger with his wife was _____ by their financial problems.

    a.   palliated
    b.   propitiated
    c.   mitigated
    d.   decimated
    e.   exacerbated

3. Considering the dire warnings by meteorologists, it was _____ that so few residents sought refuge at the shelters.

    a.   untoward
    b.   awkward
    c.   surprising
    d.   stalwart
    e.   impudent

4. Adam, who was painfully shy as a child, surprised everyone by becoming such a _____ adult.

    a.   magnanimous
    b.   garrulous
    c.   wayward
    d.   bounteous
    e.   intransigent

5. The bride's designer wedding dress was far too _____ for my simple taste.

    a.   subdued
    b.   lugubrious
    c.   ornate
    d.   bombastic
    e.   austere

6. If Julie were a true friend, she would not make _____ remarks about you behind your back.

    a.   querulous
    b.   superfluous
    c.   disparaging
    d.   unctuous
    e.   facetious

7. Despite her best efforts, Zelda was too _____ to engage in the party scene.

    a. introverted
    b. urbane
    c. prolific
    d. fulminating
    e. quaint

Directions: *The passages below are followed by questions based on their content. Answer the questions, based on what is <u>stated</u> or <u>implied</u> in the passage and any introductory material that may be provided.*

English pioneers found an instrument for colonization in companies of merchant adventurers, which had long been employed in carrying on commerce with foreign countries. Such a corporation was composed of many persons of different ranks of society--noblemen, merchants, and gentlemen--who banded together for a particular undertaking, each contributing a sum of money and sharing in the profits of the venture. It was organized under royal authority; it received its charter, its grant of land, and its trading privileges from the king and carried on its operations under his supervision and control. The charter named all the persons originally included in the corporation and gave them certain powers in the management of its affairs. When the members of the corporation remained in England, as in the case of the Virginia Company, they operated through agents sent to the colony. When they came over the seas themselves and settled in America, as in the case of Massachusetts, they became the direct government of the country they possessed. The stockholders in that instance became the voters and the governor, the chief magistrate.

12

Four of the thirteen colonies in America owed their origins to the trading corporation. It was the London Company, created by King James I in 1606, that laid during the following year the foundations of Virginia at Jamestown. It was under the auspices of their West India Company, chartered in 1621, that the Dutch planted the settlements of the New Netherland in the valley of the Hudson. The founders of Massachusetts were Puritan leaders and men of affairs whom King Charles I incorporated in 1629 under the title: "The governor and company of the Massachusetts Bay in New England." In this case, the law incorporated a group drawn together by religious ties. Far to the south, on the banks of the Delaware River, a Swedish commercial company in 1638 made the beginnings of a settlement, christened New Sweden; it was destined to pass under the rule of the Dutch, and finally as the proprietary colony of Delaware.

22

In a certain sense, Georgia may be included among the "company colonies." It was, however, originally conceived by the moving spirit, James Oglethorpe, as an asylum for poor men, especially those imprisoned for debt. To realize this humane purpose, he secured from King George II, in 1732, a royal charter uniting several gentlemen, including himself, into "one body politic and corporate," known as the "Trustees for establishing the colony of Georgia in America." In the structure of their organization and their methods of government, the trustees did not differ materially from the regular companies created for trade and colonization. Though their purposes were benevolent, their transactions had to be under the forms of law and according to the rules of business.

31

A second agency which figured largely in the settlement of America was the religious brotherhood, or congregation, of men and women brought together in the bonds of a common religious faith. The Mayflower Compact, so famous in American history, was a written and signed agreement, incorporating the spirit of obedience to the common good, which served as a guide to self-government in Plymouth until it was annexed to Massachusetts in 1691. Three other colonies, all of which retained their identity until the eve of the American Revolution, likewise sprang directly from the congregations of the faithful: Rhode Island, Connecticut, and New Hampshire They were founded by small bodies of men and women, "united in solemn covenants with the Lord," who planted their settlements in the wilderness. These pioneers agreed that "the Scriptures do hold forth a perfect rule for the direction and government of all men."

41

The third colonial agency was the proprietor, who was granted property by the king in North America to have, hold, use, and enjoy for his own benefit and profit, with the right to hand the estate down to his heirs in perpetual succession. The proprietor was a rich and powerful person, prepared to furnish or secure the capital, collect the ships, supply the stores, and assemble the settlers necessary to found and sustain a plantation beyond the seas. Sometimes the proprietor worked alone. Sometimes two or more were associated like partners in the common undertaking.

48

Five colonies, Maryland, Pennsylvania, New Jersey, and the Carolinas, owe their formal origins, though not always their first settlements, nor in most cases their prosperity, to the proprietary system. Maryland, established in 1634 under a Catholic nobleman, Lord Baltimore, and blessed with religious toleration by the act of 1649, flourished under the mild rule of proprietors until it became a state in the American union. New Jersey, beginning its career under two proprietors, Berkeley and Carteret, in 1664, passed under the direct government of the crown in 1702. Pennsylvania was, in a very large measure, the product of the generous spirit and tireless labors of its first proprietor, the leader of the Friends, William Penn, to whom it was granted in 1681 and in whose family it remained until 1776. The two Carolinas were first organized as one colony in 1663 under the government and patronage of eight proprietors, including Lord Clarendon; but after more than half a century both became royal provinces governed by the king.

60

8. What is the main point of the passage?

   a. To document the role of the King of England in the development of the thirteen colonies
   b. To explain the role of religion in the thirteen colonies
   c. To discuss the three different ways that the original thirteen colonies were established
   d. To explain the role of trading companies in colonial times
   e. To document the superiority of the proprietary system in establishing the thirteen colonies

9. In Line 1, what does "*instrument*" mean?

   a. Justification
   b. Mechanism
   c. Exception
   d. Escape
   e. Obligation

10. According to the passage, all of the following are true about charters EXCEPT:

   a. The members included nobleman, merchants, and gentleman
   b. The charter, land, and trading privileges all came from the king
   c. The king supervised and controlled all operations of the venture
   d. All profits were retained by the king
   e. The charter defined the specific powers of each member

11. According to the passage, what is the primary difference between the corporations in Virginia and Massachusetts?

   a. The members of the Massachusetts corporation were Pilgrims, while the members of the Virginia corporation were primarily merchants and noblemen
   b. The members of the Virginia corporation remained in England, while the members of the Massachusetts corporation actually settled in the colony
   c. The members of the Virginia corporation had no religious affiliation, while the members of the Massachusetts corporation were Christian
   d. The members of the Massachusetts corporation remained in England, but hired the chief magistrate to govern the colony
   e. The corporations were similar in organization and structure, but very different in size

12. Which of the following American colonies owed their origins to the trading corporation?

   a. Massachusetts, Virginia, New Hampshire, Rhode Island
   b. Virginia, Delaware, Maryland, Pennsylvania
   c. Connecticut, Virginia, New Jersey, Rhode Island
   d. Virginia, Massachusetts, Delaware, Rhode Island
   e. Virginia, Massachusetts, Delaware, Georgia

13. Which colony was once christened New Sweden?

    a. Virginia
    b. Massachusetts
    c. Delaware
    d. Georgia
    e. New England

14. Which ruler was associated with the work of James Oglethorpe?

    a. King James I
    b. King Charles I
    c. King George I
    d. Lord Clarendon
    e. King George II

15. All of the following are true about the settlement of Georgia EXCEPT:

    a. It was conceived by a moving spirit
    b. It was conceived as an asylum for poor men
    c. Its charter was issued by King Charles II in 1732
    d. It is considered a company colony
    e. The purposes of its organization were benevolent

16. Which of the following colonies were settled by the religious brotherhood?

    a. Massachusetts
    b. Massachusetts, Rhode Island, Connecticut, and New Hampshire
    c. Rhode Island, Connecticut, and New Hampshire
    d. Massachusetts, Rhode Island, Connecticut, and New Hampshire
    e. None

17. In Line 39, what does "*covenants*" mean?

    a. Scriptures
    b. Subservience
    c. Agreement
    d. Aristocracy
    e. Obligation

18. All of the following are true about proprietors EXCEPT:

    a. They were the first settlers of five of the first thirteen colonies
    b. The king granted them the right to use property in America for their own benefit
    c. They could leave their property in America to their own heirs
    d. They were required to secure the capital, collect the ships, supply the stores, and assemble the settlers onto their plantations
    e. They included Berkeley, Carteret, Lord Clarendon and William Penn

19. Which of the following colonies were affiliated with proprietors?

    a. Maryland, Pennsylvania, Virginia, New York, and the Carolinas
    b. New Jersey, Georgia, Virginia, Delaware and the Carolinas
    c. Maryland, Pennsylvania, Virginia, North Carolina, and South Carolina
    d. Pennsylvania, New Jersey, Virginia, North Carolina, and South Carolina
    e. New Jersey, Maryland, Pennsylvania, North Carolina, and South Carolina

20. **PRONE**:

    a.   Emaciated
    b.   Brisk
    c.   Viscous
    d.   Impetuous
    e.   Vertical

21. **APOGEE**:

    a.   Pinnacle
    b.   Violation
    c.   Pedestal
    d.   Commitment
    e.   Reservation

22. **HOMAGE**:

    a.   Reverence
    b.   Complacency
    c.   Affinity
    d.   Disrespect
    e.   Shame

23. **DESICCATE**:

    a.   Honor
    b.   Moisten
    c.   Repair
    d.   Admire
    e.   Capitulate

24. **AVERSE**:

    a.   Hostile
    b.   Apathetic
    c.   Erroneous
    d.   Unprepared
    e.   Inclined

Directions: Each of the following questions includes a pair of words or phrases that are separated by a colon. Likewise, each of the five answer choices also includes a pair of word or phases that are presented in a similar manner. Select the answer choice in which the <u>relationship</u> between the two words is most similar to that of the original pair.

25. **DISPARATE: INCONGRUENT::**

    a.   Troth: pledge
    b.   Mercurial: ancient
    c.   Poverty: oppression
    d.   Fidelity: conformity
    e.   Burgeoning: dwindling

26. **CARBUNCLE: BOIL::**

    a. Mark: commemorate
    b. Injury: diagnose
    c. Demur: dainty
    d. Consequence: fatal
    e. Memory: enhance

27. **HINT: DECLARE:**

    a. Marry: love
    b. Eat: gorge
    c. Run: sprint
    d. Scamper: scuttle
    e. Speak: mumble

28. **INBUE: FEELINGS::**

    a. Denigrate: praise
    b. Mitigate: injury
    c. Prove: corroborate
    d. Meander: path
    e. Inspire: confidence

29. **AEROSOL: CAN::**

    a. Spiritual: divine
    b. Liquid: bottle
    c. Beauty: splendor
    d. Powder: dry
    e. Dehydrate: flake

30. **COMPENDIUM: UNABRIDGED::**

    a. Define: explain
    b. Cement: undermine
    c. Capitulate: relent
    d. Myopic: uninformed
    e. Taper: narrow

Answer Key for Verbal Section 12

Sentence Completion

1. The correct answer means uncertain, which is choice B, tentative.

2. The correct answer means made worse, which is choice E, exacerbated.

3. The word considering indicates contrast; the correct answer choice is C, surprising.

4. The correct answer is the opposite of shy, which is choice B, garrulous.

5. The correct answer is the opposite of simple, which is choice C, ornate.

6. The correct answer means bad or insulting, which is choice C, disparaging.

7. The correct word means quiet, which is choice A, introverted.

Reading Comprehension

8. Choice C is correct. The others are too broad or narrow in scope.

9. Choice B is correct. In context, instrument means mechanism.

10. Choice D is correct. All of the other answer choices are presented in the first paragraph of the passage.

11. Choice B is correct. The answer is presented in Lines 8 – 11.

12. Choice E is correct. The answer is presented in Lines 13 - 23.

13. Choice C is correct. The answer is presented in Lines 20 – 21.

14. Choice E is correct. The answer is presented in Line 25.

15. Choice C is correct. All of the other answer choices are presented in Lines 23 – 29.

16. Choice B is correct. The answer is given in Lines 33 – 38.

17. Choice C is correct. In context, covenant means agreement.

18. Choice A is correct. All of the other answer choices are presented in Lines 42 – 59.

19. Choice E is correct. The answer is presented in Line 49.

Antonym

20. Prone means horizontal, which is the opposite of vertical. Choice E is correct.

21. An apogee is a summit or peak, which is the opposite of base or pedestal. Choice C is correct.

22. Homage means respect or honor or reverence, which is the opposite of disrespect. Choice D is correct.

23. Desiccate means to dry, which is the opposite of moisten. Choice B is correct.

24. Averse means reluctant, which is the opposite of inclined. Choice E is correct.

Analogy

25. The words are synonyms. Choice D is correct.

26. The words are synonyms. Choice A is correct.

27. The second word is a stronger version of the first. Choice B is correct.

28. You do X to Y. Choice E is correct.

29. X is contained in Y. Choice B is correct.

30. The words are antonyms. Choice B is correct.

Directions: For each question in this section, select the best answer from the choices given and fill the corresponding circle on the answer sheet.

1. There was not enough evidence to _____ the accuser's claims.

    a.   surmount
    b.   supersede
    c.   substantiate
    d.   stipulate
    e.   slander

2. If left unresolved, small issues van eventually cause a permanent _____ between marital partners.

    a.   rumination
    b.   sanguinary
    c.   rebuttal
    d.   schism
    e.   respite

3. According to Strunk and White, good writing requires clear focus and a _____ writing style, which makes the most of every word.

    a.   creative
    b.   provisional
    c.   precise
    d.   original
    e.   enigmatic

4. The _____ disease left Jason a wasted man who could barely move his legs.

    a.   myocardial
    b.   hereditary
    c.   infectious
    d.   debilitating
    e.   inflammatory

5. If used incorrectly, statistics can _____ the truth and lead researchers to _____ conclusions.

    a.   enhance - critical
    b.   summarize - concise
    c.   twist - negligent
    d.   distort - erroneous
    e.   encapsulate – spurious

6. Although Diane disliked the subcompact car, it was a more_____ choice than the sports car she originally selected.

    a.   economical
    b.   myriad
    c.   efficient
    d.   malleable
    e.   provocative

About five miles from Warwick are the ruins of Kenilworth Castle, the magnificent home of the Earl of Leicester. Geoffrey de Clinton, in the reign of Henry I, built a strong castle and founded a monastery here. It was afterwards the castle of Simon de Montfort, and his son was besieged in it for several months, ultimately surrendering, when the king bestowed it upon his youngest son, Edward, Earl of Lancaster and Leicester. Edward II, when taken prisoner in Wales, was brought to Kenilworth, and signed his abdication in the castle, being afterwards murdered in Berkeley Castle. Then it came to John of Gaunt, and in the Wars of the Roses was alternately held by the partisans of each side. Finally, Queen Elizabeth bestowed it upon her ambitious favorite, Dudley, Earl of Leicester, who made splendid additions to the buildings.

9

It was here that Leicester gave magnificent entertainment to Queen Elizabeth, including a series of pageants that lasted seventeen days and cost $5000 a day--a very large sum for those times. The queen was attended by thirty-one barons and a host of retainers, and four hundred servants, who were all lodged in the fortress. The attendants were clothed in velvet, and the party drank sixteen hogsheads of wine and forty hogsheads of beer every day, while to feed them ten oxen were killed every morning. There was a succession of plays and amusements provided, including the Coventry play of "Hock Tuesday" and the "Country Bridal," with bull-and bear-baiting, of which the queen was very fond. The display and hospitality of the Earl of Leicester were intended to pave the way to marriage, but the wily queen was not to be thus entrapped.

18

The castle is now part of the Earl of Clarendon's estate, and he has taken great pains to preserve the famous ruins. The great hall, ninety feet long, still retains several of its Gothic windows, and some of the towers rise seventy feet high. These ivy-mantled ruins stand upon an elevated rocky site commanding a fine prospect, and their chief present use is as a picnic-ground for tourists. Not far away are the ruins of the priory, which was founded at the same time as the castle. A dismantled gate-house with some rather extensive foundations are all that remain. In a little church near by the matins and the curfew are still tolled, one of the bells used having belonged to the priory.

26

Few English ruins have more romance attached to them than those of Kenilworth, for the graphic pen of the best story-teller of Britain has interwoven them into one of his best romances, and has thus given an idea of the splendors as well as the dark deeds of the Elizabethan era that will exist as long as the language endures.

30

7. What is the main point of the passage?

    a. To discuss the romantic significance of the English ruins
    b. To discuss the ownership and use of Kenilworth Castle from ancient times until modern day
    c. To discuss Queen Elizabeth's romance with the Earl of Leicester at Kenilworth Castle
    d. To explain the Earl of Clarendon's efforts to restore Kenilworth Castle to its original beauty
    e. To document the architectural genius of Geoffrey de Clinton

8. The passage mentions all of the following about Edward II EXCEPT:

    a. Taken prisoner in Wales
    b. Signed his abdication at Kenilworth Castle
    c. Murdered in Berkeley Castle
    d. Son of the Earl of Lancaster and Leicester
    e. Besieged in Kenilworth Castle

9. In Line 7, what does "*partisans*" mean?

    a. Rulers
    b. Servants
    c. Opponents
    d. Followers
    e. Clergy

10. Which of the following is NOT true about Queen Elizabeth's pageants?

    a. The pageants were designed to convince the Queen to marry the Earl of Clarendon
    b. The pageants cost $5000 per day
    c. The Queen's attendants were clothed in velvet
    d. Ten oxen were killed every morning to feed the guests
    e. The Queen's barons, retainers, and servants were lodged in the fortress

11. According to the passage, what is currently the primary use of Kenilworth Castle?

    a. A church
    b. An historic bell tower
    c. A picnic ground for tourists
    d. The current home of the Earl of Clarendon
    e. A private residence of the British royal family

12. In Line 22, what does "*priory*" mean?

    a. Tower
    b. Ruins
    c. Estate
    d. Castle
    e. Monastery

13. According to the passage, what is the most notable feature of Kenilworth Castle?

    a. It was built during the reign of Henry I
    b. It has an impressive romantic history among all English ruins
    c. It is the only castle of its time to be sufficiently preserved
    d. It is still used as a sacred monastery
    e. It has been exhaustively researched by British historians

Directions: *For each question in this section, select the answer choice that means the exact OPPOSITE of the bold-faced word.*

14. **HEADLONG:**

    a. Impetuous
    b. Vertical
    c. Callow
    d. Considered
    e. Insipid

15. **PIQUE:**

    a. Soothe
    b. Crevice
    c. Espouse
    d. Abnegate
    e. Bottom

16. **SEPULCHRAL**:

    a. Somber
    b. Jovial
    c. Banal
    d. Spiritual
    e. Sacrilegious

17. **CAPRICIOUS**:

    a. Whimsical
    b. Homely
    c. Predictable
    d. Generous
    e. Fatuous

18. **INVIDIOUS**:

    a. Odious
    b. Diseased
    c. Apocryphal
    d. Endogamous
    e. Pleasant

19. **CHORTLE**:

    a. Gurgle
    b. Cry
    c. Offend
    d. Assure
    e. Pull

20. **TRUCULENT**:

    a. Partisan
    b. Ingenuous
    c. Generous
    d. Agreeable
    e. Fractious

21. **QUIESCENT**:

    a. Active
    b. Noisome
    c. Inert
    d. Random
    e. Orderly

22. **CANNY**:

    a. Astute
    b. Fetid
    c. Boring
    d. Intransigent
    e. Dim

23. **SINUOUS**:

    a.   Lithe
    b.   Inflexible
    c.   Credulous
    d.   Fortuitous
    e.   Regrettable

Directions: *Each of the following questions includes a pair of words or phrases that are separated by a colon. Likewise, each of the five answer choices also includes a pair of word or phases that are presented in a similar manner. Select the answer choice in which the* <u>relationship</u> *between the two words is most similar to that of the original pair.*

24. **LUCKY: HAPLESS::**

    a.   Permanent: stuck
    b.   Savage: unlucky
    c.   Civilized: feral
    d.   Generous: giving
    e.   Stupendous: excessive

25. **COMPENSATE: NEUTRALIZE::**

    a.   Enormous: diminutive
    b.   Agrarian: traditional
    c.   Monolith: secondary
    d.   Prolific: fecund
    e.   Amazon: aquatic

26. **PLANT: FERN::**

    a.   Hoe: land
    b.   Grain: sorghum
    c.   Pasta: wheat
    d.   Cook: meat
    e.   Juice: orange

27. **FARMER: TILL::**

    a.   Driver: car
    b.   Salesman: quota
    c.   Engineer: spreadsheet
    d.   Archeologist: dig
    e.   Accountant: pen

28. **CLOWN: SERIOUS::**

    a.   Runner: sprint
    b.   Psychologist: analyze
    c.   Teacher: read
    d.   Policeman: unlawful
    e.   Attorney: advocate

29. **PROLIFERATION: SCARCITY::**

    a.   Peaceful: belligerent
    b.   Perplexed: tangled
    c.   Unity: concord
    d.   Ravenous: hunger
    e.   Multitude: throng

30. **CREATE: BEGET::**

    a.   Diminish: spate
    b.   Ponder: deliberate
    c.   Muse: hinder
    d.   Monster: colossal
    e.   Obvious: ambiguous

Answer Key for Verbal Section 13

Sentence Completion

1. The correct answer means prove, which is choice C, substantiate.

2. The correct answer means unresolved issue or, choice D, schism.

3. The correct word means exact, which is choice C, precise.

4. The correct word means seriously ill or immobile, which is choice D, debilitating.

5. The two words are both negative; the correct answer is choice D, distort – erroneous.

6. The correct word means the same as less expensive, which is choice A, economical.

Reading Comprehension

7. Choice B is correct. The passage discusses the ownership and use of Kenilworth Castle from ancient times until modern day

8. Choice E is correct. All of the other answer choices are mentioned in Lines 4 – 5.

9. Choice D is correct. In context, *partisans* means followers.

10. Choice A is correct. All of the other answer choices are mentioned in Lines 10 – 17. Choice A is actually a trick question, though – it contains the name of the wrong Earl (Clarendon versus Leicester).   Be careful.

11. Choice C is correct. The answer is stated directly on Line 22.

12. Choice E is correct. In context, *priory* means monastery.

13. Choice B is correct. The answer is stated directly in Line 27.

Antonym

14. Headlong means rash or hasty, which is the opposite of considered. Choice D is correct.

15. To pique is to irritate or annoy, which is the opposite of soothe. Choice A is correct.

16. Sepulchral means sad or somber, which is the opposite of jovial. Choice B is correct.

17. Capricious means impulsive or fickle, which is the opposite of predictable. Choice C is correct.

18. Invidious means unpleasant or offensive, which is the opposite of pleasant. Choice E is correct.

19. Chortle is to laugh or giggle, which is the opposite of cry. Choice B is correct.

20. Truculent means hostile or defiant, which is the opposite of agreeable. Choice D is correct.

21. Quiescent means dormant or sluggish, which is the opposite of active. Choice A is correct.

22. Canny means smart or clever, which is the opposite of dim. Choice E is correct.

23. Sinuous means lithe or supple, which is the opposite of inflexible. Choice B is correct.

Analogy

24. The words are antonyms. Choice C is correct.

25. The words are synonyms. Choice D is correct.

26. The second word is an example of the first word. Choice B is correct.

27. X does Y. Choice D is correct.

28. X does not act in Y manner. Choice D is correct.

29. The words are antonyms. Choice A is correct.

30. The words are synonyms. Choice D is correct.

Verbal Section 14:   30 minutes   30 questions

Directions: *For each question in this section, select the best answer from the choices given and fill the corresponding circle on the answer sheet.*

1. Ironically, Jennifer's efforts to make people like her only served to _____ them.

      a.   ridicule
      b.   coddle
      c.   pacify
      d.   repel
      e.   confuse

2. Although the Professor was a brilliant man, he appeared to be _____ of common sense.

      a.   cautious
      b.   full
      c.   devoid
      d.   appreciative
      e.   disdain

3. Janice was too vibrant and athletic to settle for a _____ lifestyle.

      a.   humanitarian
      b.   traditional
      c.   spiritual
      d.   sedentary
      e.   chaotic

4. His sterling reputation as a New York theatre actress was _____ by the publication of her photos on the society page.

      a.   compromised
      b.   obliterated
      c.   enhanced
      d.   disregarded
      e.   mitigated

5. Long after Gladys lost her wealth in the stock market crash, she continued to spend _____ amounts of money.

      a.   innocuous
      b.   prudent
      c.   pragmatic
      d.   exorbitant
      e.   parsimonious

6. Gloria, the office gossip, repeated personal details about her boss's life with little or no _____.

      a.   innuendo
      b.   candor
      c.   discretion
      d.   conviviality
      e.   conservation

Directions: *The passages below are followed by questions based on their content. Answer the questions, based on what is* stated *or* implied *in the passage and any introductory material that may be provided.*

Passage 1

The evolution of American democracy into a government by public opinion, enlightened by the open discussion of political questions, was in no small measure aided by a free press. That too, like education, was a matter of slow growth. A printing press was brought to Massachusetts in 1639, but it was under the control of an official censor and limited to the publication of religious works. Forty years elapsed before the first newspaper appeared, bearing the curious title, "Public Occurrences Both Foreign and Domestic," and it had not been running very long before the government of Massachusetts suppressed it for discussing a political question.

8

Publishing, indeed, seemed to be a precarious business; but in 1704 there came a second venture in journalism, "The Boston News-Letter," which proved to be a more lasting enterprise because it refrained from criticizing the authorities. Still the public interest languished. When Benjamin Franklin's brother, James, began to issue his "New England Courant" about 1720, his friends sought to dissuade him, saying that one newspaper was enough for America. Nevertheless he continued it; and his confidence in the future was rewarded. In nearly every colony a gazette or chronicle appeared within the next thirty years or more. Benjamin Franklin was able to record in 1771 that America had twenty-five newspapers. Boston led with five. Philadelphia had three: two in English and one in German.

17

The idea of printing, unlicensed by the government and uncontrolled by the church, was, however, slow in taking form. The founders of the American colonies had never known what it was to have the free and open publication of books, pamphlets, broadsides, and newspapers. When the art of printing was first discovered, the control of publishing was vested in clerical authorities. After the establishment of the State Church in England during the reign of Elizabeth, censorship of the press became a part of royal prerogative. Printing was restricted to Oxford, Cambridge, and London; and no one could publish anything without previous approval of the official censor. When the Puritans were in power, the popular party, with a zeal that rivaled that of the crown, sought, in turn, to silence royalist and clerical writers by vigorous censorship. After the restoration of the monarchy, control of the press was again placed in royal hands, where it remained until 1695, when Parliament, by failing to renew the licensing act, did away entirely with the official censorship. By that time political parties were so powerful and so active and printing presses were so numerous that official review of all published matter became a sheer impossibility.

30

In America, likewise, some troublesome questions arose in connection with freedom of the press. The Puritans of Massachusetts were no less anxious than King Charles or the Archbishop of London to shut out from the prying eyes of the people all literature "not mete for them to read;" and so they established a system of official licensing for presses, which lasted until 1755. In the other colonies, where there was more diversity of opinion and publishers could set up in business with impunity, they were nevertheless constantly liable to be arrested for printing anything displeasing to the colonial governments. In 1721, the editor of the "Mercury" in Philadelphia was called before the proprietary council and ordered to apologize for a political article, and for a later offense of a similar character he was thrown into jail.

39

A still more famous case was that of Peter Zenger, a New York publisher, who was arrested in 1735 for criticizing the administration. Lawyers who ventured to defend the unlucky editor were deprived of their licenses to practice, and it became necessary to bring an attorney all the way from Philadelphia. By this time, the tension was high, and the approbation of the public was forthcoming when the lawyer for the defense exclaimed to the jury that the very cause of liberty itself, not that of the poor printer, was on trial. The verdict for Zenger, when it finally came, was the signal for an outburst of popular rejoicing. Already the people of King George's province knew how precious a thing is the freedom of the press.

47

Thanks to the schools, few and scattered as they were, and to the vigilance of parents, a very large portion of the colonists could read. Through the newspapers, pamphlets, and almanacs that streamed from the types, the people could follow the course of public events and grasp the significance of political arguments. An American opinion was in the process of making—an independent opinion nourished by the press and enriched by discussions around the fireside and at the taverns. When the day of resistance to British rule came, government by opinion was at hand. For every person who could hear the voice of Patrick Henry and Samuel Adams, there were a thousand who could see their appeals on the printed page. Men who had spelled out their letters while poring over Franklin's "Poor Richard's Almanac" lived to read Thomas Paine's thrilling call to arms.

57

7. What is the main point of the passage?

   a. To explain the popularity of political literature in colonial America
   b. To explain the evolution of censorship in England
   c. To illustrate the legal penalties for authors and publishers who failed to honor the censorship laws in colonial America
   d. To explain the importance of literacy in colonial America
   e. To discuss the importance and evolution of the free press in colonial America

8. In Line 9, what does *"precarious"* mean?

   a. Illegal
   b. Derivative
   c. Capricious
   d. Unsteady
   e. Pedantic

9. The passage mentions all of the following newspapers EXCEPT:

   a. New England Courant
   b. The Philadelphia Times
   c. Public Occurrences Both Foreign and Domestic
   d. The Mercury
   e. The Boston News-Letter

10. According to the passage, why did official censorship end?

   a. Due to the increased availability of printed material, the government could no longer review all published material
   b. The government benefited financially from the fees that were generated by licensing printing presses
   c. The State Church relaxed its moral standards regarding published materials
   d. Royalist and clerical writers staged a coup in 1695
   e. The high literacy rate increased the demand for printed materials

11. In Line 35, what does *"impunity"* mean?

   a. Government sanctions
   b. Little or no supervision
   c. Wanton abandon
   d. Religious or spiritual fervor
   e. Exemption from punishment

12. Which of the following is NOT true about the Peter Zenger case?

   a. He was a New York publisher
   b. His original attorneys were deprived of their law licenses
   c. The final verdict was in favor of Zenger
   d. He was arrested in 1735 for criticizing the church
   e. The case was tried in King George's province

13. According to the author, what role did literacy have in the American Revolution?

    a.   It allowed people to document the events in writing for future generations
    b.   It allowed people to follow and understand the significance of political arguments
    c.   It allowed the church and government to influence people by publishing propaganda
    d.   It had little influence because people could not afford to buy printed matter
    e.   It allowed people to read the ballot when they voted in national elections

Passage 2

The most dangerous fault that any food can have is that it shall be tainted, or spoiled, or smell bad. Spoiling, or tainting, means that the food has become infected by some germs of putrefaction, generally bacteria or molds. It is the poisons, called ptomaines, or the toxins produced by these germs which cause the serious disturbances in the stomach, and not either the amount or the kind of food itself. Even a regular "gorge" upon early apples or watermelon or cake or ice cream will not give you half so bad, nor so dangerous, colic as one little piece of tainted meat or fish or egg, or one cupful of dirty milk, or a single helping of cabbage or tomatoes that have begun to spoil, or of jam made out of spoiled berries or other fruit.

8

This spoiling can be prevented by strict cleanliness in handling foods, especially milk, meat, and fruit; by keeping foods screened from dust and flies; and by keeping them cool with ice in summer time, thus checking the growth of these "spoiling" germs. The refrigerator in the kitchen prevents colic or diarrhea, ice in hot weather is one of the necessaries of life. Smell every piece of food to be eaten, in the kitchen before it is cooked, if possible; but if not, at the table avoid everything that has an unpleasant odor, or tastes odd, and you will avoid two-thirds of the colic, diarrhea, and bilious attacks which are so often supposed to be due to eating too much.

15

14. According to the passage, which of the following is NOT considered a source of dangerous food spoilage?

    a.   Moldy egg
    b.   Unclean milk
    c.   Rotting cabbage
    d.   Unripe fruit
    e.   Jam made from rotting berries

15. In Line 2, what does "*putrefaction*" mean?

    a.   Vile
    b.   Colitis
    c.   Contamination
    d.   Reproduction
    e.   Disintegration

16. According to the passage, which of the following is NOT an effective way to prevent food spoilage?

    a.   Avoiding food with unpleasant smells
    b.   Avoiding raw meat
    c.   Refrigerating milk, meat, and fruit
    d.   Protecting food from flies and dust
    e.   Extreme cleanliness while handling perishable foods

Directions: *For each question in this section, select the answer choice that means the exact OPPOSITE of the bold-faced word.*

17. **ORTHODOX**:

   a. Ethereal
   b. Forthright
   c. Spiritual
   d. Innovative
   e. Conformist

18. **INTERMINABLE:**

   a. Finite
   b. Incessant
   c. Itinerant
   d. Protracted
   e. Burgeoning

19. **DECAMP**:

   a. Glamorize
   b. Crave
   c. Approach
   d. Abandon
   e. Vilify

20. **PERIPATETIC**:

   a. Clear
   b. Wise
   c. Soiled
   d. Laconic
   e. Stationary

21. **HECTOR**:

   a. Solitary
   b. Innocent
   c. Tyro
   d. Encourage
   e. Fulsome

22. **FETTER**:

   a. Release
   b. Restrain
   c. Elevate
   d. Diminish
   e. Confuse

23. **FOIBLE**:

   a. Filial
   b. Strength
   c. Rancor
   d. Guile
   e. Nascent

24. **ASCETIC**:

    a. Frugal
    b. Emotional
    c. Fledgling
    d. Riotous
    e. Dauntless

Directions: *Each of the following questions includes a pair of words or phrases that are separated by a colon. Likewise, each of the five answer choices also includes a pair of word or phases that are presented in a similar manner. Select the answer choice in which the* <u>relationship</u> *between the two words is most similar to that of the original pair.*

25. **MIRACULOUS: EXTRASENSORY::**

    a. Sensual: fluidity
    b. Minor: scale
    c. Musical: theatre
    d. Hardware: software
    e. Pragmatic: sober

26. **QUIESCENCE: CHAOS::**

    a. Frozen: melted
    b. Morning: daylight
    c. Season: spell
    d. Diamond: graphite
    e. Sage: mystic

27. **QUIDNUNC: BUSYBODY::**

    a. Chemistry: reactionary
    b. Solitude: camaraderie
    c. Platitude: uncommon
    d. Hirsute: bald
    e. Prophylactic: infection

28. **PROFESSOR: LECTURE::**

    a. Crossing guard: waiver
    b. Scientist: book
    c. Actor: revise
    d. Stenographer: type
    e. Server: wait staff

29. **HURRICANE: THUNDERSTORM::**

    a. Cacophony: deafness
    b. Street: intersection
    c. Circuit: keyboard
    d. Library: books
    e. Blindness: myopia

30. **WEDGE: SHOE::**

    a.   Opal: necklace
    b.   Carrot: vegetable
    c.   Shampoo: hair
    d.   Belt: leather
    e.   Miami: capital

Answer Key for Verbal Section 14

Sentence Completion

1. The word ironically means that the correct word means the opposite of what Jennifer hoped to accomplish; the best answer choice is D, repel.

2. The correct word means lacking, which is choice C, devoid.

3. The correct word is the opposite of athletic, which is choice D, sedentary.

4. The correct word means enhanced, which is choice C.

5. The correct word means excessive, or choice D.

6. The correct word is discretion, or choice C.

Reading Comprehension

7. Choice E is correct. The other options are either to broad or narrow in scope.

8. Choice D is correct. In context, precarious means uncertain or unsteady.

9. Choice B is correct. All of the other answer choices are mentioned in the passage.

10. Choice A is correct. The answer is presented in Lines 26 – 29.

11. Choice E is correct. In context, impunity means exempt from punishment.

12. Choice D is correct. He was arrested for criticizing the administration, not the church. The other answer choices are all mention in Lines 40 – 46.

13. Choice B is correct. The answer is presented in Lincs 49 – 50.

14. Choice D is correct. The answer is stated in Lines 4 – 7.

15. Choice E is correct. In context, *putrefaction* means disintegration.

16. Choice B is correct. The other answer choices are presented in Lines 9 - 14.

Antonym

17. Orthodox means conventional or traditional, which is the opposite of innovative. Choice D is correct.

18. Interminable means endless, which is the opposite of finite. Choice A is correct.

19. Decamp means to escape or flee, which is the opposite of approach. Choice C is correct.

20. Peripatetic means roaming or nomadic, which is the opposite of stationary. Choice E is correct.

21. Hector means to bully or harass, which is the opposite of encourage. Choice D is correct.

22. Fetter means to bind or restrain, which is the opposite of release. Choice A is correct.

23. A foible is a fault or shortcoming, which is the opposite of a strength. Choice B is correct.

24. Ascetic means austere or abstinent, which is the opposite of riotous. Choice D is correct.

Analogy

25. The words are synonyms. Choice E is correct.

26. The words are antonyms. Choice A is correct.

27. The words are synonyms. Choice B is correct.

28. X does Y. Choice D is correct.

29. The first word is a more intense version of the second word. Choice E is correct.

30. The second word is an example of the first word. Choice B is correct.

Verbal Section 15:   30 minutes   30 questions

Directions: *For each question in this section, select the best answer from the choices given and fill the corresponding circle on the answer sheet.*

1. In a less _____ part of town, such _____ is a rarity.

    a.   chaotic - tranquility
    b.   prestigious - chicanery
    c.   sophisticated - notoriety
    d.   gregarious - duplicity
    e.   affluent - decadence

2. Jane was so _____ that she could not try on clothes in most tiny dressing rooms.

    a.   agoraphobic
    b.   bashful
    c.   claustrophobic
    d.   modest
    e.   conservative

3. Bank robbers are _____ for wearing clever disguises, which prevent them from being identified.

    a.   notorious
    b.   suspected
    c.   unseemly
    d.   sadistic
    e.   pliant

4. Although Sara tried to maintain her composure, she was clearly _____ by the horrific turn of events.

    a.   consumed
    b.   exonerated
    c.   devastated
    d.   aggrandized
    e.   expatriated

5. Although the two countries had declared a truce, their relationship continued to be _____.

    a.   sapient
    b.   terpsichorean
    c.   tractable
    d.   turbulent
    e.   convivial

6. After an extensive search for a new Corporate Treasurer, the selection committee's choice won the immediate _____ of the managers, although a few of them had _____ about her.

    a.   skepticism….apprehension
    b.   acclaim….reservations
    c.   ire…preconceptions
    d.   disapproval…repercussions
    e.   approval…..disagreements

Passage 1

Until the thirteenth century, the juggling profession was a lucrative one in most European cities. There was no public or private feast of any importance without the profession being represented. Jugglers were the principal attraction at the Cours Plénières, and, according to the testimony of one of their members, they frequently retired from business loaded with presents, such as riding-horses, carriage-horses, jewels, cloaks, fur robes, clothing of violet or scarlet cloth, and, above all, with large sums of money.

6

Jugglers are also the subject of many noble stories, both veracious and fanciful. Before the battle of Hastings, Norman Taillefer was said to have advanced alone on horseback between the two armies about to commence the engagement, and drew off the attention of the English by singing them the Song of Roland. He then began juggling, and taking his lance by the hilt, he threw it into the air and caught it by the point as it fell; then, drawing his sword, he spun it several times over his head, and caught it in a similar way as it fell. After these skilful exercises, during which the enemy were gaping in mute astonishment, he forced his charger through the English ranks, and caused great havoc before he fell, positively riddled with wounds.

14

Notwithstanding this noble instance, not to belie the old proverb, jugglers were never received into the order of knighthood. They were, after a time, as much abused as they had before been extolled. Their licentious lives reflected itself in their obscene language. Their pantomimes, like their songs, showed that they were the votaries of the lowest vices. The lower orders laughed at their coarseness, and were amused at their juggleries; but the nobility were disgusted with them, and they were absolutely excluded from the presence of ladies and girls in the châteaux and houses of the bourgeoisie. The clergy, and St. Bernard especially, denounced them in one of his sermons written in the middle of the twelfth century: "A man fond of jugglers will soon enough possess a wife whose name is Poverty. If it happens that the tricks of jugglers are forced upon your notice, endeavor to avoid them, and think of other things. The tricks of jugglers never please God."

24

Thus, throughout this period, jugglers wandered about the country with their trained animals nearly starved; they were half naked, and were often without anything on their heads, without coats, without shoes, and always without money. The lower orders welcomed them, and continued to admire and idolize them for their clever tricks, but the bourgeois class, following the example of the nobility, turned their backs upon them. In 1345 Guillaume de Gourmont, Provost of Paris, forbade their singing or relating obscene stories, under penalty of fine and imprisonment. Thus, by 1350, the lucrative days of juggling in France were all but forgotten.

30

7. Which of the following is the main point of the passage?

    a. Jugglers were the most highly compensated street entertainers in thirteenth century Europe
    b. Jugglers, although talented, were not expert swordsmen
    c. The clergy took a dim view of jugglers in thirteenth century Europe
    d. Jugglers were never respected by the bourgeois class
    e. In the thirteenth century, jugglers descended from an exalted social position to one of mockery and contempt

8. In Line 7, what does "*veracious*" mean?

    a. Dull
    b. Audacious
    c. Fallacious
    d. Truthful
    e. Objective

9. Norman Taillefer did all of the following EXCEPT:

    a. Riddled the English army with wounds
    b. Forced his charger through the English ranks
    c. Diverted the English by singing the Song of Roland
    d. Threw his lance in the air and caught it by the point as it fell
    e. Rode alone on horseback between the two armies

10. In Line 15, what does "*belie*" mean?

    a. Affirm
    b. Contradict
    c. Justify
    d. Exacerbate
    e. Extol

11. Which of the following best conveys St. Bernard's impression of the jugglers?

    a. Audacious
    b. Baneful
    c. Amusing
    d. Melodious
    e. Debauched

12. According to the author, which of the following groups always admired the jugglers?

    a. The French army
    b. The bourgeois class
    c. The lower orders
    d. The ladies and girls in the châteaux
    e. The nobility

Passage 2

In English legal practice, the written statement given to a barrister to form the basis of his case is called a brief; it was probably so-called because it was the first copy of the original writ. When a barrister assumes the responsibility for a case when it comes into the court, all of the preliminary work, such as the drawing up of the case, serving papers, and marshalling evidence, is performed by a solicitor, so that a brief contains a concise summary of the case that the counsel has to plead, with all material facts in chronological order, and frequently such observations thereon as the solicitor may think fit to make, the names of witnesses, with the "proofs," that is, the nature of the evidence which each witness is ready to give, if called upon. The brief may also contain suggestions for the use of counsel when cross-examining witnesses called by the other side.

10

Accompanying the brief may be copies of the pleadings and of all documents material to the case. The brief is always endorsed with the title of the court in which the action is to be tried, with the title of the action, and the names of the counsel and of the solicitor who delivers the brief. Counsel's fee is also marked. The delivery of a brief to counsel gives him authority to act for his client in all matters which the litigation involves. The result of the action is noted on the brief by counsel, or if the action is compromised, the terms of the compromise are endorsed on each brief and signed by the leading counsel on the opposite side. In Scotland a brief is called a memorial.

18

In the United States the word has, to a certain extent, a different meaning, a brief in its English sense not being required, for the American attorney exercises all the functions distributed in England between barristers and solicitors. A lawyer sometimes prepares for his own use what is called a "trial brief" for use at the trial. This corresponds in all essential particulars with the "brief" prepared by the solicitor in England for the use of counsel. But the more distinctive use of the term in America is in the case of the brief "in error or appeal," before an appellate court. This is a written or printed document, varying according to circumstances, but embodying the argument on the question affected. Most of the appellate courts require the filing of printed briefs for the use of the court and opposing counsel at a time designated for each side before hearing.

28

In the rules of the United States Supreme Court and circuit courts of appeals, the brief is required to contain a concise statement of the case, a specification of errors relied on, including the substance of evidence, the admission or rejection of which is to be reviewed, or any extract from a charge excepted to, and an argument exhibiting clearly the points of law or fact to be discussed. This form of brief, it may be added, is also adopted for use at the trial in certain states of the Union which require printed briefs to be delivered to the court.

35

The "brief-bag," in which counsel's papers are carried to and from court, now forms an integral part of a barrister's outfit, but in the early part of the 19th century the possession of a brief-bag was strictly confined to those who had received one from a king's counsel. King's counsel were then few in number, were considered officers of the court, and had a salary of £40 a year, with a supply of paper, pens and purple bags. These bags they distributed among rising juniors of their acquaintance, whose bundles of briefs were getting inconveniently large to be carried in their hands. These perquisites were abolished in 1830. English brief-bags are now either blue or red. Blue bags are those with which barristers provide themselves when first called, and it is a breach of etiquette to let this bag be visible in court. The only brief-bag allowed to be placed on the desks is the red bag, which by English legal etiquette is given by a leading counsel to a junior who has been useful to him in some important case.

46

13. What is the main point of the passage?

     a.   To compare and contrast a legal brief in England to one in the United States
     b.   To explain the original of "brief bags" in the British legal system
     c.   To differentiate among solicitors, barristers, and attorneys
     d.   To explain the legal definition of a brief
     e.   To compare and contrast the British and American legal systems

14. According to the passage, a brief in England is endorsed with all of the following EXCEPT:

     a.   Title of the court
     b.   Title of the action
     c.   Names of the counsel and solicitor
     d.   Name of the district or circuit judge presiding
     e.   Counsel fee

15. According to the passage, what is a brief "in error or appeal"?

     a.   A written document submitted by an attorney to the U.S. court of appeals
     b.   A written document submitted by a U.S. attorney to the opposing counsel
     c.   A written document submitted by a solicitor in England to the opposing counsel
     d.   A written document submitted by a barrister in England to the opposing counsel
     e.   A written response from the U.S. Supreme Court in response to an attorney's "trial brief"

16. In Line 41, what does "*perquisites*" mean?

     a.   Accoutrements
     b.   Privileges
     c.   Briefcases
     d.   Professional attire
     e.   Obligations

17. All of the following are true about "brief bags" EXCEPT:

     a.   They are used in England to carry counsel's papers to and from court
     b.   In the 19th century, they were only distributed to a select few by the King's counsel
     c.   They are either red or blue
     d.   It is a breach of etiquette for a blue bag to be visible in court
     e.   In England, they now form an integral part of a solicitor's outfit

Directions: *For each question in this section, select the answer choice that means the exact OPPOSITE of the bold-faced word.*

116

18. **ABERRATION**:

    a. Eccentric
    b. Normal
    c. Diurnal
    d. Wicked
    e. Superior

19. **STULTIFY**:

    a. Assuage
    b. Vilify
    c. Vindicate
    d. Accentuate
    e. Meander

20. **PROLIX**:

    a. Concise
    b. Dim
    c. Unassuming
    d. Barren
    e. Forthright

21. **ESPOUSE**:

    a. Suggest
    b. Adopt
    c. Oppose
    d. Proclaim
    e. Renege

22. **PILLORY**:

    a. Discredit
    b. Humiliate
    c. Restore
    d. Knell
    e. Commend

23. **WRAITH**:

    a. Human
    b. Anger
    c. Subterfuge
    d. Idealism
    e. Materialistic

24. **PRECURSOR**:

    a. Predecessor
    b. Descendant
    c. Ancestor
    d. Antecedent
    e. Patriarch

25. **DOG: CANINE::**

    a. Cat: feline
    b. Bird: aviary
    c. Livestock: farm
    d. Horse: equestrian
    e. Chicken: poultry

26. **PANDEMIC: ILLNESS::**

    a. Ideal: religion
    b. Metastasis: cancer
    c. Protest: riot
    d. Norm: trend
    e. Wiring: circuit

27. **CILANTRO: SPICE::**

    a. Dairy: ice cream
    b. Socks: shoes
    c. Scarf: accessory
    d. Telephone: internet
    e. Door: house

28. **NETWORK: CIRCUITRY::**

    a. Vegetarian: meat
    b. Automobile: car
    c. Ambivalent: decision
    d. Animal: mineral
    e. Daughter: son

29. **ELECTRICAL: MANUAL::**

    a. Advanced: introductory
    b. Militia: army
    c. Sword: sheath
    d. Engine: piston
    e. Ink: pen

30. **RECOVERY: CONVALESCENCE::**

    a. Opinion: consensus
    b. Warrant: deny
    c. Desperation: tranquility
    d. Pregnancy: gestation
    e. Admission: matriculation

Answer Key for Verbal Section 15

Sentence Completion

1. The correct words are synonyms; Choice E is correct.

2. The correct word means fearful of small spaces, or choice C, claustrophobic.

3. The correct word means well-known, which is choice A, notorious.

4. The correct answer means emotionally upset, which is choice C, devastated.

5. The correct answer means non-peaceful, which is choice D, turbulent.

6. In this sentence, the word won tells us that the first word is positive. Likewise, the word *although* indicates that the second word is negative. The correct choice is B.

Reading Comprehension

7. Choice E is correct. The remaining choices are not the correct scope to be the main idea of the passage.

8. Choice D is correct. In this context, veracious means truthful.

9. Choice A is correct. All of the other choices are mentioned in the third paragraph (Lines 8 – 13).

10. Choice B is correct. In this context, belie means contradict.

11. Choice E is correct. St. Bernard thought the jugglers were debauched or amoral (Lines 20 – 23).

12. Choice C is correct. The answer is presented in Line 27.

13. Choice A is correct. The other answer choices are too broad or narrow in scope.

14. Choice D is correct. The other answer choices are all mentioned in Lines 11 – 14.

15. Choice A is correct. The answer is presented in Lines 23 – 25.

16. Choice B is correct. In context, perquisites means privileges.

17. Choice E is correct. All of the other answer choices are presented in Lines 36 – 45.

Antonym

18. Aberration means deviation or anomaly, which is the opposite of normal. Choice B is correct.

19. Stultify means to reduce or dampen, which is the opposite of accentuate. Choice D is correct.

20. Prolix means wordy or verbose, which is the opposite of concise. Choice A is correct.

21. Espouse means to support or advocate, which is the opposite of oppose. Choice C is correct.

22. Pillory means to denounce or deride, which is the opposite of commend. Choice E is correct.

23. Wraith means a phantom or apparition, which is the opposite of human. Choice A is correct.

24. Precursor means forerunner or pioneer, which is the opposite of descendant. Choice B is correct.

Analogy

25. The second word is an adjective that describes the first word. Choice A is correct.

26. The first word is a more intense version of the second word. Choice B is correct.

27. The first word is an example of the second word. Choice C is correct.

28. The words are synonyms. Choice B is correct.

29. The words are antonyms. Choice A is correct.

30. The words are synonyms. Choice D is correct.

Verbal Section 16:   30 minutes   30 questions

Directions: For each question in this section, select the best answer from the choices given and fill the corresponding circle on the answer sheet.

1. Rather than participate in a fight, Sara preferred to assume a position of _____.

    a.   mediator
    b.   neutrality
    c.   arbiter
    d.   clarity
    e.   despot

2. In a less _____ society, liability insurance would be less of a necessity.

    a.   decadent
    b.   disreputable
    c.   precarious
    d.   litigious
    e.   colloquial

3. True scholars are not _____ by money or fame, but by their devotion to their fields of study.

    a.   distracted
    b.   inveighed
    c.   consoled
    d.   motivated
    e.   tempted

4. David's _____ past, including several arrests for fraud, _____ his chances at a management job.

    a.   humiliating - perpetrated
    b.   criminal - ruined
    c.   duplicitous - mitigated
    d.   lackluster - torpedoed
    e.   narcissistic – minimized

5. By failing to keep his word, Jeremy _____ the trust his parents had placed in him.

    a.   augmented
    b.   exacerbated
    c.   eroded
    d.   dispatched
    e.   recapitulated

6. The best plans are _____ in their simplicity.

    a.   erratic
    b.   coveted
    c.   embellished
    d.   elegant
    e.   authoritative

The origin of the corset is lost in remote antiquity. The figures of the early Egyptian women show clearly an artificial shape of the waist produced by some style of corset. A similar style of dress must also have prevailed among the ancient Jewish maidens; for Isaiah, in calling upon the women to put away their personal adornments, says: "Instead of a girdle there shall be a rent, and instead of a stomacher (corset) a girdle of sackcloth." Homer also tells us of the cestus of Venus, which was borrowed by the haughty Juno with a view to increasing her personal attractions, that Jupiter might be a more tractable and orderly husband. Coming down to the later times, we find the corset was used in France and England as early as the 12th century.

8

The most extensive and extreme use of the corset occurred in the 16th century, during the reign of Catherine de Medici of France and Queen Elizabeth of England. With Catherine de Medici a thirteen-inch waist measurement was considered the standard of fashion, while a thick waist was an abomination. No lady could consider her figure of proper shape unless she could span her waist with her two hands. To produce this result a strong rigid corset was worn night and day until the waist was laced down to the required size. Then over this corset was placed a steel apparatus called a corset-cover, which reached from the hip to the throat, and produced a rigid figure over which the dress would fit with perfect smoothness.

16

During the 18th century corsets were largely made from a species of leather known as "Bend," which was not unlike that used for shoe soles, and measured nearly a quarter of an inch in thickness. About the time of the French Revolution, a reaction set in against tight lacing, and for a time there was a return to the early classical Greek costume. This style of dress prevailed, with various modifications, until about 1810 when corsets and tight lacing again returned with threefold fury. Buchan, a prominent writer of this period, says that it was by no means uncommon to see "a mother lay her daughter down upon the carpet, and, placing her foot upon her back, break half a dozen laces in tightening her stays."

24

It is reserved to our own time to demonstrate that corsets and tight lacing do not necessarily go hand in hand. Distortion and feebleness are not beauty. A proper proportion should exist between the size of the waist and the breadth of the shoulders and hips, and if the waist is diminished below this proportion, it suggests disproportion and invalidism rather than grace and beauty.

29

The perfect corset is one which possesses just that degree of rigidity which will prevent it from wrinkling, but will at the same time allow freedom in the bending and twisting of the body. Corsets boned with whalebone, horn or steel are necessarily stiff, rigid and uncomfortable. After a few days wear, the bones or steels become bent and set in position, or, as more frequently happens, they break and cause injury or discomfort to the wearer.

34

About seven years ago, an article was discovered for the stiffening of corsets, which has revolutionized the corset industry of the world. This article is manufactured from the natural fibers of the Mexican Ixtle plant, and is known as Coraline. It consists of straight, stiff fibers like bristles bound together into a cord by being wound with two strands of thread passing in opposite directions. This produces an elastic fiber intermediate in stiffness between twine and whalebone. It cannot break, but it possesses all the stiffness and flexibility necessary to hold the corset in shape and prevent its wrinkling.

41

We congratulate the ladies of today upon the advantages they enjoy over their sisters of two centuries ago, in the forms and the graceful and easy curves of the corsets now made as compared with those of former times.

44

7. What is the main point of the passage?

   a.   To argue against the use of corsets for medical reasons
   b.   To justify the use of Coraline in the manufacture of corsets
   c.   To explain the historical preference for an artificially small waistline
   d.   To mock the ancient standard of beauty in European culture
   e.   To discuss the historical evolution of the corset in women's fashion

8. In Line 5, what is a "*cestus*"?

   a.   Dress
   b.   Wig
   c.   Girdle
   d.   Stocking
   e.   Wardrobe

9. The author mentions the use of corsets in all countries EXCEPT:

    a. Egypt
    b. Greece
    c. France
    d. Italy
    e. England

10. In Line 11, what does "*abomination*" mean?

    a. Disgrace
    b. Obesity
    c. Distress
    d. Menacing
    e. Uncouth

11. From Lines 9 - 15 in the passage, what we can conclude about Catherine de Medici?

    a. She was a fashion icon in Italy
    b. She used a corset-cover to attain a thirteen-inch waist
    c. She abolished the use of corsets due to their extreme discomfort
    d. She imported special leather called Bend to make her corsets
    e. She was a strong enthusiast of classic Greek costume

12. According to the author, all of the following are true EXCEPT:

    a. Corsets boned with whalebone are stiff, but comfortable
    b. Distortion and feebleness are not beauty
    c. The perfect corset prevents wrinkling, but allows the body to twist and bend
    d. Corsets and tight lacing do not necessarily go hand in hand
    e. An artificially small waist suggests disproportion and invalidism

13. Which of the following is NOT true about Coraline?

    a. Coraline is manufactured from the natural fibers of the Ixtle plant
    b. Coraline cannot break
    c. Coraline is an elastic fiber that is stiffer than whalebone
    d. Coraline revolutionized the corset industry
    e. Coraline possesses the required stiffness and flexibility to hold a corset in shape.

14. What is the tone of the passage?

    a. Ambivalent
    b. Aghast
    c. Lackadaisical
    d. Factual
    e. Incredulous

Directions: *For each question in this section, select the answer choice that means the exact OPPOSITE of the bold-faced word.*

15. **ANCILLARY**:

 a. Additional
 b. Prerequisite
 c. Outside
 d. Primary
 e. Miraculous

16. **ASPERITY**:

 a. Wealth
 b. Destitution
 c. Austerity
 d. Bland
 e. Softness

17. **TRENCHANT**:

 a. Mild
 b. Shallow
 c. Impenetrable
 d. Variable
 e. Restless

18. **ESOTERIC**:

 a. Abstruse
 b. Illuminating
 c. Regulatory
 d. Disreputable
 e. Mysterious

19. **EQUITY**:

 a. Impartial
 b. Leverage
 c. Bias
 d. Poverty
 e. Vacuum

20. **ERSATZ**:

 a. Unusual
 b. Mundane
 c. Cumbersome
 d. Overwhelming
 e. Genuine

21. **TURGID**:

 a. Hard
 b. Flexible
 c. Solemn
 d. Modest
 e. Bland

22. **CIRCUMSPECT**:

   a. Hasty
   b. Guarded
   c. Direct
   d. Undecided
   e. Surrounded

23. **PERPLEX**:

   a. Stymie
   b. Clarify
   c. Stupefy
   d. Ignore
   e. Dread

Directions: *Each of the following questions includes a pair of words or phrases that are separated by a colon. Likewise, each of the five answer choices also includes a pair of word or phases that are presented in a similar manner. Select the answer choice in which the* relationship *between the two words is most similar to that of the original pair.*

24. **PRECIPITATE: DELAY::**

   a. Supplement: adequacy
   b. Minor: percentage
   c. Miserable: decry
   d. Renaissance: resurgence
   e. Colossal: tiny

25. **PEARLS: CULTURED::**

   a. Mahogany: bedposts
   b. Steel: stainless
   c. Wisdom: knowledge
   d. Criterion: checklist
   e. Recover: diagnosis

26. **EXTINCT: ENDANGERED::**

   a. Incarceration: conviction
   b. Apathy: litigation
   c. Ignorance: proliferation
   d. Resurgence: capitulation
   e. Resonance: hydrogenation

27. **SEASON: SPRING::**

   a. Holiday: commemorate
   b. Vacation: summer
   c. Dinner: evening
   d. Grade: sophomore
   e. Leap Year: month

28. **CLANDESTINE: SURREPITIOUS::**

    a.   Stealth: intensity
    b.   Expatriate: documentation
    c.   Majority: consensus
    d.   Beleaguered: blithe
    e.   Eradication: extirpation

29. **EBONY: WHITE::**

    a.   Hue: intensity
    b.   Auburn: red
    c.   Color: clarity
    d.   Egocentric: altruistic
    e.   Explosive: volatile

30. **EMBARGO: PROHIBITION::**

    a.   Assembly: conflagration
    b.   Assiduous: lackluster
    c.   Bane: spoil
    d.   Permanent: temporary
    e.   Inferno: dysentery

Answer Key for Verbal Section 16

Sentence Completion

1. The correct answer means unbiased, which is choice B, neutrality.

2. The correct word means eager to sue, which is choice D, litigious.

3. The correct answer means inspired, which is choice D, motivated.

4. The two words are both negative; the best answer is choice B, criminal – ruined.

5. The correct word means destroyed, which is choice C, eroded.

6. The correct answer is the opposite of simple, which is choice D, elegant.

Passage-Based Reading

7. Choice E is correct. The main point of the passage is to discuss the historical evolution of the corset in women's fashion.

8. Choice C is correct. In context, cestus means girdle.

9. Choice D is correct. All of the other countries are mentioned in the passage.

10. Choice A is correct. In context, abomination means disgrace.

11. Choice B is correct. The answer is stated directly in Lines 9 – 15.

12. Choice A is correct. All of the other answer choices are mentioned in the passage.

13. Choice C is correct. All of the other answer choices are mentioned in Lines 35 – 40.

14. Choice D is correct. The author presents his case in a clear and factual manner.

Antonym

15. Ancillary means auxiliary or supplementary, which is the opposite of primary. Choice D is correct.

16. Asperity means roughness, which is the opposite of softness. Choice E is correct.

17. Trenchant means sharp or incisive, which is the opposite of mild. Choice A is correct.

18. Esoteric means obscure or cryptic, which is the opposite of illuminating. Choice B is correct.

19. Equity means fair and impartial, which is the opposite of bias. Choice C is correct.

20. Ersatz is fake or artificial, which is the opposite of genuine. Choice E is correct.

21. Turgid means pompous or self-important, which is the opposite of modest. Choice D is correct.

22. Circumspect means cautious or prudent, which is the opposite of hasty. Choice A is correct.

23. Perplex means to confuse or baffle, which is the opposite of clarify. Choice B is correct.

Analogy

24. The words are antonyms. Choice E is correct.

25. The second word is an adjective that describes the first word. Choice B is correct.

26. The first word is the consequence of the second word. Choice A is correct.

27. The second word is an example of the first word. Choice D is correct.

28. The words are synonyms. Choice E is correct.

29. The words are antonyms. Choice D is correct.

30. The words are synonyms. Choice C is correct.

Verbal Section 17: 30 minutes   30 questions

Directions: For each question in this section, select the best answer from the choices given and fill the corresponding circle on the answer sheet.

1. Although the physician had _____ credentials, the patient was convinced he was a(n) _____.

     a.   dubious - maverick
     b.   impressive - humanitarian
     c.   contradictory - fraud
     d.   prestigious - charlatan
     e.   mediocre- advocate

2. The _____ woman actually believed that she was Joan of Arc, despite all evidence to the contrary.

     a.   innovative
     b.   delusional
     c.   provocative
     d.   vainglorious
     e.   temerarious

3. The _____ citizens angrily protested the tax increase.

     a.   multifarious
     b.   forlorn
     c.   reprehensible
     d.   misguided
     e.   irate

4. After years of dealing with a(n) _____ boss, who favored rumor and innuendo to direct conversation, Joan found her new boss's _____ to be downright refreshing.

     a.   non-communicative - ego
     b.   evasive - candor
     c.   dishonest - ardor
     d.   talkative - timidity
     e.   flippant – altruistic

5. Alicia's efforts to sound sophisticated, including her tendency to adopt a British accent, merely made her seem _____.

     a.   disingenuous
     b.   parsimonious
     c.   multifarious
     d.   fastidious
     e.   plebian

6. After missing three car payments, Jason knew that repossession was _____.

     a.   contraindicated
     b.   diffident
     c.   avoidable
     d.   disdainful
     e.   imminent

Directions: *The passage below is followed by questions based on its content. Answer the questions, based on what is stated or implied in the passage and any introductory material that may be provided.*

Despite the worldwide progress of the women's rights movement, women in all nations continue to face an uphill battle to achieve an equal measure of legislative representation. Although the percentage of women in political office differs from country to country, current research indicates that their likelihood of being elected depends on three factors: quotas, party ideology and districting.

5

Some state governments and political parties facilitate female legislative representation by using quotas, or affirmative action, to guarantee that a certain percentage of women are represented in the legislature. In India, for example, the ruling Congress party has mandated that 15 percent of its candidates in state elections be women. Likewise, political parties in Venezuela, Sweden, Norway and Germany maintain similar requirements. Quotas for women have a greater impact in the Proportional Representation (PR) system, in which seats in parliament are allotted in proportion to the votes each party receives, which creates an incentive for a political party to broaden its appeal to the public by including more women on its list of candidates. As a result of these mandated quotas, twice as high a proportion of women are elected to public office in PR systems than in Single Member District (SMD) electoral systems, in which the electorate typically favors the incumbent, who is usually male.

16

Existing poll data suggest that party ideology, particularly leftism, may also facilitate female legislative representation. In European countries with a strong Marxist-Socialist or Communist tradition, leftist parties take the lead in nominating and electing women. Although European leftist parties have always placed a greater emphasis on equality, after surviving numerous political, economic, and religious upheavals, other European countries have also become receptive to philosophies or ideologies that promote social justice. Ironically, although leftist parties took the lead in nominating women to political office, their historical performance indicates that they elect only slightly more women than parties on the right. This overall gain for women may be attributed to the party's fear of losing an electoral advantage.

25

Districting may also help women obtain greater legislative representation. Recent research suggests that women are uncomfortable with the adversarial political culture fostered by the single-member district systems, in which parties do not have to negotiate with each other to implement their legislative programs. In such a highly competitive environment, candidates often resort to using negative campaigns against each other. Historically, women have lacked the confidence and desire to participate in the gladiatorial contests that characterize these elections. Even if they triumph, women are likely to be adversely judged because such confrontational behavior contradicts the underlying social expectations that they be peacemakers, rather than gladiators. Instead, women tend to prefer the PR system, which fosters a consensus-seeking political culture in which parties must negotiate to pass legislation. Women tend to thrive in this type of interactive environment, in which they can use their communications skills and interpersonal strengths the same way they do in their family relationships.

37

Quotas, party ideology, and districting are only three of the complex factors that help to facilitate female representation in legislatures across the globe. Ironically, although women comprise fifty percent of every country's population, scholars have only recently begun to examine the different electoral arrangements on a worldwide basis, to determine the implications for women in their quest for political office. As the research continues, the results will inevitably provide women with a greater voice in government, where they can bring attention to critical issues that have been ignored by male-dominated legislatures. An influx of feminine dignity and intelligence will unquestionably benefit the governments in which women participate and the communities in which they live.

46

7. What is the main idea of the passage?

    a. Socialist countries are more committed to equality than democracies.
    b. Quotas, party ideology and districting have dramatically improved female representation in government.
    c. Although women are under-represented in most legislatures, they have much to offer the political process.
    d. Equality for women will never be achieved in legislative representation.
    e. Women are temperamentally unsuited for an adversarial political culture.

8. According to the author, what countries use affirmative action to guarantee a certain percentage of women in the legislature?

    a. Sweden, Germany, Bolivia, India, Pakistan
    b. Venezuela, Germany, Sweden, Norway, Bolivia
    c. Bolivia, Venezuela, Sweden, India, Norway
    d. Pakistan, India, Norway, Germany, Venezuela
    e. India, Norway, Sweden, Germany, Venezuela

9. What reason does the author give to explain the higher percentage of women in the PR electoral system (SMD electoral system?

    a. countries that use the PR system are more committed to sexual equality.
    b. the PR system favors parties that champion social justice.
    c. the PR system favors incumbents, who are mostly women.
    d. the PR system creates an incentive for a party to broaden it appeal by electing women.
    e. The SMD system is ripe with corruption, which has turned most voters away.

10. According to the author, why do Socialist countries tend to have a higher percentage of women in the legislature?

    a. the party's fear of losing an electoral advantage
    b. women are less likely to accept bribes
    c. women outnumber men in Socialist countries
    d. women are wealthier and better educated in Socialist countries
    e. the party believes that women representatives are more easily manipulated than men

11. In Line 30, what does "*gladiatorial*" mean?

    a. effusive
    b. intrepid
    c. negotiable
    d. adversarial
    e. corrupt

12. According to the author, which of the following does NOT explain why women are uncomfortable with political campaigns?

    a. Lack of confidence
    b. Tend to be peacemakers
    c. Thrive in interactive environments
    d. Fear adverse judgments
    e. Poor educational credentials

13. The author's tone suggests that his attitude toward women in the legislature is:

    a. scornful
    b. apathetic
    c. enthusiastic
    d. pessimistic
    e. dismissive

14. The author cites all of the following as feminine strengths EXCEPT:

    a.   intelligence
    b.   strong analytical skills
    c.   good communication skills
    d.   peacemakers
    e.   dignity

Directions: *For each question in this section, select the answer choice that means the exact OPPOSITE of the bold-faced word.*

15. **NOMINAL**:

    a.   Original
    b.   Derivative
    c.   Actual
    d.   Anonymous
    e.   Unexpected

16. **OBLIQUE**:

    a.   Muscular
    b.   Circuitous
    c.   Opaque
    d.   Concave
    e.   Upright

17. **PLIABLE:**

    a.   Rigid
    b.   Supple
    c.   Essential
    d.   Original
    e.   Respectable

18. **DISPASSIONATE**:

    a.   Detached
    b.   Fiery
    c.   Unbiased
    d.   Insensitive
    e.   Obtuse

19. **COLLOQUIAL**:

    a.   Modern
    b.   Garish
    c.   Unexpected
    d.   Formal
    e.   Idiomatic

20. **AUTONOMY**:

    a. Self-sufficiency
    b. Confusion
    c. Reliance
    d. Generosity
    e. Sovereignty

21. **SUMMON**:

    a. Beckon
    b. Gather
    c. Arrest
    d. Notify
    e. Dismiss

22. **MALADROIT**:

    a. Evil
    b. Awkward
    c. Innocent
    d. Poised
    e. Gauche

23. **EGRESS**:

    a. Entrance
    b. Progress
    c. Relapse
    d. Compensate
    e. Digress

Directions: Each of the following questions includes a pair of words or phrases that are separated by a colon. Likewise, each of the five answer choices also includes a pair of word or phases that are presented in a similar manner. Select the answer choice in which the relationship between the two words is most similar to that of the original pair.

24. **MAINSTREAM: AVANT-GARDE::**

    a. Collaborative: mutual
    b. Perishable: preserved
    c. Monsoon: rain
    d. Democratic: president
    e. Independent: fierce

25. **QUINTESSENTIAL: ARCHETYPAL::**

    a. Preponderance: scanty
    b. Myth: proven
    c. Intact: unbroken
    d. Island: oceanic
    e. Collective: open

26. **CROISSANT: PASTRY::**

   a. Fish: ocean
   b. Doughnuts: sugar
   c. Bakery: dairy
   d. Cheddar: cheese
   e. Tire: rubber

27. **SCULPTOR: MOLD::**

   a. Hobbyist: model
   b. Collector: stamps
   c. Pen: easel
   d. Maitre d: wine
   e. Longshoreman: fish

28. **CRIMINAL: BEHAVE::**

   a. Stoic: cry
   b. Author: outline
   c. Poet: haiku
   d. Prosecutor: trial
   e. Decorator: sew

29. **FLAVOR: TASTELESS::**

   a. Hero: brave
   b. Droll: humorless
   c. Maritime: ocean
   d. Salt: sodium
   e. Bewilder: bamboozle

30. **OGRE: TROLL::**

   a. Yardstick: ungraded
   b. Wooden: awkward
   c. Kingdom: planet
   d. Corresponding: alternative
   e. Countenance: head

Answer Key for Verbal Section 17

Sentence Completion

1. The words will be opposites of each other; the correct choice is D, prestigious- charlatan.

2. The correct choice means mentally unbalanced or confused, which is choice B, delusional.

3. The correct answer is a synonym for angry, which is choice E, irate.

4. The two words are opposites; the first means indirect, while the second means honest. The correct answer choice is, B, evasive – candor.

5. The correct word means artificial or dishonest, which is choice A, disingenuous.

6. The correct word means soon, which is choice E, imminent.

Reading Comprehension

7. Choice C is correct. The other choices are too broad or narrow to be the main idea.

8. Choice E is correct. The answer countries are listed in Line 9 of the passage.

9. Choice D is correct. The answer is presented in Lines 11 –12 of the passage.

10. Choice A is correct. The answer is presented in Line 24 of the passage.

11. Choice D is correct. In this context, *gladiatorial* means adversarial.

12. Choice E is correct. The answer is presented in Lines 31 – 36 of the passage.

13. Choice C is correct. In the final paragraph, the author expressly states the benefits that women will bring to the legislature.

14. Choice B is correct. The passage includes all of the other answer choices.

Antonym

15. Nominal means supposed or ostensible, which is the opposite of actual. Choice C is correct.

16. Oblique means slanted or tilted, which is the opposite of upright. Choice E is correct.

17. Pliable means elastic or supple, which is the opposite of rigid. Choice A is correct.

18. Dispassionate means calm or cool, which is the opposite of fiery. Choice B is correct.

19. Colloquial means informal or slang, which is the opposite of formal. Choice D is correct.

20. Autonomy means independence, which is the opposite of reliance. Choice C is correct.

21. Summon means to call or beckon, which is the opposite of dismiss. Choice E is correct.

22. Maladroit means awkward or clumsy, which is the opposite of poised. Choice D is correct.

23. Egress means a way out, which is the opposite of an entrance. Choice A is correct.

Analogy

24. The words are antonyms. Choice B is correct.

25. The words are synonyms. Choice C is correct.

26. The first word is an example of the second word. Choice D is correct.

27. X does Y. Choice E is correct.

28. X does not show Y emotion/activity. Choice A is correct.

29. The words are antonyms. Choice B is correct.

30. The words are synonyms. Choice B is correct.

Quantitative Section 1: 28 questions   45 minutes

Each question has two quantities to be compared: one in Column A and one in Column B. Compare the quantities taking into consideration any other information given and choose
Answer A - if the quantity in Column A is greater
Answer B - if the quantity in Column B is greater
Answer C - if the two quantities are equal
Answer D - if the relationship cannot be determined without further information.

1. 700 college students were asked to name their favorite color. One hundred students said red, 225 said blue, 125 said green, and 50 students each said yellow, orange and white, respectively. The remaining students were undecided.

Column A	Column B
The % of students who were undecided	15%

2. Three workers can clean eighteen hotel rooms in one day.

Column A	Column B
The number of rooms eleven workers can clean in one day	66

3. On a snowy Sunday night, Sam and Joe decided to compare CD collections. Sam has 12 less than four times the number of CDs that Joe has.

Column A	Column B
62	The number of Joe's CDs

4. Jill's boyfriend asked her to bring four DVDs from her collection of eight to a weekend party.

Column A	Column B
1680	The number of different combinations

5. A rectangular box has a width of ½ foot, a length of 18 inches and a height of 2 feet.

Column A	Column B
3,000 cubic inches	The volume of the box (in cubic inches)

6. The difference between $(X + Y)$ and $(X - Y)$ is 12. XY is 90.

Column A	Column B
15	The smaller number

7. A retiree places $50,000 in a CD that pays an attractive rate of interest. She also places $75,000 in a second CD that pays an annual interest rate that is 3% lower than the first CD. The total return on the retiree's two CDs is $10,000.

Column A   **Column B**

The interest rate on the $50,000 CD   8%

Directions: *For each problem, decide which answer is the best of the choices given.*

8. $(1/36)(44 + 22)^2 =$

    a. 0.02776
    b. 0.1666
    c. 1.8333
    d. 120
    e. 121

9. If x + 7 is an even integer, the sum of the next three even integers is:

    a. 3x + 4
    b. 3(x +7)
    c. 3x + 28
    d. 3x + 33
    e. $(x + 7)^3$

10. If 4x + 9y = 55 and 2x + 7y = 11, what is the value of (x+y)/2?

    a. 4
    b. 7
    c. 9
    d. 11
    e. 22

11. Which of the following sets of numbers *cannot* represent the lengths of the sides of a right triangle?

    a. 10, 24, 26
    b. 3.7, 11.9, 12.5
    c. 9, 26, 31
    d. 4, 15, 15.5
    e. 15, 36, 39

12. If a square of side 9 and a circle of radius r have equal areas, what is the value of the radius, r (use π = 3.1416)?

    a. 5
    b. 6
    c. 9
    d. 12
    e. 18

13. The perimeter of a rectangle is 25x. If one side has a length of x/4, what is the area of the rectangle?

    a. $125x^2/16$
    b. $5x^2/2$
    c. $100x$
    d. $100x^2$
    e. $49x^2/8$

14. A line segment has endpoints of (6, 14) and (8, 21), What are the coordinates of its midpoint?

    a.   (7, 17)
    b.   (7, 17.5)
    c.   (6, 17)
    d.   (6, 17.5)
    e.   (17, 7)

15. What is the largest integer that will divide evenly into 63 and 117?

    a.   1
    b.   7
    c.   9
    d.   11
    e.   13

16. What is the product of (3/8)(4/5)(9/3)?

    a.   106/120
    b.   54/64
    c.   108/122
    d.   9/10
    e.   54/56

17. Two individual price reductions of 10% and 15% are equal to a single price reduction of:

    a.   12.5%
    b.   20%
    c.   24.5%
    d.   25%
    e.   27.5%

18. Sara is completely broke when she receives a $74 parking ticket. When Sara's brother gives her $125 for her birthday, she pays the ticket and buys $26 in gas. How much money does Sara have left?

    a. $25
    b. $26
    c. $51
    d. $99
    e. $101

19. How many positive integers less than 75 are evenly divisible by 3, 5 and 6?

    a.   1
    b.   2
    c.   3
    d.   4
    e.   5

20. Gina decides to save money by making her bridal outfit from scratch. She buys 5 yards of a beautiful silk fabric that costs $35 per yard. After studying her pattern, Gina concludes that she will need 6/4 yards of the fabric for her dress, 5/2 yards for her jacket, and 1/3 yard for her veil. How many yards of material will Gina have left over?

        a.   2/5
        b.   1/2
        c.   2/3
        d.   1
        e.   5/2

21. A buffet table contains 7 entrees, 3 soups and 2 specialty salads. The remaining ¼ of the items are desserts. What percent of the items on the buffet table are specialty salads?

        a.   3.125%
        b.   6.25%
        c.   12.5%
        d.   16.67%
        e.   20%

22. If it takes a robot thirty-six minutes to travel the 18 blocks between the police station and the fire house, how long will it take the same robot (in minutes), traveling at the same rate per block, to travel from the police station to the train station that is 64 blocks away?

        a.   10
        b.   32
        c.   128
        d.   648
        e.   2304

23. For three consecutive integers, three times the sum of the first and second is 27 more than twice the third. What is the smallest of these three integers?

        a.   6
        b.   7
        c.   8
        d.   9
        e.   11

24. Nathan is seven years older than his sister Claire, who is three years younger than Jayne, who is 28 years old. How old is Nathan?

        a.   22
        b.   25
        c.   28
        d.   29
        e.   32

25. The Big Red Boat and the Carnival Cruise Ship left Port Canaveral at the same time and sailed in opposite directions. If the Big Red Boat traveled 35 miles per hour slower than the Carnival Cruise Ship, and they were 490 miles apart after sailing for 10 hours, how fast was the Carnival Cruise Ship sailing (in miles per hour)?

    a.   7
    b.   15
    c.   40
    d.   42
    e.   50

Refer to the following tables for questions 26 – 28.

Number of Items Sold (in thousands)

	Macys	Dillard's
Clothes	425	550
Furniture	375	300
Jewelry	421	400

Total Sales (in millions)

	Clothes	Furniture	Jewelry
Macys	19.125	56.250	25.250
Dillard's	22.750	60.000	12.000

26. Which items sell for the twice as much at Macys than at Dillard's?

    a.   Clothes
    b.   Furniture
    c.   Jewelry
    d.   None
    e.   Cannot be determined from the information given

27. Which item commands the highest price per unit?

    a.   Furniture at Macys
    b.   Furniture at Dillard's
    c.   Clothes at Macys
    d.   Clothes at Dillard's
    e.   Jewelry at Dillard's

28. If both stores earn 35% profit on all jewelry sales, how much profit did Macy and Dillard's both earn from jewelry in the time period this table represents?

    a. $4,200,000
    b. $8,400,000
    c. $8,837,500
    d. $10,037,500
    e. $13,037,500

Answer Key for Quantitative Section 1

1. 700 – 100 – 225 – 125 – 50 – 50 – 50 = 100. 100/700 = 14.28% = **14% were undecided**. Choice B is correct.

2. We can solve this problem by using a proportion: 3/18 = 11/x, Solve for **x =66**. Choice C is correct.

3. Choice D is correct. We do not have enough information to determine how many CDs Joe has.

4. In this case, order does not matter. We can use the factorial formula to solve: 8! / {4!(8! - 4!)} = 8!/{(4!)(4!)} = (8 x 7 x 6 x 5 x 4 x 3 x 2 x 1) / {(4 x 3 x 2 x 1)(4 x 3 x 2 x 1)} = (8 x 7 x 6 x 5)/ (4 x 3 x 2 x 1) = 1680/24 = **70**. Choice A is correct.

5. V = L x W x H = 6 x 18 x 24 = **2,592 cubic inches**. Choice A is correct.

6. The easiest way to solve this problem is to try the value of the number in Column A in the equation XY = 90 and solve for the other number. When we do, we discover that (15)(6) = 90; the two numbers also satisfy the other equation (15 + 6) – (15 – 6) =12. Hence, the smaller number is **6**. Choice A is correct.
7. First, we must draw a table with the information that we know.

CD	Amount	Interest Rate	Total Return
First	$50,000	x	50,000x
Second	$75,000	x – 3	75,000(x – 3)
Total	125,000		10,000

Here, we are asked to determine the interest rate for one CD, based on the initial investment in each CD and the total rate of return. We can do this by writing an equation that represents the sum of the interest from both CDs. First, let's assign our variables. We will let x = the rate for the $50,000 CD. Therefore, the rate for the $75,000 CD = x - 3. Next, we can use these variables to write expressions for the total return for each CD. Finally, we can use these expressions to write an equation for the total return:

Return from $50,000 CD + Return from $75,000 CD = Total Return
50,000x + 75,000 (x - 0.03) = 10,000
50000x + 75000X – 2,250 = 10,000
125,000x = 12,250
x = 0.098 = **9.8%** = Interest Rate for $50,000 CD. Choice A is correct.

8. (1/36) $(44 + 22)^2$ = 1/36 $(66)^2$ = 4356/36 = **121**. Choice E is correct.

9. (x + 9) + (x + 11) + (x + 13) = **3x + 33**. Choice D is correct.

10. 4x + 9y = 55 and 2x + 7y = 11. After subtracting the two equations, we have 2x + 2y = 44, or x + y = 22, so (x + y) / 2 = **11**. Choice D is correct.

11. According to the Pythagorean theorem. *The squares of the two shorter sides MUST equal the square of the third side.* For these five answer choices, run through the calculations as quickly as you can. When you do, you will discover that they are all correct answer choices, except for choice C. If we square 9 and 26 and add those numbers together, they do NOT equal the square of 31. Since the question asks us to identify the *one incorrect answer*, we must choose C.

12. Area of square is 81, or S^2 Area of circle = πr^2 Thus, 81 = πr^2 · Radius r = the square root of $(81/\pi)$= 5.08 = **5**. Choice A is correct.

13. The perimeter 25x = sum of all 4 sides. Two of the sides are x/4 + x/4, or x/2. This means that the other two sides add up to 25x – x/2, or 50x-1x = 49x. One side, therefore, is 49x/2. Area = (x/4)(49x/2) = **$49x^2$/8**. Choice E is correct.

14. (6,14), (8, 21). Midpoint = (6+8)/2, (14 +21)/2 = 14/2, 35/2 = **7, 17.5** Choice B is correct.

15. The fastest way to solve this problem is to try each answer choice. Choice C is correct.

16. (3/8)(4/5)(9/3) = 108/120. Choice D is correct, **9/10**.

17. Two price reductions = 0.9 x 0.85 = 0.765, which is **24.5%.** Choice C is correct.

18. To answer this question, subtract the amount of money that Sara spent from the total amount she had available. 125 – 74 – 26 = **25.** Choice A is correct. The trap in this question is the inclusion of alternative

answer choices that match the answers you WOULD have gotten if you had subtracted incorrectly.

19. The question asks us to determine how positive integers less than 75 are divisible by 3, 5 and 6. First, we will list the integers that are evenly divisible by our largest number, which is 6: 6, 12, 18, 24, 30, 36, 42, 48, 54, 60, 66, 72. (Note: Because they are all multiples of 6, they are also divisible by 3.)

In this group, we must then select the numbers that are ALSO evenly divisible by 5, which are 30 and 60. Our correct answer is Choice B. There are **two** positive integers less than 75 that are divisible by 3, 5, and 6.

20. First, we must determine how much fabric Gina will need to sew her entire outfit, which is 6/4 + 5/2 + 1/3 yards. To add these fractions together, they must all have the same denominator. In this case, the least common denominator (which is evenly divisible by 2, 3, and 4) is 12, which makes our equation:

18/12 + 30/12 + 4/12 = 52/12 = 4- 4/12 yards = 4 -1/3 yards.   Now, we must determine how many yards of fabric Gina will have left over. If she has purchased 5 yards of the fabric, she will have 5 – 4- 1/3 = **2/3** yards left over. Choice C is correct.

As far as the price of the fabric ($35 per yard), you didn't need to know it. It's completely extraneous information.

21. 7 + 3 + 2 = 12 items = ¾ of the total number of items. Hence, the overall total is 16.   2/16 = 1/8 = **12.5%.** Choice C is correct.

22. We can solve this using a proportion. 36/18 = x/64.   x = **128** minutes. Choice C is correct.

23. The three consecutive integers are x, x + 1 and x + 2. From the problem, we can write the following equation: 3 {x + (x + 1)} = 2 (x + 2) + 27. Thus, 6x + 3 = 2x + 31. 4x = 28
x = **7**, x + 1 = 8 x + 2 = 9. Choice B is correct.

24. In this case, we can start with Jayne, whose actual age we are given. Then, we can work backwards to determine Nathan's age. Jane = 28. Claire = 28 – 3 = 25. Nathan = 25 + 7 = **32**. Choice E is correct.

25. The first step for this type of problem is to draw a quick chart of what we know:

Driver	Distance	Rate	Time
Big Red Boat	10(x - 35)	x - 35	10
Carnival Cruise	10x	x	10

In this case, we will let x = the rate (or speed) of the Carnival Cruise ship, which is what we are asked to find. The speed of the Big Red Boat is therefore x - 35. Since they both travel for 10 hours, we can complete the Distance entry for the Big Red Boat and the Carnival Cruise ship as 10(x - 35) and 10x, respectively.

Next, we must write our equation to solve for the speed of the Carnival Cruise ship. Although both ships started in the same place and sailed for the same amount of time, they traveled at different speeds. The 490 miles distance is the TOTAL distance that the two of them sailed. Mathematically, it can be represented by the SUM of the Big Red Boat's distance, 10(x - 35), and the Carnival Cruise ship's distance, 10x. Hence, our equation becomes: 10x + 10(x - 35) = 490. 20x – 350 = 490. 20x = 840. X =**42** miles per hour = speed of the Carnival Cruise ship. Choice D is correct.

26. Jewelry at Dillard's sells for $30 per unit ($12,000,000/400,000 = $30), while jewelry at Macys sells for $15 per unit ($25,250,000/421,000 = $60). Choice C is correct.

27. Choice B is correct. Furniture at Dillard's costs $200 per unit ($60,000,000/300,000 = $200).

28. Macys profit from jewelry = ($25,250,000)(0.35) = $8,837,500
Dillard's profit from jewelry = ($12,000,000)(0.35) = $4,200,000
Total profit = $8,837,500 + $4,200,000 = **$13,037,500**. Choice E is correct.

Quantitative Section 2: 28 questions   45 minutes

Each question has two quantities to be compared: one in Column A and one in Column B. Compare the quantities taking into consideration any other information given and choose
Answer A - if the quantity in Column A is greater
Answer B - if the quantity in Column B is greater
Answer C - if the two quantities are equal
Answer D - if the relationship cannot be determined without further information.

1. Six hundred guests will either eat shrimp or roast beef at a wedding reception. The ratio of shrimp eaters to roast beef eaters is 6:4.

Column A	Column B
250	The # of guests who will eat roast beef

2. **Column A**

| Column B |

Eleven less than eleven times eleven   111

3. Joe borrowed $25,000 from the bank at 5% simple interest and agreed to pay it back over two years.

Column A	Column B
$1041.67	Joe's monthly payment (principal plus interest)

4. A general admission ticket to the symphony costs $32, while a student ticket costs $10.00. Eight hundred people attended a Saturday concert that generated $12,400 in total ticket sales.

Column A	Column B
The number of student tickets sold	200

5. Eighty students are attending summer school courses at Beaver Falls High School. Fifty have registered for Spanish, 20 have registered for Math, and 15 have registered for neither Spanish nor Math.

Column A	Column B
5	The # registered for BOTH Spanish and Math

6. The difference between two positive consecutive integers, when each is squared, equals 29.

Column A	Column B
14	The smaller number

7. A scientist has a 10-ounce solution that is 15% acid. Later, he adds 5 ounces of pure acid to the solution.

Column A   **Column B**

The percentage of acid in the resulting mixture   35%

Directions: _For each problem, decide which answer is the best of the choices given._

8. Equilateral triangle XYZ has an area of 36. If U is the midpoint of XY and V is the midpoint of XZ, what is the area of triangle XUV?

    a.   3
    b.   6
    c.   9
    d.   12
    e.   18

9. In quadrilateral ABCD, the sum of angles B, C and D = 5A. What is the value of angle A?

    a.   15
    b.   20
    c.   36
    d.   45
    e.   60

10. Line Q contains five points: A, B, C, D and E. How many different line segments do these five points form?

    a.   4
    b.   5
    c.   6
    d.   10
    e.   11

11. If $x \wedge y = xy - y + y^2$, then $2 \wedge 4 =$

    a.   4
    b.   16
    c.   20
    d.   24
    e.   68

12. On her way to the Post Office, Claire spent 10 minutes in her car, 11 minutes at the drugstore and another 11 minutes talking on her cell phone to her boyfriend. If she arrived at the Post Office at exactly 11:04 am, what time did Claire leave for the Post Office?

    a.   10:22 am
    b.   10:32 am
    c.   10:33 am
    d.   10:34 am
    e.   10:35 am

13. What is the largest integer that will divide evenly into 97 and 117?

    a.   1
    b.   7
    c.   9
    d.   11
    e.   13

14. Ken listed his car for sale on EBay for $8,000 but did not receive any bids. Later, he re-listed it for $6,400. What fraction of the original price does this represent?

    a.   2/3
    b.   3/4
    c.   4/5
    d.   5/6
    e.   7/8

15. Eight hundred people answered a newspaper ad to audition for American Idol. Forty percent of them were assigned Whitney Houston songs. Of this 40%, one-quarter of the people sang "I Will Always Love You." How many people sang "I Will Always Love You?"

    a.   40
    b.   60
    c.   80
    d.   120
    e.   160

16. What is the sum of the following fractions: 1/15, 2/10, 2/5, 1/3, 3/30

    a.   11/10
    b.   29/30
    c.   14/15
    d.   31/30
    e.   32/30

17. The sum of two numbers is 18. When three times the larger number is subtracted from 5 times the smaller number, the difference is 2. What is the larger number?

    a.   7
    b.   8
    c.   9
    d.   10
    e.   11

18. Jocelyn weighs 60% as much as Connie. If Jocelyn gains 8 pounds, she will weigh 75% as much as Connie. What is Jocelyn's weight (in pounds)?

    a.   32.0
    b.   35.5
    c.   40.0
    d.   43.3
    e.   53.3

19. A US Air commercial jet and a Sea Hawk helicopter left the Chicago airport at the same time and headed in opposite directions. If the US Air jet flew at an average rate of 500 miles per hour and the Sea Hawk helicopter flew at an average rate of 100 miles per hour, how many hours would it take the two flights to be 4,200 miles apart (assuming no stops to re-fuel)?

     a.   7
     b.   8
     c.   10
     d.   12
     e.   20

20. The Zippy Cheese Company has established a quality control program to minimize the number of underweight bars of cheese that leave their plant. During the first six weeks of the program, the number of bars that failed, by week, was 324, 119, 267, 219, 553, and 189. If management's goal is to have an overall average of 300 failing bars or less during the first seven weeks of the program, what is the highest number of bars that can fail during week seven?

     a.   297
     b.   307
     c.   359
     d.   429
     e.   548

21. How much greater than $11 - 9y$ is $7y + 4$?

     a. $16y - 7$
     b. $-2y - 7$
     c. $2y + 15$
     d. $6y - 15$
     e. $-16y + 1$

22. $(3/6 + 4/2)^3 =$

     a.   6.25
     b.   8
     c.   15.625
     d.   16.525
     e.   48

23. Which of the following is a multiple of 10, 15 and 35?

     a.   70
     b.   150
     c.   350
     d.   525
     e.   1050

24. Jenny has twice as many swimming medals as Cindy. If the sum of the squares of each number is 180, how many medals does Jenny have?

     a.   6
     b.   8
     c.   12
     d.   16
     e.   24

25. A pet shop had an inventory of 150 animals - 105 of the animals were cats and the rest were dogs. If 85 of the animals are female and 80% of the dogs are female, how many of the pets are male cats?

    a. 9
    b. 36
    c. 45
    d. 49
    e. 56

Refer to the following chart for questions 26 – 28.

Number of Items Sold (in thousands)

	Macys	**Dillard's**
Clothes	425	550
Furniture	375	300
Jewelry	421	400

Total Sales (in millions)

	Clothes	**Furniture**	**Jewelry**
Macys	19.125	56.250	25.250
Dillard's	22.750	60.000	12.000

26. If Macy's sells 50% additional furniture items next year and earns 30% profit on them, how much total profit from furniture will Macys earn (assuming the price per unit does not change)?

    a. $1,687,500
    b. $20,250,000
    c. $25,312,500
    d. $21,167,500
    e. $84,375,000

27. What is the difference between the average cost of a piece of clothing at Macys and Dillard's?

    a. The average price of an item of clothing at Macys is $10 higher than at Dillard's
    b. The average price of an item of clothing at Dillard's is $10 higher than at Macys
    c. The average price of an item of clothing at Dillard's is $5 higher than at Macys
    d. The average price of an item of clothing at Macys is $5 higher than at Dillard's
    e. It cannot be determined from the information given.

28. To sell the same dollar amount of clothing as Dillard's without increasing the number of units they sell, Macys will have to increase the average price of its clothing items to what amount?

    a. $50.00
    b. $53.50
    c. $55.00
    d. $57.50
    e. $60.50

Answer Key for Quantitative Section 2

1. For a 6:4 ratio, the whole is 10. 4/10 of 600 is **240**. Choice A is correct,

2. From the problem, we can easily write the following equation to solve for the unknown:
$11(11) – 11 = 121 – 11 = $ **110.** Choice B is correct.

3. To solve this problem, we must first calculate the total interest that Joe will pay on the loan. To do so, we use the basic formula, Interest = Principal x Rate x Time. In this case, the Principal = $25,000, the Rate = 0.05 and the Time = 2 years. Hence, Interest = ($25,000)(0.05)(2) = $2,500 in total interest over 2 years. Now, we must convert this number to a monthly basis. If Joe pays $2,500 in total interest over 2 years, then she pays $2,500/24 = $104.17 in interest per month.

But we aren't done yet. Joe also pays 1/24 of his $25,000 principal each month, which is $25,000/24 = $1,041.67. His total monthly payment (principal plus interest) is therefore $104.17 + $1041.67 = **$1,145.84.** Choice B is correct.

4. Let x = the number of general tickets; therefore, the number of student tickets is 800 − x. The total ticket sales equal the sum of general and student tickets, so: 32.00x + 10.00(800 − x) = 12,400. 32 x + 8000 − 10x = 12400. 22x = 4400.   x = 200 general tickets; 800 − 200 = **600 student tickets**. Choice A is correct.

5. To avoid counting students twice, we must divide them into four categories according to the following equation: Spanish + Math + Neither − Both = 80.   50 + 20 + 15 - Both = 80. Both = **5.** Choice C is correct.

6. In this case, the fastest way to solve this problem is to plug in the value in Column A and test it. When we do, we discover that 14 and 15 fit the criteria: (15)(15) - (14)(14) = 225 − 196 = **29**. Choice C is correct.

7. First, we must draw a table with the information we know.

Solution	Quantity (oz)	Percent Acid	Amount Acid (oz)
Original	10	15	10(0.15) = 1.5
Added	5	100	5(1.0) = 5
Final	15		1.5 + 5 = 6.5

In this case, the tabulated data tells us the entire story. The final 15-ounce solution contains 6.5 ounces of acid. 6.5/15 = **43.3%** acid. Choice A is correct.

8. The area of the triangle formed by the midpoints is ¼ of the original triangle XYZ. Therefore, the area is 36/4 = 9. Choice C is correct.

9. A + B + C + D = 360. Here, A + 5A = 360. Therefore, A = **60** degrees. Choice E is correct.

10. Choice D is correct. There are **10** possible segments: AB, AC, BC, AC, BD, CD, AE, BE, CE, DE.

11. If x ^ y = xy − y + y^2, then 2 ^ 4 = (2)(4) − 4 + 16 = **20.** Choice C is correct.

12. Add the minutes that Claire spent in the car; then, subtract them from the time she arrived at the Post Office. 10 + 11 + 11 = 32 minutes en route. 11:04 − 32 minutes = **10:32 am**. Choice B is correct.

13. The fastest way to solve this problem is to try each of the answer choices. When we do, we discover that the largest one that divides evenly into 97 and 117 is **1**. Choice A is correct.

14. If the original price was $8,000 and the new price is $6,400, then the relationship can be represented by $6,400/$8,000 = 8/10 = **4/5.** Choice C is correct.

15. 800 x 0.4 = 320. 320 x 0.25 = **80**. Choice C is correct.

16. Convert all fractions to the form with an LCD of 30. The sum is: 2/30 + 6/30 + 12/30 + 10/30 + 3/30 = 33/30 = **11/10**. Choice A is correct.

17. First, let's define our variables. We will let x = the smaller number and 18 − x equal the larger number. Five times the smaller number is therefore 5x. Three times the larger number is 3(18 − x). Further, we know that the difference between these two quantities is equal to 2. We must therefore solve the following equation: 5x − 3(18-x) = 2, so 5x −54 + 3x = 2, or 8x =56, or x = 7 and 18 − 7 = **11.** Choice E is correct.

18. First, we must summarize our data in a table:

Name	Current Weight	Hypothetical Weight
Connie	x	-
Jocelyn	0.6x	0.6x + 8

In this case, Connie's weight does not change. Our equation is simply the relationship between the two weights if Jocelyn gains eight pounds: $0.6x + 8 = 0.75x$. Solving for x, Connie's weight = 53.3 lbs and Jocelyn's weight = **32** lb. Choice A is correct.

19. The first step for this type of problem is to draw a quick chart of what we know.

Driver	Distance	Rate	Time
US Air	500x	500	x
Sea Hawk	100x	100	x

In this case, we will let x = the time it takes for the jet and the helicopter to travel 4,200 miles. We can also enter the rates for each plane and write an expression for their respective distances. Next, we must use this information to solve for x.

The US Air jet and the Sea Hawk helicopter each traveled *a portion* of the total distance, which is 4,200 miles. Our equation, therefore, is: Jet's Distance + Helicopter's Distance = Total Distance
$500x + 100X = 4,200$. $600x = 4,200$. $X = 7$ hours. Choice A is correct

20. For this problem, we can simply use the equation for simple averages to find the missing number: $300 = (324 + 119 + 267 + 219 + 553 + 189 + x) / 7$, So $300 = (1671 + x) / 7$, so $2100 = 1671 + x$, so x = **429.** Choice D is correct.

21. Here, we are simply being asked to find the difference between the two quantities: $7y + 4 - (11 - 9y) = 7y + 4 - 11 + 9y = $ **16y – 7**.   Choice A is correct.

22. $(3/6 + 4/2)^3 = $ $(5/2)(5/2)(5/2) = 125/8 = $ **15.625**. Choice C is correct.

23. Choice E, 1050.

24. First, let's define our variables.   We will let x = the number of Cindy's medals and 2x = the number of Jenny's medals. Therefore, the squares of the two numbers are x^2 and $4x^2$. Our equation therefore becomes: $x^2 + 4x^2 = 180$. $5x^2 = 180$. $x^2 = 180/5 = 36$. $x^2 = 36$.   x = +6 and – 6
Cindy has 6 medals. Jenny has 2(6) = **12** medals. Choice C is correct.

25. The best way to attack this type of problem is to summarize the data you are given in a simple table. Once you do, the answer will either be obvious – or surprisingly easy to calculate. In this case, we have cats and dogs in a pet shop; some are male, while others are female. When we put the information into our chart, we get:

	Cats	Dogs	Total
Male	56	9	65
Female	49	36	85
Total	105	45	150

From the table, we can answer the question; the number of male cats is **56**. Choice E is correct.

26. Macys currently sells 375,000 units of furniture per year. If they sell 50% more, they will sell (375,000)(1.5) = 562,500 units. From the chart, we know that the price per unit is $150 ($56,250,000 / 375,000).   Thus, for 562,500 units, Macys total furniture sales will be (562,500)($150) = $84,375,000. If 30% of this is profit, Macys will earn **$25,312,500** in profit from furniture. Choice C is correct.

27. At Macys, the average cost of an item of clothing = $19,125,000/425,000 = $45
At Dillard's, the average cost of an item of clothing = $22,000,000/ 550,000= $40
Thus, the average price of an item of clothing at Macys is **$5 higher** than at Dillard's. Choice D is correct.

28. Dillard's sold $22,750,000 in clothing last year, while Macys sold 425,000 clothing items. For Macys to generate $22,750,000 from 425,000 units, they will need to sell each unit for $22,750,000/425,000 = **$53.50**. Choice B is correct.

Quantitative Section 3:   28 questions   45 minutes

Each question has two quantities to be compared: one in Column A and one in Column B. Compare the quantities taking into consideration any other information given and choose
Answer A - if the quantity in Column A is greater
Answer B - if the quantity in Column B is greater
Answer C - if the two quantities are equal
Answer D - if the relationship cannot be determined without further information.

1. Rick earns $6,000 per month, but pays 1/3 of his gross income in taxes. He saves 1/7 of his take-home pay each month, but he receives no interest on the money.

Column A	Column B
The dollar amount that Rick saves per year	$6,750

2.

Column A	Column B
The ratio of fifteen minutes to eight hours	1/32

3. David scored the following number of baskets during his first six basketball games: 5, 6, 9, 12, 4, and 8.

Column A	Column B
The number of baskets David must score in game 7 to have an average of 8 baskets per game for the entire 7-game season	10

4. In quadrilateral ABCD, the sum of angles A, B and C = 7D.

Column A	Column B
The value of angle D (in degrees)	48

5. Tina splits her three thousand dollar lottery prize evenly with her two parents, after 20% is deducted from the winnings in taxes.

Column A	Column B
The dollar amount each person receives	$800

6. One number is six times a smaller number. Four times their difference is equal to 60.

Column A	Column B
18	The larger number

7. If x = 5, y = 2 and z = 3, what is the value of $3x^3 + 5y^4 - 2z^2$?

    a. 357
    b. 375
    c. 393
    d. 437
    e. 455

8. What are the y-intercepts of the graph for the following equation: $(x + 6)^2 + (x + 3)^2 = 1$

    a. (6, 0) (3, 0)
    b. (-6, 0) (-3, 0)
    c. (0 –6) (0, -3)
    d. (0, 6) (0, 3)
    e. There are no y-intercepts

9. Find the area of a square with a diagonal of 8.

    a. 32
    b. 36
    c. 49
    d. 64
    e. 96

10. If x = 3, calculate $5^x - (x^3)^{x-1}$

    a. -604
    b. 44
    c. 98
    d. 104
    e. 604

11. Simply the following expression: $(3x + y)(x + 3y) - 10xy =$

    a. 0
    b. $3x^2 - 11xy + y^2$
    c. $-21xy$
    d. $3x^2 + 3y^2$
    e. $3x^2 - 3y^2$

12. The inequality $5x - 78 > 6x + 80$ is true for what values of x?

    a. $x < 2$
    b. $x > 158$
    c. $x > -158$
    d. $x < -158$
    e. $x < 158$

13. A wholesaler shipped seven dozen roses to a flower shop for use in a window display. If Jane takes three roses for her own use, and nineteen are discarded because they are wilted, but Barb adds back an additional half-dozen roses to the group, how many roses were available for the window display?

      a. 61
      b. 64
      c. 68
      d. 71
      e. 74

14. Which of the following is the smallest integer that leaves a remainder of 1 when divided by 8?

      a. 131
      b. 137
      c. 145
      d. 153
      e. 168

15. A year ago, Julie had 62 recipes for her country cookbook. This year, she has 329 recipes. What percentage increase does this number represent?

      a. 4.306%
      b. 43.06%
      c. 430.6%
      d. 4306%
      e. none of the above

16. The larger of two numbers is 11 more than the smaller. Double the small number equals 14 more than the larger number. What is the small number?

      a. 24
      b. 25
      c. 26
      d. 35
      e. 36

17. Over the summer, Bill borrowed $6,500 from the bank at 8% simple interest. If he pays the money back over three years, what total amount of interest will Bill pay on the loan?

      a. $156
      b. $520
      c. $1040
      d. $1560
      e. $2080

18. Grace had $124.50 in her cookie jar, which consisted of nickels, dimes, and quarters. If Grace had 50 more nickels than quarters and 30 more dimes than nickels, how many quarters did Grace have?

      a. 285
      b. 315
      c. 335
      d. 345
      e. 365

19. If the perimeter of an isosceles triangle is 64 and its base is 16, find the length of one of the equal sides.

    a.   18
    b.   20
    c.   24
    d.   26
    e.   28

20. If $f(p) = p/7 + 10 - (7^3)/p$, what is $f(14)$?

    a.   −12.5
    b.   -12
    c.   0
    d.   7
    e.   343

21. What is the next term in the following series?   85, 84, 82, 79, 75.......

    a.   71
    b.   70
    c.   69
    d.   68
    e.   64

22. Which of the following is equal to 0.0000321?

    a. 32.1×10^7
    b. $32.1 \text{ c } 10^{-7}$
    c. 321×10^{-8}
    d. 3.21×10^{-6}
    e. 3.21×10^{-5}

23. Which of the following expressions is equivalent to $(a + b - 1)(a - b - 1)$?

    a. $a^2 + 2a - 2b - b^2 + 1$
    b. $a^2 - 2a + 2b + b^2 + 1$
    c. $a^2 - 2a + 2b - b^2 + 1$
    d. $a^2 - 2a - b^2 + 1$
    e. $a^2 + 2a - b^2 + 1$

24. A research lab has a new hand pump, which can fill a bucket in 32 seconds. It also has an older pump that can fill the same bucket in 48 seconds. If both pumps are used at the same time, how many seconds will it take to fill the bucket?

    a.   18.0
    b.   19.2
    c.   28.5
    d.   36.4
    e.   40.0

25. What is the probability of getting a white jelly bean from a dispenser that contains 28 red jelly beans, 48 green ones, 36 purple ones, 26 pink ones, 30 blue ones and 28 white ones?

    a. 1/8
    b. 1/7
    c. 1/6
    d. 1/5
    e. ¼

26. Heidi bought U wedding favors at a bridal shop at a price of V per favor. Afterwards, Heidi had W dollars left over. Assuming that she made no other purchases, how much money (in dollars) did Heidi bring to the bridal shop for favors?

    a. UVW
    b. UV + W
    c. (U/V) + W
    d. UV – W
    e. It cannot be determined from the information given.

Refer to the chart below for questions 27 & 28.

Number of Hospitals per Million Residents

Atlanta	56
Boston	94
Chicago	87
Detroit	79
Los Angeles	99
Miami	48
Sacramento	61

27. If the population of Los Angeles decreases from 10 million to 7.5 million, how many fewer hospitals will be needed in the city?

    a. 190
    b. 240
    c. 247
    d. 743
    e. 790

28. If there are 5 million people in Miami and 20 X-ray technicians per hospital, how many X-ray technicians work in hospitals in Miami?

    a. 240
    b. 1,200
    c. 2,400
    d. 2,600
    e. 4,800

Answer Key for Quantitative Section 3

1. First, we must determine Rick's take-home pay, which is $6,000 (2/3) = $4,000 per month. If he saves 1/7 of it each month for one year, he will save $4,000(1/7)(12) = **$6,857.14**. Choice A is correct.

2. Fifteen minutes = ¼ hour = **1/32** of 8 hours. Choice C is correct.

3. 8 = (5 + 6 + 9 + 12 + 4 + 8 + x)/7, So, 8 = (44 + x)/7, so 56 = 44 + x, or x = 12. David must score **12 baskets** in the final game. Choice A is correct.

4. A + B + C + D = 360. Here, D + 7D = 360, or 8D = 360. D = **45 degrees**. Choice B is correct.

5. The first step is to determine the actual amount that Tina won after taxes are deducted, which is $3000 – $600 = $2,400. Next, we must divide this figure by the total number of recipients, which is 3, to get **$800**. Choice C is correct.

6. Let's call the two numbers x and 6x. We also know that 4(x – 6x) = 60. If we solve for x, we find:
4x -24x = 60
 -20x = 60
 x = -3
6x = -18. The larger number is **–3**. Choice A is correct

7. If x = 5, y = 2 and z = 3, then $3x^3 + 5y^4 – 2z^2$ = (3)(5)(5)(5) + (5)(2)(2)(2)(2) – (2)(3)(3) = 375 + 80 – 18= **437**. Choice D is correct.

8. None. Choice E is correct.

9. The square is the sum of two right triangles that share the diagonal as their hypotenuse. Therefore, the sum of the squares of the other two sides must equal 64. Therefore $2x^2 = 64$, where x = a side of the square. To calculate the area of the square, which is L x W, we get (5.65)(5.65) =**32**. Choice A is correct.

10. 125 – 729 = **-604**. Choice A is correct.

11. $(3x + y)(x + 3y) – 10xy = 3x^2 + 9xy + xy + 3y^2 – 10xy$ = **$3x^2 + 3y^2$**. Choice D is correct.

12. Choice D is correct. When we simplify the expression, we get **x < -158**

13. First, determine the total number of roses. Then, add and subtract according to the details in the question stem. If we do, we get: 12(7) = 84 roses - 3 – 19 + 6 = **68**. Choice C is correct. This problem requires you to add and subtract a string of numbers. As long as you convert the "dozen" terms to individual roses, and keep the signs correct when you add, you will obtain the right answer.

14. The easiest way to solve this problem is to try the answer choices in the order they are presented. When we do, we discover that 137 = **8(17) + 1**. Choice B is correct.

15. 329 - 62 = 267/62 = 4.306 x 100 = **430.6% increase**. Choice C is correct.

16. Let x = the smaller number. Therefore, the larger number = x + 11. We also know that:
2x = (x + 11) + 14
2x = x + 25
x = **25.** Choice B is correct.

17. This is a straightforward problem that we can solve using the formula, Interest = Principal x Rate x Time. In this case, the Principal = $6500, the Rate = 0.08 and the Time = 3 years. Hence, Interest = ($6500)(0.08)(3) = **$1,560** in total interest. Choice D is correct.

18. To solve, we must first define our variables. In this case, x = the number of quarters, x + 50 = the number of nickels, and x + 80 = the number of dimes. Since the sum of the coins = $124.50, our equation becomes:

Quarters + Dimes + Nickels = Total
25x + 10(x + 80) + 5(x + 50) = 12450
25x + 10x + 800 + 5x + 250 = 12450
40x = 11400
x = **285** quarters. Choice A is correct.

19. Perimeter = sum of all three sides = 16 + 2x = 64. Therefore, 2x = 48. x = **24**. Choice C is correct.

20. If f(p) = p/7 + 10 – (7^3)/p , then f (14) = 14/7 + 10 – 343/14 = 2 + 10 – 24.5 = **-12.5** Choice A is correct.

21. The first term decreases by 1, the second decreases by 2, the third decreases by 3, etc. The next term would be 75 –5 = **70**. Choice B is correct.

22. **3.21 x 10^{-5}**. Choice E is correct.

23. $(a + b - 1)(a - b - 1) = a^2 -ab -a + ab - b^2 -b -a +b + 1 = a^2 - 2a - b^2 + 1$. Choice D is correct.

24. For this problem, our unknown x is the total time required to fill the bucket if both pumps are used. Hence, our equation becomes $1/32 + 1/48 = 1/x$. To solve, we must multiply both sides of the equation by 96x, which is our least common denominator: 3x + 2x = 96, so 5x = 96 and x = **19.2** seconds. Choice B is correct.

25. First, we must determine the total number of jelly beans: 28 + 48 + 36 + 26 + 30 + 28 = 196.   Then, we can determine the probability of choosing one of a specific color: 28/196 = **1/7**.   Choice B is correct.

26. We can solve this problem by plugging in numbers or by doing a few simple "backwards" calculations. First, let's plug- in numbers. Let's assume that Heidi bought 10 favors at a price of 2 dollars per favor. Let's also assume that she had 5 dollars left over. Hence, U = 10, V = 2 and W = 5. Heidi therefore spent (10)(2), which is UV. If she had 5 dollars left over, then her original amount of money was **UV + W**. Choice B is correct.

Option 2. If you don't want to plug in numbers, you can just reason the problem through.   If Heidi bought U wedding favors, which cost V dollars each, then she spent UV. Finally, she had W cents left over, which we must add to her total amount of money. When we do, we get the same answer as we did with the plug-in method: UV + W.

27. (99)(10) = 990. (99)(7.5) = 743. 990 – 743 = **247**. Choice C is correct.

28. (48)(5)(20) = **4,800**. Choice E is correct.

Quantitative Section 4: 28 questions   45 minutes

Each question has two quantities to be compared: one in Column A and one in Column B. Compare the quantities taking into consideration any other information given and choose
Answer A - if the quantity in Column A is greater
Answer B - if the quantity in Column B is greater
Answer C - if the two quantities are equal
Answer D - if the relationship cannot be determined without further information.

1. Robert bought a condo with an unusual financing plan. He paid a down payment of $5,000, which was 1/12 of the cost of the condo, and agreed to pay the balance in 60 equal installments (with no interest).

Column A	Column B
Robert's monthly installment payment	$900

2. A chef has a wonderful recipe for meatloaf, which uses 8 oz of garlic for a loaf that serves 12 people. She plans to quadruple the recipe to feed 48 people.

Column A	Column B
32 oz.	The additional garlic she will need

3. American Airlines is recording the number of on-time flights into and out of the Miami airport. The daily totals for one particular week are 1135, 1059, 1432, 2310, 1587, 1986, and 2131.

Column A	Column B
1578	The median of this data set

4. The sum of the interior angles of a polygon is 1,980 degrees.

Column A	Column B
17	The number of sides of the polygon

5. The sum of five consecutive integers is 410.

Column A	Column B
86	The largest of the five integers

6. Rachel is 2 years older than Lisa. The product of their ages is 120.

Column A	Column B
Rachel's age	10

Directions: For each problem, decide which answer is the best of the choices given.

7. How many 4-inch sections of ribbon can be obtained from a roll of ribbon that is 30 yards long?

    a.   108
    b.   270
    c.   360
    d.   810
    e.   1,080

8. One hundred vacationers on a cruise ship have signed up for the ship's activities. Sixty sign up for ballroom dancing lessons. Thirty-five sign up for aerobics class. Twenty sign up for neither ballroom dancing nor aerobics class. How many have signed up for BOTH ballroom dancing and aerobics class?

    a.   5
    b.   10
    c.   12
    d.   15
    e.   18

9. Joe's monthly budget includes $1,200 for rent, $400 for his car payment, $150 for insurance, $250 for utilities, and $200 for groceries. Assuming that Joe' monthly take-home pay is $3,300, what fraction of it is left for discretionary spending?

    a. 1/5
    b. 1/4
    c. 1/3
    d. 2/5
    e. 2/3

10. What is the area of a square with a side of length 5?

    a.   5
    b.   25
    c.   50
    d.   100
    e.   125

11. The first term in a sequence is -50. Every consecutive term is 25 greater than the term that immediately preceded it. What is the value of the 75th term in the sequence?

    a. 1,750
    b. 1,775
    c. 1,800
    d. 1,825
    e. 1,850

12. Which of the following numbers is closest in value to 3/8?

    a.   3/10
    b.   4/13
    c.   5/16.
    d.   7/19
    e.   0.395

13. Jason has 1,489 nickels in a large jar in his bedroom. If he adds 324 nickels on Monday, and adds another 112 nickels on Tuesday, but removes 117 nickels on Wednesday, how much money (in dollars) does Jason have left in the jar on Thursday, assuming that there are no other additions or subtractions?

      a. $90.40
      b. $94.80
      c. $108.80
      d. $180.80
      e. $188.00

14. What is the least positive integer that is divisible by both 2 and 9 and leaves a remainder of 4 when divided by 5?

      a.   18
      b.   36
      c.   45
      d.   49
      e.   54

15. If the 6% hotel tax on a room is $4.32, what was the total price of the room (including tax)?

      a. $70.32
      b. $72.00
      c. $76.00
      d. $76.32
      e. $78.00

16. If 25 less than eight times a number is equal to 215, find the number.

      a.   20
      b.   25
      c.   30
      d.   35
      e.   40

17. Ronda borrowed $15,000 from the bank at 9% simple interest. If she pays the money back over four years, how much will she pay each month in interest?

      a. $37.50
      b. $112.50
      c. $375.00
      d. $450.00
      e. $5,400.00

18. Ben found a jar with 320 coins, all dimes and quarters, which were worth $77.90. How many of the coins were dimes?

      a.   14
      b.   15
      c.   32
      d.   210
      e.   306

19. Each of the equal sides of an isosceles triangle is four less than three times its base. If the perimeter is 90, what is the base of the triangle?

    a. 12
    b. 14
    c. 15
    d. 18
    e. 28

20. If $3x + 4y = 12$ and $x + 8y = 46$, what is the value of $2x + 6y$?

    a. 15
    b. 24
    c. 29
    d. 68
    e. 112

21. If $11 - 4x = 3$, what is the value of $6 - 4x$?

    a. -8
    b. -2
    c. 0
    d. 2
    e. 8

22. Pipe A can fill a tank in 40 hours. Pipe B can fill the same tank in 72 hours. Pipe C can empty the tank in 96 hours. If all three pipes are open at the same time, how many hours will it take to fill the tank?

    a. 20
    b. 35
    c. 40
    d. 56
    e. 60

23. If you roll a 6-sided die, which sides are numbered 1 through 6, what is the probability that you will roll a 3?

    a. 1/6
    b. 1/5
    c. 1/4
    d. 1/3
    e. ½

24. The cost to park at Yankee Stadium is J dollars for the first eight hours and P dollars for each additional hour. How much did Grace pay to park at the stadium for S hours (assuming that S is greater than eight)?

    a. $J + PS$
    b. $J + 1/JPS$
    c. $J + P(S - 8)$
    d. $JPS - P(S - 8)$
    e. $J + \{(S - 8)/P\}$

25. What positive integer is 40% less than 15,600?

    a. 4,680
    b. 6,240
    c. 6,864
    d. 8,680
    e. 9,360

26. What is the largest integer that will divide evenly into 57 and 399?

    a. 7
    b. 13
    c. 17
    d. 19
    e. 21

Refer to the chart below for questions 27 and 28.

Percentage of Diabetics (By Age)

	China	Italy	France	Germany
Under 10	5	5	2	0
10 – 18	20	30	15	13
19 – 30	35	30	28	29
31 – 50	30	30	40	48
Over 51	10	5	15	10

27. If there are 15 million diabetics in China, how many of them are less than 31 years old?

    a. 750,000
    b. 3 million
    c. 5.25 million
    d. 9 million
    e. 10 million

28. If there are 8 million diabetics in France, and they each purchase two insulin pumps per year, how many pumps are needed by the diabetics who are 51 or older?

    a. 1.0 million
    b. 1.2 million
    c. 2.4 million
    d. 4 million
    e. 4.8 million

Answer Key for Quantitative Section 4

1. If the $5000 down payment is 1/12 the cost of the house, then the total cost is ($5000)(12) = $60,000. The remaining balance of $55,000 will be paid in 60 equal installments of 55,000/60 = $916.67 = **$917**. Choice A is correct.

2. We first must use a proportion to solve for the total amount of garlic needed. 8/12 = x/48. x = 32. 32 - 8 = **24 additional ounces**. Choice A is correct.

3. First, arrange the numbers in ascending order: 1059, 1135, 1432, 1587, 1986, 2131, 2310. The middle number, **1587**, is the median. Choice B is correct.

4.180 $(X - 2) = 1,980$, so $X - 2 = 11$, or $X = $ **13 sides**. Choice A is correct.

5. In this problem, we know that 5 consecutive numbers, when added together, equal 410. We will let the smallest of the 5 numbers = x. Therefore, the second, third, fourth and fifth consecutive numbers are equal to $x + 1$, $x + 2$, $x + 3$, and $x + 4$, respectively. Mathematically, we can represent their relationship by the following equation: $x + (x + 1) + (x + 2) + (x + 3) + (x + 4) = 410$
$5x + 10 = 410$
$x = 400/5 = 80$ = the smallest number.
The largest number is $x+4 = $ **84**.   Choice A is correct.

6. First, let's define our variables. We will let x = Lisa's age. Therefore, Rachel's age = x + 2. Since the product of their ages is 120, our equation becomes: $x(x + 2) = 120$, or $x^2 + 2x - 120 = 0$ $(x - 10)(x + 12)= 0$

Therefore, $x = - 12$ and $+10$. Since a person's age cannot be negative, we can discard the -12 root. Therefore, Lisa's age = 10 and Rachel's age = $10 + 2 = $ **12**. Choice A is correct.

7. 30 yards x 3 feet/yard x 12 inches/foot = 1,080 inches / 4 = **270** 4-inch segments. Choice B is correct

8. The relationship of the groups is defined as follows: Group 1 + Group 2 + Neither – Both = 100. Once we establish this simple equation, we can plug in numbers to solve for the unknown, which in this case is the group defined as Both.

Group 1 + Group 2 + Neither – Both = 100
60 + 35 + 20 – Both = 100
Both = **15**, which is answer choice D.

9. Total expenses = 1200 + 400 + 150 + 250 + 200 = 2200. 2200/3300 = 2/3, which leaves 1/3 for discretionary spending. Choice C is correct.

10. Area = L x W = 5 x 5 = **25**.   Choice B is correct.

11. For an arithmetic sequence in which the first term is A and the difference between the terms is D, the *nth* term is: $An = A1 + (n - 1)D$. In this case, the first term in the sequence is -50. The difference in terms is 25 and n = 75. The 75th term = $-50 + (75 - 1)25 = -50 + 1,850 = 1,800$. Choice C is correct.

12. 3/8 = 0.375. The closest answer choice is D, **7/19**, which is 0.368.

13. This is a simple addition and subtraction problem, with a final conversion to dollars at the end. When we add and subtract the terms, we get: 1489 + 324 + 112 – 117 = 1808 nickels x ($1.00/20 nickels) = **$90.40**. Choice A is correct.

14.   To solve this problem, we must check our answer choices against both criteria in the problem. First, they must be divisible by 2 and 9. Second, they must leave a remainder of 4 when they are divided by 5. Choices C and D are not divisible by 2, so we do not need to examine them further. Of the remaining choices, only Choice E (54) meets both criteria.

15. If 0.06x = $4.32, then x = $72. Total price = **$76.32.** Choice D is correct.

16. This can be solved by a simple equation: $8x - 25 = 215$. $x = $ **30**. Choice C is correct.

17. To solve this problem, we must first calculate the total interest that Ronda will pay on the loan. To do so, we use the basic formula, Interest = Principal x Rate x Time. In this case, the Principal = $15000, the Rate = 0.09 and the Time = 4 years. Hence, Interest = ($15000)(0.09)(4) = $5,400 in total interest over 4 years. Now, we must convert this number to a monthly basis. If Ronda pays $5,400 in total interest over 4 years, then she pays $5,400/48 = **$112.50** in interest per month. Choice B is correct.

18. First, we must define our variables. In this case, x = the number of dimes. Therefore, 320 – x = the number of quarters.   Since the value of these two coins is $77.90, our equation becomes:

$10x + 25(320 - x) = 7790$
$10x + 8000 - 25x = 7790$
$--15x = -210$

x = **14** dimes. Choice A is correct.

19. Let x be the length of the base. Perimeter = sum of all three sides = 90 = x + 2(3x - 4) = 7x – 8. Thus, 7x = 98. x = **14**. Choice B is correct.

20. Add the equations together, then divide by 2: 2x + 6y = **29**. Choice C is correct.

21. If 11 – 4x = 3, then x = 2. 6 – (4)(2) = **-2**. Choice B is correct.

22. Our unknown is the total amount of time needed to fill the tank, which is the sum of the intake pipes, minus the drain pipe. Hence, our equation is 1/40 + 1/72 – 1/96 = 1/x

To solve, we must multiply both sides of the equation by 4320x, which is our least common denominator:

108x + 60x – 45x = 4320
123x = 4320
x = **35.12** hours. Choice B is correct.

23. The probability is **1/6**, or Choice A.

24. This is a simple problem if we substitute numbers for letters. Let's assume that Yankee Stadium charges $20 for the first 8 hours and $5 for each additional hour. Let's also assume that Grace parked for 12 hours. If we do, then J = 20, P = 5, and S = 12. Grace's total cost will be the basic charge for 8 hours, plus the additional cost for every hour over 8. The basic cost = 20 = J. The additional cost per hour = 5(12 – 8) = P(S – 8). Therefore, Grace's total cost = 20 + 5(12 – 8) = **J + P(S – 8).** Choice C is correct.

25. (0.6) 15,600= **9,360**. Choice E is correct.

26. The easiest way to solve this problem is to try each answer choice. The largest one that divides evenly into 57 and 399 is **19,** which is Choice D.

27. (15 million)(0.05 + 0.20 + 0.35) = 9 million. Choice D is correct.

28. If France has a total of 8 million diabetics, then the number of them who are 51 or older is (8 million)(0.15) = 1.2 million. If all of these patients purchase 2 insulin pumps per year, they will require a total of 2.4 million. Choice C is correct.

Quantitative Section 5: 28 questions   45 minutes

Each question has two quantities to be compared: one in Column A and one in Column B. Compare the quantities taking into consideration any other information given and choose
Answer A - if the quantity in Column A is greater
Answer B - if the quantity in Column B is greater
Answer C - if the two quantities are equal
Answer D - if the relationship cannot be determined without further information.

1. American Idol invited the top ten finalists to perform on their national tour. Only the top three would be offered a chance to sing solos.

Column A	Column B
The number of possible ways to order the top three finalists	750

2. Joe and Candy have a $100 gift certificate for a local restaurant, which must cover the complete cost of their meal, plus tax and tip. They will pay 6% sales tax for the meal and leave a 20% tip.

Column A	Column B
$79.50	The maximum amount their food can cost

3. A hospital is conducting an efficiency study to determine the number of thermometers that are broken on any given day. For the first three weeks in July, the following daily values have been recorded: 5, 3, 7, 3, 6, 4, 8, 3, 7, 10, 3, 5, 9, 5, 3, 7, 2, 6, 5, 3, 7.

Column A	Column B
The mode of the data set	3

4. A decorator wishes to cover a rectangular floor that measures 6 feet by 10 feet with pieces of tile, which each measure 6 inches by 9 inches.

Column A	Column B
The # tiles needed to complete the job	164

5. Dina drove 240 miles round trip to visit her family for Thanksgiving. Her car averages 30 miles per gallon of gas and Dina paid an average price of $2.85 per gallon of gas.

Column A	Column B
The amount Dina spent for gas on her trip	$22.50

6. Walter put $150,000 into an investment account, which he left untouched for eleven years and three months. At that time, he withdrew the entire amount, plus all of the simple annual interest he had earned. The total balance in Walter's account was $272,514.

Column A   **Column B**

The simple rate of annual interest   7%
the account earned

Directions: **For each problem, decide which answer is the best of the choices given.**

7. Which of the following is not a factor of 420?

    a.   10
    b.   15
    c.   40
    d.   42
    e.   60

8. In triangle ABC, AB = 3 and BC = 5. Which of the following could possibly be the length of side AC?

    a.   6
    b.   9
    c.   10
    d.   either a, b or c
    e.   none of the above

9. Which of the following polygons has all sides of equal length and all angles of identical measure?

    a.   hexagon
    b.   octagon
    c.   nonagon
    d.   pentagon
    e.   None of the above

10. The line represented by $3x - 9y = 12$ is parallel to which of the following lines?

    a. $y = 3x + 5$
    b. $y = 12x + 1$
    c. $y = 1/3x - 8$
    d. $y = 4/3 \, x - 3$
    e. $y = 3x + 4/3$

11. What is the value of x if $xy + xz = 15$ and $y + z = 3$?

    a.   1/2
    b.   1
    c.   3
    d.   5
    e.   15

12. Which of the following are the solutions to the following equation? $x^2 -7x + 10 = 0$

    a.   5, 2
    b.   2, -5
    c.   -2, -5
    d.   -2, 5
    e.   5, ½

13. Stephanie has a certain amount of money invested at 4% and three times that amount invested at 7%. If the total annual interest from her two investments is $17,500, how much does Stephanie have invested at 7%?

    a. $35,000
    b. $70,000
    c. $135,000
    d. $170,000
    e. $210,000

14. The base of a triangle is 16 more than the height. If the area of the triangle is 256 square inches, what is its base?

    a.   4
    b.   8
    c.   16
    d.   32
    e.   36

15. What is 5/4 divided by 7/6?

    a.   15/30
    b.   24/28
    c.   24/35
    d.   14/15
    e.   15/14

16. Three hundred entertainers will perform at a talent show. The group contains only singers and dancers. If the ratio of singers to dancers is 2:1, how many dancers are there?

    a.   50
    b.   100
    c.   150
    d.   175
    e.   200

17. Carla owed her university $585 in tuition. When she receives her paycheck of $116, she pays it all to the university, along with $219 that she has borrowed from a friend. Later in the day, Carla wins $947 in the lottery, and immediately pays off the rest of her tuition bill and her friend. How much money does Carla have left?

    a. $250
    b. $362
    c. $478
    d. $697
    e. $728

18. If Q is 25% of R and S is 30% of R, what is the ratio of Q to S?

    a. 3/20
    b. 1/5
    c. 11/20
    d. 3/4
    e. 5/6

19. Five consecutive even integers have a sum of 370. What is the largest of the five integers?

    a. 70
    b. 76
    c. 78
    d. 80
    e. 82

20. The length of a rectangular gift box is 4 inches shorter than its width. If the area of the box is 572 square inches, what is its length?

    a. 18
    b. 20
    c. 22
    d. 26
    e. 28

21. At a local hospice with 200 patients, 120 have HIV and the rest have cancer. If 70 of the patients are under 18 and one quarter of the cancer patients are over 18, how many of the patients are under 18 with HIV?

    a. 10
    b. 20
    c. 60
    d. 70
    e. 80

22. In a jar containing dimes and nickels, the ratio of nickels to dimes is 3:5. If there are 80 coins, what is value of the nickels (in dollars)?

    a. $0.10
    b. $0.50
    c. $1.00
    d. $1.50
    e. $2.50

23. Professor Davis can write a book manuscript in 5 days. His graduate student Miguel can write the same manuscript in 10 days. After working alone for 3 days, Professor Davis was called away on urgent business, which left Miguel alone to finish the manuscript. How many days did it take Miguel to finish it?

    a. 2
    b. 3
    c. 4
    d. 5
    e. 6

24. If the following series continues in the same pattern, what will the next term be?

5, 9, 6, 11, 7, 13, 8, 15…..

a. 7
b. 9
c. 11
d. 12
e. 13

25. What is the total cost (in cents) of W watermelons, which cost X dollars each, and Y apples, which cost Z cents each?

a. WXYZ/100
b. 100WX + YZ
c. WX + 100YZ
d. W + YZ/100
e. 100WX/YZ

Refer to the following charts to answer questions 26 – 28.

Number of Financial Products Sold

	Traditional Brokerage	Online Brokerage
CD	200	350
Annuity	50	105
401-K	85	409

Total Value of Financial Product Sold (in millions)

	CD	Annuity	401-k
Traditional Brokerage	54	23	10
Online Brokerage	92	27	31

26. For the time period represented by these charts, what was the average value of an Annuity sold at the traditional brokerage house (in millions of dollars)?

a. 0.23
b. 0.25
c. 0.46
d. 0.50
e. 0.75

27. For the time period represented by these charts, what was the average value of a 401-K sold at an online brokerage house (in millions of dollars)?

a. 0.076
b. 0.088
c. 0.100
d. 0.295
e. 0.358

28. For the time period represented by these charts, what was the total value of all financial products sold by the online brokerage (in millions of dollars)?

        a.   87
        b.   146
        c.   150
        d.   237
        e.   864

Answer Key for Quantitative Section 5

1. For situations in which the *order matters*, the correct formula is $10!/(10-3)! = 10! / 7! =$

$(10 \times 9 \times 8 \times 7 \times 6 \times 5 \times 4 \times 3 \times 2 \times 1) / (7 \times 6 \times 5 \times 4 \times 3 \times 2 \times 1) = 720$. Choice B is correct.

2. The total bill, which can be no more than $100, include the cost of the meal, 6% sales tax and a 20% tip. If we let x = the cost of the food, then the tax = 0.06x. The tip is 20% of the total cost of the food and the 6% tip. Algebraically, we can represent the tip as 0.20 (x + 0.06x) = 0.212x.

Since the total bill can be no more than $100, our final equation for the meal is:
Meal + Tax + Tip = 100, or x + 0.06x + 0.212x = 100, or 1.272x = 100. Solving for x, the cost of the meal must be less than **$78.62**. (Tax = $4.72, Tip = 16.67). Choice A is correct.

3. First, arrange the values in ascending order: 2, 3, 3, 3, 3, 3, 3, 4, 5, 5, 5, 5, 6, 6, 7, 7, 7, 7, 8, 9, 10. Then, find the value that occurs most often; in this case, it is **3,** which is the mode. Choice C is correct.

4. The area of the floor is 6 feet x 10 feet, or 60 square feet. The area of one tile is 6 inches x 9 inches = 54 square inches. First, for simplicity, we must convert the units of the tiles from square inches to square feet: 54 square inches (1 square foot/ 144 square inches) = 0.375 square feet.

Next, we must multiply the total area of the wall by the area of one tile to determine how many tiles we need: 60 square feet (1 tile/0.375 square feet) = **160 tiles**. Choice B is correct.

5. 240 miles/30 miles per gallon x $2.85 per gallon = **$22.80**. Choice A is correct.

6. In this problem, we know the beginning and ending amounts and are being asked to calculate the rate of simple annual interest that was earned over 11.25 years. To solve, we will use the basic equation:

Interest = Principal x Rate x Time. The trick is to work backwards from our final total to determine the rate of interest that was paid. In this case, our total of $272,514 represents the initial deposit of $150,000 plus the interest that was earned.

Mathematically, $272,514 = $150,000 + PRT = $150,000 + ($150,000)(X)(11.25), so
$272,514 = $150,000 + (1,687,500)X, or X = 122514/1,687,500 = 0.0726 = **7.26%.** Choice A is correct.

7. Choice C, **40**.

8. The length of the third side of the triangle must be less than the sum of the other two sides. Thus, the length must be less than 5 + 3 = **8.** Choice A is correct.

9. Octagon. Choice B is correct.

10. Parallel lines have the same slope. In this case, the slope of 3x −9y = 12 is 1/3, because the equation simplifies to 9y = 3x − 12, or y = 1/3x − 4/3. Choice C also has a slope of **1/3.**

11. xy + xz = 15, so x (y + z) = 15. Since (y + z) = 3, 3x = 15 and x = **5.** Choice D is correct.

12. If x^2 -7x + 10= 0, then (x − 2)(x - 5) = 0. So, x = 5, or **2**. Choice A is correct.

13. To solve, we must first determine how much interest Stephanie earns on each investment separately. For simplicity, we will x = the amount she has invested at 4%. Therefore, 3x = the amount that she has invested at 7%. The interest on the account that pays 4% = 0.04x. The interest on the account that pays 7% = (0.07)3x = 0.21x.

According to the problem, 0.04x + 0.21x = $17,500.
Therefore, 0.25x = $17,500, so x = $70,000 = amount invested at 4%.
3x = **$210,000** = the amount invested at 7%. Choice E is correct.

14. Area = ½(Base)(Height). Here, we will let x = the height and x+16 = the base. Therefore,
$256 = ½ x(x + 16)$
$512 = x^2 + 16x$
$0 = x^2 + 16x - 512$
$0 = (x - 16)(x + 32)$. The height = 16 inches. The base = X + 16 = **32** inches. Choice C is correct.

15. Choice E is correct, **15/14**.

16. For a 2:1 ratio, the whole is 3. 2/3 of 300 = 200 singers; 1/3 of 300 = **100** dancers. Choice B is correct.

17. The easiest way to solve this problem is to keep a running total of what Carla has. When she pays the first part of her tuition bill, she winds up owing 250 (585 – 116 – 219 = 250). Then, after Carla wins the lottery and settles up with both the school and her friend, she has 947 – 250 – 219 = **478**. Choice C is correct.

18. Q = 0.25R. S = 0.3R. Thus, Q/S = 0.25/0.30 = 5/6. Choice E is correct.

19. From the data in the problem, we can write the following equation: x + (x + 2) + (x + 4) + (x + 6) + (x + 8) = 370, so 5x + 20 = 370, so 5x = 350, x = 70. x + 8 = **78**. Choice C is correct.

20. First, let's define our variables. We will let x = the length of the gift box. Therefore, its width = x + 4 and its area (Length x Width) = x(x + 4). Our equation becomes:

$x(x + 4) = 572$
$x^2 + 4x - 572 = 0$
$(x - 22)(x + 26) = 0$
Therefore, x = 22 and -26. Since a length cannot be negative, we can discard the -26 root. The length of the rectangle is **22** and the width is 22 + 4 = 26. Choice C is correct. .

21. The best way to attack this type of problem is to summarize our data in a simple table.
In this case, the hospice patients either have HIV or cancer. Some of the patients are under 18, while others are over 18. When we put the information into our chart, we get:

	HIV	Cancer	Total
Under 18	10	60	70
Over 18	110	20	130
Total	120	80	200

From the table, we can answer the question; the number of HIV patients under 18 is **10**. Choice A is correct.

22. In this case, the test writers have thrown us a curveball by presenting the number of nickels to dimes as a ratio. Don't be intimidated by it – just use the information to define the variables. In this case, since the ratio of nickels to dimes is 3:5, we will let 3x = the number of nickels and 5x = the number of dimes. Since their total is 80, our equation becomes:

3x + 5x = 80
8x = 80
x = 10
Therefore, the number of nickels is 3(10) = 30; their value is 5(30) = **$1.50**. Choice D is correct.

23. To solve, we must first calculate the amount of work that Professor Davis did in 3 days, which is (1/5)(3) = 3/5. Miguel, therefore, only had to complete 2/5 of the book. Since Miguel's rate is 1/10, our equation

becomes 1/10 = (1/x)(2/5), or 1/10 = 2/5x
1/10 = 2/5x
x = **4** days. Choice C is correct

24. This problem is a combination of two sub-series. In the first one, each number increase by 1 (5, 6, 7, 8); in the second, each number increases by 2 (9, 11, 13, 15). The next number would be **9**. Choice B is correct.

25. Let's substitute numbers for the variables and see what we get. Let's assume that we have 10 watermelons that cost $3.00 each and 5 apples that cost 60 cents each. Hence, W = 10, X = 3.00, Y = 5 and Z = 0.60.

The total cost of W watermelons is 100(10)(3) = 100WX
The total cost of C apples is (5)(60) = YZ
Therefore, the total cost of the watermelons and apples is 100(10)(3) + (5)(6) = **100WX + YZ**. Choice B is correct.

26. The average value = 23/50 = **0.46** million dollars. Choice C is correct.

27. The average value = 31/409 = **0.076** million dollars. Choice A is correct.

28. Total value of financial products sold by online brokerage = 92 + 27 + 31 = **150** million. Choice C is correct.

Quantitative Section 6: 28 questions   45 minutes

Each question has two quantities to be compared: one in Column A and one in Column B. Compare the quantities taking into consideration any other information given and choose
Answer A - if the quantity in Column A is greater
Answer B - if the quantity in Column B is greater
Answer C - if the two quantities are equal
Answer D - if the relationship cannot be determined without further information.

1. Sam is five times as old as Greg. Lori is 15 years older than Sam. Their combined age is 81.

Column A	Column B
Greg's age	5

2. Stenographer 1 can type four times as fast as Stenographer 2.

Column A	Column B
The number of pages Stenographer 2 will type, if they both spend and equal amount of time typing 1000 pages of data	250

3. At a church raffle, the pastor selects one ticket randomly for a prize out of 40 tickets in the raffle bowl.

Column A	Column B
The probability (in percent) that any one ticket will be selected	2%

4. In triangle FHG, one angle is equal to 60 degrees, the second angle is equal to x, and the third angle is equal to 3x.

Column A	Column B
x	45

5. The ratio of the areas of Circle A and Circle B is 16π to 36π.

Column A	Column B
The ratio of the circumference of Circle A to Circle B	2/3

6. A retiree needs to earn $25,000 in interest per year from her three investments to make ends meet. She already has $200,000 invested at 8% interest and $80,000 invested at 3% interest.

Column A	Column B
The additional amount money must she invest at 5% interest to reach her $25,000 total	$135,000

7. In the xy-plane, a circle is centered at the origin and passes through the point (-7,0). What is the area of the circle?

    a. $49/\pi$
    b. $3.5\,\pi$
    c. $7\,\pi$
    d. $49\,\pi$
    e. $81\,\pi$

8. If f (a) = a^2 - 4a + 3, what is f(-1) ?

    a.   -2
    b.   0
    c.   7
    d.   8
    e.   9

9. What is the mean of the following set of numbers? 44, 33, 58, 22, 16, 66

    a.   35.8
    b.   38.5
    c.   38.9
    d.   39.8
    e.   39.9

10. 23/42 – 35/84 =

    a.   −12/84
    b.   −11/84
    c.   11/84
    d.   12/84
    e.   12/42

11. For the repeating decimal 0.04321043210432104321....., what is the 49th digit to the right of the decimal point?

    a.   0
    b.   1
    c.   2
    d.   3
    e.   4

12. If p =3 and q is 2, what is $(9^p)(27^q)$ =

    a. 3^9
    b. 3^{14}
    c. $(729)^2$
    d.   6561 x 2
    e. 9^5

13. If   m (8)(10)(12)(14)= (4)(5)(6)(7), what is the value of m?

    a.   1/16
    b.   1/8
    c.   ½
    d.   8
    e.   16

14. Which of the following are the solutions to the following equation? $x^2 + 3x - 18 = 0$

    a.   −2, 9
    b.   2, -9
    c.   -3, 6
    d.   3, -6
    e.   3, -9

15. 12.67 =

    a.   37/4
    b.   38/3
    c.   72/6
    d.   72.5
    e.   100/6

16. Which of the following expresses the ratio of 12 ounces to 6 pounds?

    a.   1/16
    b.   1/12
    c.   1/8
    d.   1/6
    e.   ¼

17. If 86,868,686 is divided by 6,868, what is the remainder?

    a. 2222
    b. 3434
    c. 4343
    d. 6832
    e. 12648

18. The Glenview Airport offers two parking lots: long-term and short-term. Long-term parking costs a flat rate of $7.00 per day. Short-term parking costs $1.00 for the first two hours, and 50 cents for each additional hour. If a visitor plans to park for 6 hours at the airport, what will be the additional cost of parking in long-term parking versus short-term parking?

    a. $1.00
    b. $3.00
    c. $4.00
    d. $6.00
    e. $7.00

19. What is the product of the prime numbers between 10 and 20?

    a.   60
    b.   3,536
    c.   4,199
    d.   46,189
    e. 508,079

20. Carrie added M coins to her large collection, which gave her a total of N coins. Then, Carrie sold M – 180 of her coins to a local collector. How many coins did Carrie have left?

    a. M - N + 180
    b. N + M - 180
    c. N - M + 180
    d. N - M - 180
    e. (M + N – 180)/2

21. A stock decreases in value by 20 percent. By what percent must the stock price increase to reach its former value?

    a.   20%
    b.   25%
    c.   30%
    d.   40%
    e.   50%

22. The amount of sugar in a cake batter varies directly as the weight of the batter. If there are 42 pounds of sugar in a one-ton quantity of batter, how many pounds of sugar would there be in 325 pounds of batter?

    a.   3.412
    b.   6.825
    c.   13.650
    d.   27.30
    e.   54.60

23. The sum of two numbers is 238. Their difference is 46. What is the smaller number?

    a.   96
    b.   104
    c.   136
    d.   142
    e.   150

24. What is the thirteenth even positive integer minus the twelfth odd positive integer?

    a. 1
    b. 2
    c. 3
    d. 12
    e. 13

25. The mean of two numbers is 11d + 5. If one of the numbers is d, what is the other number?

    a. $(11g - 5)/d$
    b. $(g + 5)/d$
    c. $(g - 5)/10$
    d. $(g - 5)/(10 - d)$
    e. it cannot be determined from the information given

Refer to the chart below for questions 26– 28

Ribbons Won by Warren High School Football Team

	2006	2007
September	21	18
October	56	29
November	34	35
December	12	26

26. According to the table, what was the % increase in the number of ribbons won by the football team in November 2006 vs. November 2007?

    a. 1.03%
    b. 2.17%
    c. 10.3%
    d. 21.7%.
    e. 217%

27. According to the table, what was the % change in the number of ribbons won by the football team in September 2006 vs. September 2007?

    a. 3% decrease
    b. 14.3% decrease
    c. 16.7% decrease
    d. 14.3% increase
    e. 16.7% increase

28. According to the table, what was the overall % change in the number of ribbons won by the football team in 2006 and 2007?

    a. There was no change
    b. 4% decrease
    c. 12.2% decrease
    d. 16.7% decrease
    e. 87.8% decrease

Answer Key for Quantitative Section 6

1. In this problem, we know the relationship among the ages of Sam, Lori, and Greg – and their combined age. We can use this information to build an equation to solve for Greg's age. We will let Greg's age = x. Thus, Sam's age is 5x, while Lori's age 5x + 15. Since the sum of their ages is 81, our equation becomes:
x + 5x + (5x +15) = 81
11x + 15 = 81
11x = 66
x = **6** = Greg's age. Choice A is correct.

2. Let x = # of pages that Stenographer 2 types. 4x = # pages that Stenographer 1 types. x + 4x = 1,000, so x= **200 pages**. Choice B is correct.

3. 1/40 = 0.025 x 100 = **2.5%**. Choice A is correct.

4. The sum of the angles must be 180, so 180 = 60 + x + 3x, or 4x = 120, so x = **30**. Choice B is correct.

5. The ratio of the areas of Circle A to Circle B is $16\pi/36\pi$. Since the area of each circle is πr^2, then the radius of Circle A = 4 and the radius of Circle B is 6. We can use this information to calculate the circumference of each.

The circumference of Circle A =$2\pi r = 2\pi(4) = 8\pi$
The circumference of Circle B =$2\pi r = 2\pi(6)= 12\pi$
The ratio of the circumferences of Circle A to Circle B = 8/12 or **2/3**. Choice C is correct.

6. In this problem, the interest payments from all three investments must equal $25,000 per year. To solve, we will let x = the amount of money that the retiree must invest at 5%. Our equation becomes:

8%($200,000) + 3%($80,000) + 5%(x) = $25,000
(0.08)($200,000) + (0.03)($80,000) + (0.05)(x) = $25,000
16,000 + 2,400 + 0.05x = $25,000
0.05x = $6,600
x = **$132,000**. Choice B is correct.

7. A circle that is centered at the origin and passes through point (-7, 0) has a radius of 7. Therefore, its area is **49 π,** which is answer Choice D.

8. If f (a) = a^2 - 4a + 3, then f(-1) = (-1)(-1) - 4(-1) + 3 = 1 + 4 + 3 = **8**. Choice D is correct.

9. The mean is **39.8**, or Choice D.

10. Choice C is correct, **11/84**.

11. The repeating pattern is 04321, which includes 5 digits. The 49th digit is **2**, or Choice C.

12. If p =3 and q is 2, then $(9^p)(27^q)$ = (9)(9)(9) (27)(27) = 531,441, which is **(729)^2**. Choice C is correct.

13. m =**1/16**. Choice A is correct.

14. If x^2 + 3x – 18= 0, then (x + 6)(x - 3) = 0. So, **x = 3, -6**. Choice D is correct.

15. 12.67 = **38/3**. Choice B is correct.

16. 6 pounds = 96 oz. 12/96 = **1/8**. Choice C is correct.

17. We can solve this problem by dividing the two quantities: 86868686/6868 = 12648.323529. 0.323529 x 6868 = 2222. Choice A is correct. To check: 12648 x 6,868 = 86866464 + **2222**

18. Short-term parking for 6 hours costs $1.00 + 4(0.50) = $3.00. Long-term parking costs $7.00, which is **$4.00** more. Choice C is correct.

19. The prime numbers between 10 and 20 are 11, 13, 17, and 19. Their product is (11)(13)(17)(19)= **46,189**. Choice D is correct.

20. The fastest way to solve this problem is to substitute numbers for the variables. Then, we can convert the relationship back to letters. Let's say M = 200 and N = 500. Therefore, (M – 180) = 20.

When Carrie sold the coins, she reduced her collection by the following amount: 500 – (M – 180) = 500 – M + 180. Converting this back to letters, she had **N – M + 180** coins left. Choice C is correct.

21. Let's solve this by using $100 as the initial price of the stock: The 20% decrease reduced the stock price

to $80. For the stock to reach $100 again, there must be a $20 increase. $20 is what % of $80? 20/80 x 100 = 25%. Choice B is correct.

22. 42 / 2000 = x / 325. x = **6.825** lb. Choice B is correct.

23. First, let's define our variables. We will let one number = x. Therefore, the second unknown is x – 46. The sum of these two numbers is 238. Hence, our equation becomes:

x + (x – 46) = 238
2x = 284
x = 142
x – 46 = 142 – 46 = **96**. Choice A is correct.

24. We can solve this using the formulas for arithmetic sequences:

13th even: 2 + (13-1)(2) = 2 + 24 = 26.
12th odd: 1 + (12 – 1)(2) = 1 + 22 = 23.
26 – 23 = **3**. Choice C is correct.

25. In this case, we know that there are two numbers being averaged, one of which is d. We do not know the value of the other number, so we must "assign" an arbitrary value. Since the answer choices all include a term with the variable g, let's use g to represent our unknown. By definition, their sum divided by two = the average. Mathematically,

(d + g) / 2 = 11d + 5
2d + 2g = 22d + 10
2g -10 = 20d
g – 5 = 10d
d = (g - 5)/10. Choice C is correct.

26. 35/34 x 100 = **1.03%** increase. Choice A is correct.

27. 18/21 = 85.4%, which is a **14.3%** decrease from the previous year. Choice B is correct.

28. The team won 123 ribbons in 2006; 108 ribbons in 2007. 108/123 = 87.5%, which is a **12.2 %** decrease. Choice C is correct.

Quantitative Section 7: 28 questions   45 minutes

Each question has two quantities to be compared: one in Column A and one in Column B. Compare the
quantities taking into consideration any other information given and choose
Answer A - if the quantity in Column A is greater
Answer B - if the quantity in Column B is greater
Answer C - if the two quantities are equal
Answer D - if the relationship cannot be determined without further information.

1. **Column A**   **Column B**

The number of two-digit positive integers   2
that are multiples of both 7 and 9?

2. George earns a base salary of $300 each week, plus a 20% commission on all sales. During the week of
July 1, George sold $15,000 in merchandise

Column A   **Column B**

George's total earnings the week of July 1 $3,300

3. Five consecutive odd integers have a sum of 785.

Column A   **Column B**

159   The largest of the five integers

4. For a circle whose center is F, arc GH contains 40 degrees.

Column A   **Column B**

140   The number of degrees in angle GFH

5. In Triangle XYZ, the angles are in a ratio of 2:3:5.

Column A   **Column B**

18   The degrees in the smallest angle

6. Jade placed a large sum of money in a bank CD that pays 8% simple interest per year. Then, she
deposited the same amount, plus an additional $5000, in a real estate investment trust (REIT) that paid 12%
simple annual interest. Jade's total annual return from both investments is $26,000.

Column A   **Column B**

The amount that Jade places in the bank CD $125,000

__Directions__: For each problem, decide which answer is the best of the choices given.

178

7. A parallelogram has an interior angle of 60 degrees. What is the measure of the adjacent angle?

  a. 90
  b. 120
  c. 180
  d. 300
  e. It cannot be determined from the information given

8. What is the diameter of a circle with an area of 144π

  a. 7
  b. 12
  c. 15
  d. 24
  e. 48

9. Find the number of sides in a polygon if the measure of an interior angle is twice as great as the measure of an exterior angle.

  a. 4
  b. 5
  c. 6
  d. 7
  e. 8

10. If $f(j) = j^2 + 0.001j$, what is $f(0.05)$?

  a. 0.00025
  b. 0.00250
  c. 0.00255
  d. 0.00300
  e. 0.00350

11. Which of the following numbers CANNOT be even?

  a. The sum of two odd numbers
  b. The sum of an odd number and an even number
  c. The product of two even numbers
  d. The product of an odd number and an even number
  e. The sum of two even numbers

12. Reduce the following fraction to its simplest form: 50,000 / 5 million

  a. 1/1000
  b. 5/1000
  c. 1/100
  d. 5/100
  e. 1/10

13. What number, when cubed, is equal to the square of 125?

  a. 5
  b. 15
  c. 25
  d. 35
  e. 50

14. Solve for x: (x + 5) – (4/2)(6/3) = 12

        a. -2
        b. 4/5
        c. 8
        d. 11
        e. 13

15. Solve the following equations for y: 2x + 4y = 18, 4x – 6y = 8.

        a. 2
        b. 3
        c. 4
        d. 5
        e. 6

16. What is the value of (x + 2)(x + 5) – (x + 1) (x + 3)?

        a. 3x + 7
        b. 3x - 7
        c. 5x - 10
        d. 5x + 10
        e. 5x - 7

17. If $6x$ < 1,000, what integer is the largest possible value of x?

        a. 1
        b. 2
        c. 3
        d. 4
        e. 5

18. A shopkeeper reduced the price of a refrigerator from $1000 to $500. A week later, he reduced the sales price by an additional 15%. What was the new price for the refrigerator?

        a. $350
        b. $375
        c. $400
        d. $425
        e. $450

19. After decreasing by 23% after a tsunami, the population of Sri Lanka is now 578,845. What was the original population?

        a. 445,710
        b. 548,224
        c. 674,315
        d. 711,979
        e. 751,746

20. An online store sells two products: a hardcover and soft cover book of sonnets. Altogether, the company earned $65,000 in profits last year on the sale of 5000 units. If their profit on the hardcover book is $5 and their profit on the soft cover version is $15, how many soft cover books did they sell?

    a.   1000
    b.   1500
    c.   2000
    d.   3500
    e.   4000

21. Adam earns twice as much per hour as Josh. Josh earns $5 more per hour than Connie. Together, they earn $75 per hour. What is Adam's hourly wage?

    a. $15
    b. $20
    c. $25
    d. $30
    e. $40

22. A Greyhound bus drove down the highway at 60 miles per hour. Three hours later, a second Greyhound bus traveled the same route at 40 miles per hour. How many hours will it take the second bus to reach the first?

    a.   4
    b.   5
    c.   6
    d.   8
    e.   9

23. Gina and Hillary have a small web design business. Gina can design a web site for Client A in 2 hours. Hillary can design the same site in 3 hours. How long will it take them (in minutes) to design the site if they both work at the same time?

    a.   60
    b.   66
    c.   72
    d.   90
    e.   100

24. To dilute 300 qts of a 25% solution of garlic to a 20% solution, how many qts of water should a chef add?

    a.   15
    b.   60
    c.   75
    d.   120
    e.   125

25. What is the value of $c\,(\,c^{a+b}\,)\,/\,c^{a}$?

    a. c^{a+b}
    b. $2c^{b}$
    c. c^{1+b}
    d. c^{2b}
    e. $c\,/\,c^{b}$

Refer to the following charts to answer questions 26 – 28.

Number of Financial Products Sold

	Traditional Brokerage	**Online Brokerage**
CD	200	350
Annuity	50	105
401-K	85	409

Total Value of Financial Product Sold (in millions)

	CD	**Annuity**	**401-k**
Traditional Brokerage	54	23	10
Online Brokerage	92	27	31

26. What was the total number of Annuities sold at both brokerage houses for the time period represented by these charts?

        a.   23
        b.   27
        c.   50
        d.   105
        e.   155

27. What was the total number of financial products sold at the online brokerage for the time period represented by these charts?

        a.   150
        b.   155
        c.   335
        d.   864
        e.   1199

28. CDs account for what percentage of the total dollar value of financial products sold at the traditional brokerage house (for the time period represented by these charts)?

        a.   27.0%
        b.   37.0%
        c.   59.7%
        d.   62.1%
        e.   70.2%

Answer Key for Quantitative Section 7

1. The two-digit positive integers that are multiples of 9 are 18, 27, 36, 45, 54, 63, 72, 81, 90, and 99. Of these, only 63 is *also* a multiple of 7. Hence, the correct answer is **1.** Choice B is correct.

2. George's total earnings = base salary + commissions = $300 + $15,000(0.20) = **$3,300.** Choice C is correct.

3. Our equation is: $x + (x + 2) + (x + 4) + (x + 6) + (x + 8) = 785$. Thus, $5x + 20 = 785$, or $5x = 765$. $x = 153$, $X + 2 = 155$, $X + 4 + 157$, $X + 6 = 159$, $x + 8 = 161$. The largest number is **161.** Choice B is correct.

4. According to the problem, angle F = 40 degrees. Since it is a central angle, it creates an isosceles triangle within the circle, with GF and FH as equal sides. Angles G and H are therefore equal, with a sum of 180 - 40 = 140 degrees. Angle GFH is therefore **70 degrees**. Choice A is correct.

5. The sum of all interior angles is 180 degrees. In this case, we can represent the three angles by 2x, 3x, and 5x, respectively. Therefore, our equation becomes 2x + 3x + 5x = 180, so 10x = 180 and X = 18. The smallest angle is 2x = **36.** Choice B is correct.

6. Let x = the amount in the bank CD; x + 5000 = the amount in the REIT
Interest = Principal x Rate x Time. In this case, we know the total amount that Jade earned per year, which is the sum of the two individual investments. So, X(0.08)(1) + (x + 5000)(0.12)(1) = 26,000
8x + 12(x + 5000) = 2,600,000, so 20x = 2540000
x = **$127,000** in bank CD. Choice A is correct.

7. The adjacent angle is 180 – 60 =**120.** Choice B is correct.

8. Area of circle = πr^2. In this case, the radius is the square root of 144, or 12. The diameter is 12 x 2 = **24.** Choice D is correct.

9. For a hexagon, an exterior angle = 360/6 = 60; interior angle = 180 - 60 = **120.** Choice C is correct.

10. If f(j) = j^2 + 0.001j, then f (0.05) = (0.05)(0.05) + (0.001)(0.05) = 0.0025 + 0.00005 = **0.00255.** Choice C is correct.

11. The correct answer choice MUST be odd. By plugging in numbers to test each answer choice, we can quickly determine that choice B, the sum of an odd number and an even number, is the only one that cannot produce an even number. It is therefore the correct answer.

12. 50,000 / 5, 000, 000 = 5/500 = **1/100.** Choice C is correct.

13. 25 x 25 x 25 = **125 x 125**. Choice C is correct.

14. (x + 5) – 4 = 12, thus x = **11.** Choice D is correct.

15. To solve the equations for y, we must eliminate x and add the equations together. To do so, we must multiple the first equation by two and subtract the second equation from it:

4x + 8y = 36
4x – 6y = 8
14y = 28 or y = 2. Choice A is correct.

16. (x + 2)(x +5) – (x + 1) (x + 3) = $(x^2 + 7x + 10)$ - $(x^2 + 4x +3)$ = 3x + 7. Choice A is correct.

17. 6 x 6 x 6 = 216, while 6 x 6 x 6 x 6 = 1296. Hence, **3** is the largest integer value of x. Choice C is correct.

18. The trick to this question is to ignore the initial reduction from $1000 to $500, which is extraneous information. What we are being asked to determine is a 15% reduction of a refrigerator that is marked at $500. Our answer is 500 - (500)(0.15) = 500 – 75 = **$425.** Choice D is correct.

19. Let x = the original population. 0.77x = 578,845. Thus, x = **751,746**. Choice E is correct.

20. Let x = # of soft cover books and 5000 – x = the # of hardcover books. The sum of their individual profits equals the total annual profit, or: 15x + 5(5000 – x) = 65000. To simplify: 15x + 25000 –5x = 65000 or 10x = 40000. x = **4000** soft cover books. Choice E is correct.

21. Let x = Connie's hourly wage. Josh's wage = x + 5. Since Adam earns twice as much as Josh, his hourly wage is 2 (x + 5). Therefore: x + (x + 5) + 2 (x + 5) = 75. To simplify: 4x + 15 = 75 or 4x = 60. x = Connie's wage = $15, Josh's wage = $20. Adam's wage = $40.
As a check, we can verify that $15 + $20 + $40 = **$75**. Choice E is correct.

22: The first step for this type of problem is to draw a quick chart of what we know.

Bus	Distance	Rate	Time
One	60(x + 3)	60	x + 3
Two	40x	40	x

In this case, the buses travel the same distance at different speeds. Our equation is: $60(x + 3) = 40x$. $60x + 180 = 40x$, so $-180 = 20x$. $x = $ **9 hours** = amount of time it will take the second bus to reach the first bus. Choice E is correct.

23. The problem asks us to determine the total amount of time that is needed for both girls to complete the job. First, we must figure the amount of work that each girl does as a percentage of the total amount:

Gina   Work = Rate x Time $(1/2)$ x T = $\frac{1}{2}$ T
Hillary   Work = Rate x Time $(1/3)$ x T = $1/3$T

Now, we must add them together to figure the total time for the job: $\frac{1}{2}$ T + $1/3$ T = 1. So, $3/6$T + $2/6$T =1 $3T + 2T = 6$, or $5T = 6$, so T = $6/5$ hours, or 1.2 hours
Solving for T, we find that they can complete the job in 1.2 hours if they work together, or **72** minutes. Choice C is correct.

24. First, we must draw a table with the information that we know.

Quantity of Solution (qt)	% Garlic	Amount of Garlic (qt)
300	25	300(0.25)
x	0	0
x + 300	20	0.20(x + 300)

In this case, we will let x = the amount of water to be added. Therefore, the volume of the final solution (in which the water has been added) will equal x + 300.

Once we have these variables, we can complete the rest of the chart, and derive our expressions for the AMOUNT of garlic in each solution. We can then use the information to write an equation to solve for our unknown. Since our only change is to add water – and to dilute the amount of garlic – our equation is: $300(0.25) + 0 = 0.20(x + 300)$, or $75 = 0.20x + 60$. This simplifies to $0.20x = 15$. x = **75** quarts of water. Choice C is correct.

25. $c \, (\, c^{a+b} \,) \, / \, c^a = (c^{1})(c^{a+b})(c^{-a}) = c^{1+a+b-a} = \mathbf{c^{1+b}}$. Choice C is correct.

26. Total Annuities = 50 + 105 = **155**. Choice E is correct.

27. Total number of products sold = 350 + 105 + 409 = **864**. Choice D is correct.

28. 54 / (54+ 23 + 10) = 54/87= **62.1%.** Choice D is correct.

Quantitative Section 8: 28 questions   45 minutes

Each question has two quantities to be compared: one in Column A and one in Column B. Compare the quantities taking into consideration any other information given and choose
Answer A - if the quantity in Column A is greater
Answer B - if the quantity in Column B is greater
Answer C - if the two quantities are equal
Answer D - if the relationship cannot be determined without further information.

1. Clare earns $675 per week as an accountant, but she pays 15% of her earnings in taxes.

Column A	Column B
$29,895	Claire's yearly take home pay

2.

Column A	Column B
The average of five consecutive even integers whose sum is 850	170

3. Two delivery trucks are 640 miles apart. At midnight, they start to travel toward each other at rates of 50 and 30 miles per hour, respectively.

Column A	Column B
The number of hours before they pass each other	10

4.

Column A	Column B
The number of 3-inch segments in 35/7 yards	15

5. A local hotel employs 285 men and 15 women.

Column A	Column B
The probability that one employee picked at random will be a woman	1/20

6.

Column A	Column B
$3^5 \times 9^3$	3^{10}

Directions: _For each problem, decide which answer is the best of the choices given._

7. For a line with the equation x + 3y = 6, what is the slope?

     a.   −6
     b.   −1/3
     c.   −1/6
     d.   1/6
     e.   1

8. Find the number of sides in a polygon if the measure of an interior angle is three times as great as the measure of an exterior angle.

     a.   4
     b.   5
     c.   6
     d.   7
     e.   8

9. What is the length of the hypotenuse in an equilateral right triangle with an area of 121?

     a. $7\sqrt{2}$
     b.   7
     c. $11\sqrt{2}$
     d.   11
     e.   15

10. Which of the following quantities is greater than 1/7?

     a.   0.1399
     b.   2/15
     c.   3/19
     d.   0.141
     e.   4/29

11. $(4x^2)^2(3x^3)^3 =$

     a. $12x^{10}$
     b. $144x^{13}$
     c. $288x^{10}$
     d. $432x^{13}$
     e. $1296x^{13}$

12. If (d)(3)(5) = (10)(e)(3), and neither d nor e are 0, what is the value of e/d?

     a.   1/3
     b.   1/2
     c.   2/3
     d.   2
     e.   3

13. For the following system of equations, what are the possible values of a? ab = 1, a = 4b

     a.   ½ or −1/2
     b.   1 or -1
     c.   2 or -2
     d.   4 or -4
     e.   There is no solution to the equations

14. Rectangle CDEF has a length of 6 and a width of 2. What is its perimeter?

    a. 8
    b. 12
    c. 16
    d. 40
    e. 64

15. Find the equation of the line that is parallel to y = 14 and containing the point (9, 7).

    a. y = 7 x + 2
    b. y = 7
    c. x = 14
    d. y = -7/9 x + 14
    e. y = 7/9 x + 14

16. 15 / (3/6) =

    a. 3
    b. 5
    c. 30
    d. 90
    e. 300

17. Sheila can wear her 100% linen suit four times before she needs to have it dry cleaned. She wears the suit to church every Sunday and to meetings at her bridge club on the first Tuesday of every month. If it costs $8.00 for each individual cleaning, and Sheila does not wear the suit on any other occasions, how much will Sheila pay to dry clean the suit each year?

    a. $48.00
    b. $64.00
    c. $96.00
    d. $104.00
    e. $128.00

18. If the diameter of a circle increases by 100%, by what percent will the area of the circle increase?

    a. 50%
    b. 100%
    c. 150%
    d. 200%
    e. 300%

19. A jeweler has 62 garnet rings in stock. The only color choices for the bands are gold and silver. Which of the following is a possible ratio of gold to silver bands for this selection of rings?

    a. 12/31
    b. 12/54
    c. 27/35
    d. 27/62
    e. 12/13

20. Liz is 42 years old and Amelia is 24. How many years ago was Liz three times as old as Amelia?

      a.   9
      b.   10
      c.   15
      d.   18
      e.   20

21. In a hospital with 39 patients, the average (mean) temperature of the male patients was 101.7 F. If the average (mean) temperature of the 23 female patients was 98.5 F, what was the average temperature of all 39 patients (in degrees F)?

      a.   98.0
      b.   98.8
      c.   99.0
      d.   99.8
      e.   100.1

22. The clock at the Capitol Building has an hour hand that is 12 feet long. How many feet will the top of the hand move between the hours of midnight and eight am?

      a. 16π
      b. 18π
      c. 24π
      d. 36π
      e. 48π

23.   The Wilson family measured their rectangular backyard for a privacy fence. If the ratio of the length to width was 15:36, what was the diagonal of the enclosed area (in feet)?

      a.   24
      b.   36
      c.   39
      d.   48
      e.   It cannot be determined from the information given.

24. Argon gas is pumped into a tank at a rate of 42 cubic inches per second. If the chamber's dimensions are 12 inches by 24 inches by 42 inches, how many minutes will it take for the tank to be completely filled with gas (to the nearest tenth of a minute)?

      a.   4.8
      b.   9.6
      c.   28.8
      d.   57.6
      e.   288.0

25. To adhere to local zoning laws, an architect must reduce the size of a square building by 800 square yards. When she does, the area of the building is equal to five times its perimeter. What was the original area of the building (in square yards)?

      a.   20
      b.   40
      c.   400
      d.   1,600
      e.   3,200

Use the following table to answer questions 26 – 28.

Percentage of Diabetics (By Age)

	China	Italy	France	Germany
Under 10	5	5	2	0
10 – 18	20	30	15	13
19 – 30	35	30	28	29
31 – 50	30	30	40	48
Over 51	10	5	15	10

26. A leading economic journal recently estimated the number of diabetics in China and Germany at 8 million and 14 million, respectively. If these numbers are accurate, what is the total number of people in both nations between 19 and 30 who are diabetics?

    a.   2.8 million
    b.   4.06 million
    c.   6.08 million
    d.   6.86 million
    e.   Cannot be determined from the information given

27. If there are currently 18 million diabetics in Italy, and the Italian government offers free insulin to those who are under 10 and over 51, then how many remaining diabetics will still have to buy insulin?

    a.   900,000
    b.   1.8 million
    c.   3.6 million
    d.   12.6 million
    e.   16.2 million

28. Physicians in China recently announced that all diabetics who are younger than 19 will be required to use automatic insulin pumps, rather than traditional injections. If the total number of diabetics in China is 56 million, how many of them will be required to use the automatic insulin pumps?

    a.   2.8 million
    b.   5.6 million
    c.   11.2 million
    d.   14 million
    e.   28 million

Answer Key for Quantitative Section 8

1. Clare's total earnings are $675 (52) = $35,100(0.85) = **$29,835.00** Choice A is correct.

2. The average is simply 850/5 = **170.** Choice C is correct.

3. The first step for this type of problem is to draw a quick chart of what we know:

Truck	Distance	Rate	Time
A	50x	50	x
B	30x	30	x

Here, we can use the rate equation to determine the time at which the two delivery trucks will pass each other. By definition, they are traveling the same distance, which is 640 miles. Also by definition, that distance equals the SUM of the quantities (Rate x Time) for each truck. Hence, our equation becomes:

50x + 30x = 640
80x = 640. Thus, x = 8. They will pass after **8 hours.** Choice B is correct.

4. 35/7 yards is equal to 5 yards. Each yard is equal to 12 inches, or four 3-inch segments. Therefore, 5 yards = (5)(4) = **20** 3-inch segments. Choice A is correct.

5. Probability = Number of Women/Number of People = 15/300 = **1/20**. Choice C is correct.

6. $3^5 \times 9^3$ = 177,147, which is 3^{11}. Choice A is correct.

7. The slope is **–1/3.** Choice B is correct.

8. For an octagon, an exterior angle = 360/8 = 45; interior angle = 180 – 45 = **135**. Choice E is correct.

9. In an equilateral right triangle, x^2 = 121, so the two side lengths are 11. The hypotenuse is 15.56, or **11 √2.** Choice C is correct.

10. 3/19 is greater than **1/7.** Choice C is correct.

11. $(4x^2)^2(3x^3)^3$ = $(16x^4)(27x^9)$ = **432x^{13}.** Choice D is correct.

12. The equation reduces to d = 2e, so e/d. = ½. Choice B is correct.

13. If ab = 1 and a = 4b, then b = 1/a. Therefore, a = 4/a or a^2 = 4. Hence, **a = 2 or –2**. Choice C is correct.

14. Perimeter = 2(6) + 2(2) = **16**. Choice C is correct.

15. y = 14 is horizontal, which means that a line parallel to it must also be horizontal. Hence, the answer is **y = 7**. Choice B is correct.

16. 15 / (3/6) = **30**. Choice C is correct.

17. To solve, we must first calculate the total number of times that Sheila wears the suit each year, which is 52 + 12 = 64. Then, we must calculate the total number of times that she needs to have it cleaned per year, which is 64/4 = 16. If the cost per cleaning is $8.00, then Sheila's annual cost of dry cleaning it will be (16)($8.00) = **$128**. Choice E is correct.

18. The fastest way to solve is to select values for the diameter of the circle and determine the effect on the area. If the diameter is 4, the radius is 2 and the area is 4π. Increasing the diameter by 100% to 8 makes the new radius 4 and the new area 16π. The percent increase is (16 - 4)/4 = 12/4, or **300%.**

Let's confirm our answer with another set of numbers. If the diameter is 10, the radius is 5 and the area is 25π. Increasing the diameter by 100% to 20 makes the new radius 10 and the new area 100π. The percent increase is (100 - 25)/25 = 75/25, or 300%. Choice E is correct.

19. The sum of the numerator and denominator must be a factor of 62, which is the total number of rings in stock. This limits the possibilities to 1, 2, 31 and 62. The correct answer choice, C, is the only one in which the terms add up to one of these factors (**27/35**, the sum is 62). The others are mathematically impossible.

20. Here, we are given the current ages of two women and asked to calculate a time when those numbers met a specified set of criteria. Currently, Liz = 42 and Amelia = 24. Therefore, X years ago, Liz = 42 – x and Amelia = 24 – x.

The correct equation to express the relationship between their ages x years ago is therefore:
42 – x = 3 (24 – x)
42 – x = 72 – 3x
2x = 30. x = **15** Choice C is correct. Fifteen years ago, Liz was 27 and Amelia was 9.

21. Because the number of male and female patients is not the same, we must take a *weighted average* for each of the two groups.

Average =(Sum of Males' Temperatures + Sum of Females' Temperatures/Total # Patients
Average = {(16)(101.7) + (23)(98.5)} / 39 = {1627.2 + 2265.5}/39 = 3892.7/39 = **99.8° F** Choice D is correct.

22. The clock at the Capitol building is a circle with a radius of 12 feet. The total circumference is $2\pi r = 2\pi$ (12) = 24π. In eight hours, the hand will move across two-thirds of the circumference of the circle, which is (2/3)24π = **16π**. Choice A is correct.

23. This is one of those annoying "trick" questions for which the GRE is notorious. Most students scramble furiously to calculate an area by using the numbers in the ratio, but it is not necessary.   If the ratio of the length to width is 15:36, then the diagonal will be **39**, because it is a multiple of a 5-12-13 special triangle. Choice C is correct.

24. Volume = (12)(24)(42) = 12,096 cubic inches/42 cubic inches per second = 288 seconds = **4.8** minutes. Choice A is correct.

25. First, let's define our variables.   We will let x = the side length of the building. Therefore, the perimeter = 4x. Therefore, our equation becomes:
x^2 – 800 = 5(4x)
x^2 – 20x – 800 = 0
(x + 20)(x - 40)= 0
Therefore, x = - 20 and +40. Since the length of a building cannot be negative, we can discard the -20 root. Therefore, the side length of the building is 40 yards and its area is (40)(40) = **1,600** square yards. Choice D is correct.

26. China: 8 million diabetics x (0.35) = 2.8 million between 19 and 30
Germany: 14 million diabetics x (0.29) = 4.06 million between 19 and 30

Therefore, the total number of people in both nations between 19 and 30 who wear contact lenses = 2. 8 + 4.06 = **6.86** million. Choice D is correct.

27. 18 million (0.05) = 900,000 under age 10; 8 million (0.05) = 900,000 over age 51.

900,000 + 900,000 = 1,800,000 people will get free insulin. The remaining **16.2** million will still need to purchase insulin. Choice E is correct.

28. 56 million (0.20 + 0.05) = **14** million diabetics under age 19. Choice D is correct.

Quantitative Section 9: 28 questions 45 minutes

Each question has two quantities to be compared: one in Column A and one in Column B. Compare the quantities taking into consideration any other information given and choose
Answer A - if the quantity in Column A is greater
Answer B - if the quantity in Column B is greater
Answer C - if the two quantities are equal
Answer D - if the relationship cannot be determined without further information.

1. Acme Grocery sells organic sesame seeds for 52.5 cents per ounce. A wholesale customer purchases 50 pounds of the organic sesame seeds at a 20% discount.

Column A	Column B
The total price the wholesaler paid for the seeds	$340

2. A cook is mixing 75% chocolate liqueur with 1,200 gallons of 50% chocolate liqueur to produce a mixture containing 60% chocolate liqueur.

Column A	Column B
The gallons of 75% chocolate liqueur needed	800

3. The following sequence continues indefinitely.

4,5,6,7,8,9,4,5,6,7,8,9,4,5,6,7,8,9,4,5,6,7,8,9,4,5,6,7,8,9,……..

Column A	Column B
The sum of the 500th term through the 505th term	27

4. A cube and a rectangular solid are equal in volume. The lengths of the edges of the rectangular solid are 8, 9, and 24.

Column A	Column B
The length of an edge of the cube	16

5. An octagon has seven interior angles that measure 85, 95, 115, 120, 125, 140 and 145.

Column A	Column B
The measure of the eighth internal angle (in degrees)	205

6. Bridget has 75 coins that are worth $16.50. The coins are all quarters and dimes.

Column A	Column B
The number of quarters Bridget has	65

Directions: For each problem, decide which answer is the best of the choices given.

7. What is the sum of the measure of the interior angles of a polygon having 13 sides?

    a.   360
    b.   780
    c.   1,560
    d.   1,980
    e.   2,340

8. If a wholesale dealer can buy K HD-TVs for V dollars, how much will P HD-TVs cost (in dollars)?

    a. 1/PVK
    b. (100/K)PV
    c. PK/V
    d. PV/K
    e. PVK

9. If x#y = 2xy + y, what is 3#7?

    a.   6
    b.   11
    c.   19
    d.   27
    e.   49

10. Which of these statements is/are true?

    I. The sum of the angles of a polygon is 360 degrees.
    II. In a scalene triangle, two angles may be equal.
    III. On the x-axis, all values of y are equal to 0.

    a.   I
    b.   II
    c.   III
    d.   I and II
    e.   I, II and III

11. If the prime numbers between 80 and 90 are added together, what is their sum?

    a.   81
    b.   89
    c.   164
    d.   172
    e.   176

12. Triangles with equal angles but unequal sides are called

    a. Similar triangles
    b. Congruent triangles
    c. Scalene triangles
    d. Isosceles triangles
    e. Equilateral triangles

13. What is the circumference of a circle with a diameter of 2/(9π)?

    a.   3
    b.   2/9
    c.   4/9π
    d.   18
    e.   18/π

14. $6 + 1/3 - (4/9)^2 - (3/2)(5/6) =$

    a.   4.73
    b.   4.89
    c.   5.73
    d.   5.89
    e.   6.20

15. Donna and David both decided to participate in a race for charity. Donna had eleven sponsors who promised to donate $5 for every mile that she ran. David had fifteen sponsors who promised to donate $3 for every mile that he ran. If Donna ran six miles and David ran five miles, how much ADDITIONAL money did Donna raise for the charity than David?

    a. $105
    b. $210
    c. $225
    d. $330
    e. $555

16. Dan brought his car to the mechanic to have his engine fixed. The mechanic quoted him the following prices for parts: $350 for a new alternator, $150 for the battery and $25 for miscellaneous parts. Assuming that the minimal charge for labor is $45 per hour (rounded to the nearest half-hour) and that the shop can complete all repairs in 3.5 hours, what is the minimum amount that Dan will have to pay to have his car fixed?

    a. $157.50
    b. $525.00
    c. $682.50
    d. $705.00
    e. $727.50

17. How many positive integers less than 100 are evenly divisible by 4, 6, 8 and 12?

    a.   1
    b.   2
    c.   3
    d.   4
    e.   5

18. A tour bus at Disney World holds 124 people. If the park requires one adult for every five children on the tour bus, how many children can fit on the bus?

    a.   20
    b.   22
    c.   24
    d.   30
    e.   32

19. In a large lecture hall containing 540 female students, 27 were on birth control pills, 110 were taking antibiotics, and 220 were taking antihistamines. The remaining 193 students were not taking any medication. In simplest terms, what is the ratio of female students taking birth control pills to the total number of students in the lecture hall?

    a.   1: 100
    b.   1 : 193
    c.   1: 27
    d.   1 : 20
    e.   1 : 5

20. The cost for a pen and notebook at the campus bookstore is $10.50.   If the notebook costs $10.00 more than the pen, what does the pen cost (assuming there is no sales tax)?

    a.   25 cents
    b.   50 cents
    c.   75 cents
    d. $1.00
    e. $1.50

21. Jill and Kim leave school at the same time and drive in opposite directions. After two hours, they are 100 miles apart. How fast is Jill driving, if Kim is driving 10 miles per hour faster?

    a.   20
    b.   30
    c.   35
    d.   40
    e.   50

22. Six hundred and fifty employees at a software company have registered for classes at the corporate health center. Two hundred and seventy five have signed up for karate. Five hundred and eighty have signed up for low calorie cooking. Three hundred employees have signed up for both karate and low calorie cooking. How many employees have signed up for NEITHER karate and low calorie cooking?

    a.   95
    b.   105
    c.   125
    d.   150
    e.   200

23. A bookstore is preparing a display with five different novels by a best-selling author. How many possible arrangements are there in the display (assume no title is repeated)?

    a.   25
    b.   120
    c.   125
    d.   500
    e.   600

24. The mean of seven numbers is 77. If 12 is subtracted from each of five of the numbers, what is the new mean?

    a.   65.00
    b.   66.66
    c.   68.43
    d.   70.15
    e.   72.00

Use the following table to answer questions 25 – 28.

Percentage of Contact Lens Wearers (By Age)

	U.S.	U.K.	France	India
Under 10	2	5	1	0
10 – 18	21	30	15	3
19 – 30	38	35	29	19
31 – 50	29	25	40	66
Over 51	10	5	15	12

25. If there are 18 million contact lens wearers in the U.S., how many of them are less than 18 years old?

    a.   3.24 million
    b.   3.78 million
    c.   4.14 million
    d.   21 million
    e.   23 million

26. If the number of contact lens wearers in France is 5 million, and they each own exactly three pairs of lenses, how many of the pairs belong to wearers who are 51 or older?

    a.   450,000
    b.   750,000
    c.   1,500,000
    d.   2,250,000
    e.   4,500,000

27. Which of the following best explains the small percentage of teenage contact lens wearers in India, compared to those in the U.S., the U.K, and France?

    a.   They are unsafe for use
    b.   They are unavailable
    c.   They are astronomically expensive
    d.   They are legally prohibited for minors
    e.   They are not advertised on Indian television

28. Which country has the largest number of contact lens wearers between 19 and 30?

    a.   U.S.
    b.   U.K.
    c.   France
    d.   India
    e.   Cannot be determined from the information given

Answer Key for Quantitative Section 9

1. Sesame seeds are 0.525 dollars per ounce. The cost for 50 pounds = (50)(16)(0.525) = $420 x 0.80 = **$336**. Choice B is correct.

2. First, we must draw a table with the information we know.

Amount of Syrup	% Chocolate	Amount of Chocolate
x	75	75x
1,200	50	50(1,200)
1,200 + x	60	60(1200 + x)

The problem asks us to calculate the amount of syrup containing 75% chocolate liqueur that should be blended with syrup that is 50% chocolate liqueur to create a blend that is 60% chocolate liqueur. We will let x = the gallons of 75% syrup needed. Therefore, the total amount of syrup is = 1200 + x.

Since the total amount of chocolate liqueur in the blend is the sum of the amounts in the two original syrups, we can write an equation to solve for x:
75x + 50(1,200) = 60(1,200 + x)
75x + 60,000 = 72,000 + 60x
15x = 12,000
x = **800** gallons of syrup containing 75% chocolate liqueur are needed. Choice C is correct.

3. The series includes 6 digits that repeat indefinitely in the order: 4,5,6,7,8,9. The *sum of any six consecutive digits* will therefore be the sum of 4+5+6+7+8+9 =**39**. Choice A is correct.

4. Volume of rectangular solid = 8 x 9 x 24 = 1,728 = also the volume of the cube. So, the length of an edge of the cube is the cubic root of 1728, or **12**. Choice B is correct.

5. For an octagon, the sum of the interior angles is equal to 180(8 − 2) = 1,080 total degrees, so 85 + 95 + 115 + 120 + 125 + 140 + 145 + X = 1080. X = **255** degrees. Choice A is correct.

6. First, we must define our variables. In this case, x = the number of quarters. Therefore, 75 − x = the number of dimes. Since the total value of these two coins is $16.50, our equation becomes:

25x + 10(75 − x) = 1650
25x + 750 − 10x = 1650
15x = 900
x **= 60 quarters**. Choice B is correct.

7. To solve, we use the equation 180 (13-2) = **1,980.** Choice D is correct.

8. To solve, let's plug in random numbers for each variable. In this case, let's assume that the dealer bought 20 HD-TVs (K) for 100 dollars (V). The cost for a single HD-TV is therefore 100/20 or V/K or 5 dollars. The cost for any value of P will simply be that number times 5, which, in symbols, is **PV/K**. Choice D is correct.

9. If x#y = 2xy + y, then 3#7: (2)(3)(7) + 7 = **49**. Choice E is correct.

10. Only III is true. Choice C is correct.

11. Choice D is correct. 83 + 89 = **172.**

12. Triangles with equal angles but unequal sides are **similar**. Choice A is correct.

13. Circumference is π x Diameter, or $2\pi/9\pi$= **2/9**. Choice B is correct.

14. 6 + 1/3 - (4/9)^2 - (3/2)(5/6) = 6 + 1/3 − 0.1975 − 1.25 = **4. 89**. Choice B is correct.

15. The problem asks us to calculate the difference between the amount of money raised by Donna and David. Eleven sponsors paid $5 for each mile that Donna ran. Since she ran six miles, Donna raised (11)(5)(6) = $330. In David's case 15 sponsors paid $3 for each mile. Since he ran five miles, David raised (15)(3)(5) = $225. Therefore, Donna raised **$105 more** than David. Choice A is correct.

16. The cost of repairs = Total cost of parts + Total cost of labor. The total for the parts is $350 + $150 + $25 = $525. The total cost for labor = ($45) (3.5) = $157.50. The total cost to fix the car is $525 + $157.50 = **$682.50**, or Choice C.

17. The question asks us to determine how positive integers less than 100 are evenly divisible by 4, 6, 8, and 12. First, we will list the integers that are evenly divisible by our largest number, which is 12: 12, 24, 36,

48, 60, 72, 84, and 96. (Note: Because they are all multiples of 12, these numbers are also evenly divisible by 6.)

Next, we eliminate numbers from this group that are NOT evenly divisible by 8, which leaves us with 24, 48, 72, and 96. (Note: Because they are all multiples of 8, they are also evenly divisible by 4.) Thus, there are **4** positive integers that meet the criterion: they are 24, 48, 72, and 96. Choice D is correct.

18. If there is one adult for every five children, we must divide the capacity of the bus by 6, 124/6 = 20.6. Therefore, there can be no more than **20** children on the tour bus (4 groups, each of which contains one adult and 20 children). Choice A is correct.

19. 27 / 550 = **1 / 20**. Choice D is correct.

20. Most students read this problem too quickly and simply choose Choice B, 50 cents. Not so fast. This problem contains a psychological trick that can easily convince you to select the wrong answer. First, let's define our variables. We will let the cost of the pen = x. Therefore, the cost of the notebook = x + $10.00. If the cost of both items is $10.50, our equation becomes: Cost of Pen + Cost of Notebook = Total Cost
x + (x + $10.00) = $10.50
2x + $10.00 = $10.50
2x = $0.50
X = **$0.25** = Choice A

21. The first step is to draw a quick chart of what we know:

Girl	Distance	Rate	Time
Jill	2x	x	2
Kim	2 (x + 10)	x + 10	2

Next, we must define our variables. In this case, we will let Jill's speed = x. Therefore, Kim's speed = x + 10. We also know that both girls drive for the same amount of time, which is 2 hours. We can now write an equation to solve for Jill's time based on the distance they travelled: Jill's Distance + Kim's Distance = Total Distance: 2x + 2(x + 10) = 100, so 2x + 2x + 20 = 100, which simplifies to 4x = 80 or X = **20** = Jill's speed. Choice A is correct.

22. In this case, we have four groups of employees (650 total): Taking Karate: 275; Taking a cooking class: 580; Taking karate AND a cooking class: 300; Taking neither activity: ? Hence, our equation is Karate + Cooking + Neither – Both = 650.
275 + 580 + Neither - 300 = 650
Neither = **95**. Choice A is correct.

23. For permutations, the correct formula is 5!/(5- 5)! = (5 x 4 x 3 x 2 x 1) / 1 = **120**. Choice B is correct.

24. For the original numbers, (7)(77) = 539 = sum. New sum= 539 – (12)(5) = 479. 479/7=**68.43.** Choice C is correct.

25. (18 million)(0.02 + 0.21) = **4.14 million**. Choice C is correct.

26. If France has a total of 5 million contact lens wearers, then the number of them who are 51 or older is (5 million)(0.15) = 750,000. If all of these patients own 3 pairs each, then the number of pairs is **2,250,000**. Choice D is correct.

27. Choice D is correct. Contact lenses are obviously available and affordable in India, because older patients wear them. The more logical explanation for the large discrepancy in use is that the law restricts their use to those who are 18 and over.

28. Choice E is correct. The chart only gives the % of contact lens wearers in each nation; it does not reveal the actual numbers. Without them, we cannot answer this question.

Quantitative Section 10: 28 questions   45 minutes

Each question has two quantities to be compared: one in Column A and one in Column B. Compare the quantities taking into consideration any other information given and choose
Answer A - if the quantity in Column A is greater
Answer B - if the quantity in Column B is greater
Answer C - if the two quantities are equal
Answer D - if the relationship cannot be determined without further information.

1. Carla bought several items for her new house, including a bed for $550, two chairs for $125 each, three sets of curtains for $45 per set, and an area rug for $225. Carla paid 5% sales tax for her purchases.

Column A	Column B
$1,218	The total amount that Carla spent

2. After announcing the availability of the Forever stamp, which costs 41 cents, the US Post Office recorded $2,313,716.10 in sales for the stamps at the Glendale office in a single day.

Column A	Column B
The number of Forever stamps sold that day	564,321

3. Luke purchased a new Mercedes for $65,000. The value of the car decreases by 12% each year.

Column A	Column B
The # years that must elapse before the Mercedes is worth $34,302	8

4. Gary and Bill have a lawn mowing business. Gary can mow a one-acre lawn in 3 hours. Bill can mow the same lawn in 4 hours.

Column A	Column B
The # of minutes it will take them to mow the lawn if they both work together	110

5. A cube has a volume of 27 cubic centimeters.

Column A	Column B
Its surface area (in square centimeters)	54

6. Tracy collected $6,500 in donations from 200 people to benefit a local charity. Each person gave her either $20 or $50.

Column A	Column B
The number of people who donated $50	120

7. Which of the following equations will have a horizontal line as its graph?

    a. $x = 2 - y$
    b. $x = 2 + y$
    c. $x/y = 2$
    d. $x = 2$
    e. $y = 2$

8. Which of the following relations is a function?

    a.   {(s, d), (v, z), (v, e)}
    b.   {(k, m), (v, x), (k, 9)}
    c.   {(4, 7), (5j 6), (4, 3)}
    d.   {(4, 3), (7, 6), (7, 8)}
    e.   {(4, 5), (5, 6), (7, 8)}

9. What is the next term in the following series: 11, 12, 13, 24, 15, 48.......

    a.   14
    b.   17
    c.   36
    d.   96
    e.   None of the above.

10. Which of the following answer choices correctly lists the prime numbers between 60 and 80?

    a.   61, 63, 67, 71, 73
    b.   61, 67, 71, 73, 77, 79
    c.   61, 67, 69, 71, 73, 77
    d.   61, 67, 71, 73, 79
    e.   67, 71, 73, 77, 79

11. If X is between 0 and –1, which of the following quantities is the largest?

    a. X^3
    b. X^5
    c. X^6
    d. X^7
    e.   It cannot be determined from the information given

12. If $(7b - 4)/2 = 16 - b$, then $b =$

    a.   1/2
    b.   2
    c.   3
    d.   4
    e.   9

13. If H = {6, 7, 8}, J = {9, 5, 7} and K = {7, 3, 4}, what is (H∩J)∩K?

    a. {7}
    b. {7, 5, 9}
    c. {5, 6, 7, 8, 9}
    d. {3, 4, 7}
    e. {5, 6, 7, 8}

14. If $4y \le 56$ and $3y \ge 36$, which of the following could be a value of y?

    a. 8
    b. 9
    c. 10
    d. 11
    e. 12

15. Diane has 18 errands to run, which take 14 minutes each, before she can go home. If Diane needs to be home by 5:00 pm, what is the latest time that she can start the errands?

    a. 11:40 am
    b. 11:48 am
    c. 12:40 pm
    d. 12:48 pm
    e. 1:40 pm

16. When x is divided by 17, the remainder is 9. What is the remainder when 5x is divided by 17?

    a. 3
    b. 7
    c. 9
    d. 11
    e. 13

17. A computer science curriculum includes 8 courses on hardware and 4 courses on software. The remaining ¼ of the courses are on web design. What fraction of the courses is devoted to software?

    a. 1/4
    b. 1/3
    c. 2/5
    d. 1/2
    e. 5/8

18. In the past year, Brad's coin collection increased from 214 to 328. What percentage increase does this number represent?

    a. 27%
    b. 33%
    c. 53%
    d. 72%
    e. 114%

19. A hallway that is 90 feet long is divided into two sections that are in the ratio of 3:2. What is the length of the shorter section?

       a. 9
       b. 18
       c. 21
       d. 27
       e. 36

20. Sue is twice as old as Grace. Lee is 5 years older than Grace. If their combined age is 65, how old is Grace?

       a. 12
       b. 15
       c. 16
       d. 18
       e. 24

21. Two motorcyclists are 540 miles apart. At 10:00 am they start traveling toward each other at rates of 65 and 70 miles per hour. At what time will they pass each other?

       a. 1:00 pm
       b. 1:30 pm
       c. 2:00 pm
       d. 3:30 pm
       e. 4:00 pm

22. Students at St. Agnes Academy either study French, Spanish or both. Sixty percent of the students study French, while fifteen percent study both Spanish and French. What percentage of the students only study Spanish?

       a. 10%
       b. 15%
       c. 20%
       d. 25%
       e. 30%

23. What is the probability that a card chosen at random from a standard deck of 52 cards is a King?

       a. 1/52
       b. 1/26
       c. 1/13
       d. 1/12
       e. 4/12

24. What is the sum of the first 150 positive integers?

       a. 10,500
       b. 11,250
       c. 11,325
       d. 11,400
       e. 15,000

25. The church must replace 6 stained glass windows that were destroyed by a hurricane. The windows are squares that measure 13 feet on each side. If the stained glass costs $5.86 per square foot, how many of the windows can the church afford to replace if they have budgeted $4000 for the project?

        a. 2
        b. 3
        c. 4
        d. 5
        e. 6

26. Investments A, B, and C yield $22,000 in total annual interest. Investment B. which earns 7% interest, is $25,000 larger than investment A, which earns 5% interest. In contrast, Investment C, which earns 9% interest, is $7,500 less than three times Investment A. How much is Investment A?

        a. $50,192.31
        b. $53,653.85
        c. $93,214.29
        d. $99,642.86
        e. $100,384.62

Refer to the following table for questions 27 and 28.

Joe's Budget for August 2009 (in dollars)

Rent	700
Car Payment	350
Utilities	185
Cell Phone	80
Insurance	55
Food	100
Credit Card	240
Clothes	75
Miscellaneous	321
Savings	35

27. Financial experts recommend that people Joe's age allocate at least 10% of their budget for savings. How much additional money would Joe have to save each month to reach this percentage?

        a. $35
        b. $79
        c. $150
        d. $179
        e. $214

28. To buy a house, Joe will have to assume a mortgage payment that is $300 per month higher than his current rent. Which expenses, if eliminated, will allow him to achieve this goal?

        a. Cell phone, Food and Clothes
        b. Credit card and Insurance
        c. Credit card and Savings
        d. Clothes and Credit card
        e. Savings, Clothes, Cell phone and Food

1. Carla spent $550 + $125(2) + $45 (3) + $225 = 550 + 250 + 135 + 225 = 1160 + (1160)(0.05)= **$1218.** Choice C is correct.

2. To answer, simply divide the total amount of sales by the cost per stamp: $2,313,716.10/0.41 = **5,643,210.** Choice A is correct.

3. Each year the car decreases by 12%. We can solve the problem by recording the depreciation in a chart:

Original value $65,000
First year ($65,000)(0.88) = $57,200
Second year ($57,200)(0.88) = $50,336
Third year ($50,336)(0.88) = $44,296
Fourth year ($44,296)(0.88) = $38,980
Fifth year ($38,980)(0.88) = **$34,302**. Choice B is correct

4. In this case, we must solve for the total time that is needed to complete the job. First, we figure the amount of work that each man does as a percentage of the total amount:

Gary   Work = Rate x Time (1/3) times T = 1/3 T
Bill   Work = Rate x Time (1/4) times T = 1/4T

Now, we can add these amounts together to figure the total time for the job:
1/3 T + 1/4 T = 1, so 4/12T + 3/12T = 1. When we solve for t, we get 7T = 12, or T = 1.71 hours = 60 minutes + 42.8 minutes = 102.8 minutes = **103 minutes**. Choice B is correct.

5. The volume = s^3, where s is the length of a side. Thus, a side length is the cubic root of 27, or 3 centimeters.   If the side of the cube is 3 cm, the area of one of its faces is (3)(3) = 9 square centimeters. Since a cube has 6 faces, its surface area is 6 x 9 = **54** square centimeters. Choice C is correct.

6. First, we must define our variables. In this case, we will let x = the number of $50 donations. Therefore, 200 – x = the number of $20 donations. Since the total value of these two types of donations is $6,400 our equation becomes: $50x + $20(200 – x) = $6,400, so $50x + $4000 – $20x = $6,400, or $30x = $2,400 and x = **80** $50 donations. Therefore, the number of $20 donations is 200 – 80 = **120**. Choice B is correct.

7. Choice E is correct. y = **2**

8. To be a function, a relation must not repeat any of the first elements of its ordered pairs. Only Choice E meets this criterion.

9. If you look carefully, you will see that this example is actually a combination of TWO sub-series. The odd numbers (11, 13, 15 ....) increase by two, while the even numbers double (12, 24, 48, ...). The next number in the series will be 15 + 2, or **17**. Choice B is correct.

10. Choice D is correct.

11. x^6 must be the largest, because it is the only answer choice that is positive. Choice C is correct.

12. (7b – 4)/2 = 16 - b, so 7b – 4 = 32 – 2b, or 9b – 36, or b =**4**. Choice D is correct.

13. (H∩J)∩K is the set of elements that are in all three sets. In this case, only **7** is in H,J, and K, which means that (H∩J)∩K = **{7}.** Choice A is correct.

14. Of the answers listed, only **12** fits both equations. Choice E is correct.

15. First, we must calculate the total number of minutes that Diane needs to complete her errands, which is 18 x 14 = 252 minutes, or 4.2 hours, which is 4 hours and 12 minutes. Therefore, Diane must leave home by **12:48** pm to complete the errands by 5:00 pm.   Choice D is correct.

16. To solve this problem, simply choose a number that meets the original condition: it leaves a remainder of 9 when it is divided by 17. In this case, the number **26** meets the condition. Next, let's submit the number 26 to the second condition and see what happens. $(26)(5)/17 = 130 = (17)(7) + 11$. **130** leaves a remainder of 11 when it is divided by 17. Choice D is correct.

17. 12 courses (8 + 4) comprise ¾ of the curriculum, which means that there are 16 total courses. Of these, 4, or **1/4,** are on software. Choice A is correct.

18. $328 – 214 = 114/214 =$ **53.27%** increase. Choice C is correct.

19. For a ratio of 3:2, the whole is 5. The shorter section is therefore 2/5 of the whole. 2/5 of 90 = **36**, which is Choice E.

20. In this problem, we know the relationship among the ages of Sue, Grace, and Lee – and their combined age. We can use this information to build an equation to solve for Grace's age. For simplicity, we will let Grace's age = x. Thus, Sue's age is 2x, while Lee's age is x + 5. Since the sum of their ages is 65, our equation becomes: $x + 2x + (x + 5) = 65$ or $4x + 5 = 65$. Thus, $4x = 60$ and X = **15** = Grace's age. Choice B is correct.

21. The first step for this type of problem is to draw a quick chart of what we know:

Motorcycle	Distance	Rate	Time
A	65x	65	x
B	70x	70	x

Here, we can use the rate equation to determine the time at which the two motorcyclists will pass each other. By definition, they are traveling the same distance, which is 540 miles. Also by definition, that distance equals the SUM of the quantities (Rate x Time) for each motorcycle. Hence, our equation becomes: $65x + 70x = 540$, or $135x = 540$. x = **4**. They will pass after 4 hours, which will be 2:00 pm. Choice C is correct.

22. In this case, we have three distinct groups, which must add up to 100%. Since the original two groups are 60% and 15%, the remaining group must be $100 – 60 – 15 =$ **25%** of the total. Choice D is correct.

23. There are four kings in a deck of 52 cards. Thus, the probability of choosing a king is 4/52, or **1/13**. Choice C is correct.

24. The fastest way to solve this problem is by using the formula for the sum of the numbers in an arithmetic series: Sum = Number of Items (First Item + Last or Desired Item) / 2
Sum = $150(1 + 150)/2 = (150)(151)/2 =$ **11,325**. Choice C is correct.

25. Area of each window = $(13)(13) = 169$ square feet x $5.86 = $990.34 per window. The church can replace **4** windows for $3,961.36. Choice C is correct.

26. To solve this problem, we must first define our variables:

Investment A = x; Investment B = x + $25,000; Investment C = 3x - $7,500

Next, we must write expressions to define the amount of interest that each investment earns:
Investment A = (0.05)x; Investment B = (0.07)(x + $25,000); Investment C = (0.09)(3x – $7,500)

Finally, we must add these amounts, which – by definition – are equal to $22,000.
$(0.05)x + (0.07)(x + \$25,000) + (0.09)(3x – \$7,500) = \$22,000$
$(0.05)x + (0.07)x + \$1,750 + (0.27)x - \$675 = \$22,000$
$(0.39)x = \$20,925$
x = **$53,653.85**. Choice B is correct.

27. 10% of $2141 = $214 – 35 = $179. Choice D is correct.

28. Credit Card + Clothes = $ 240 + $75 = $315. Choice D is correct.

Quantitative Section 11:   28 questions   45 minutes

Each question has two quantities to be compared: one in Column A and one in Column B. Compare the
quantities taking into consideration any other information given and choose
Answer A - if the quantity in Column A is greater
Answer B - if the quantity in Column B is greater
Answer C - if the two quantities are equal
Answer D - if the relationship cannot be determined without further information.

1. Employees at McDonalds either cook, clean or both. Ten percent of the employees cook, while twenty
percent of the employees clean.

Column A	Column B
The percentage of employees that cooks and cleans	75%

2. A coin with one side heads and the other side tails is tossed four times.

Column A	Column B
1/32	The probability of getting four consecutive tails

3. The following series continues in the same pattern. 1, 1, 6, 36, 41.....

Column A	Column B
The next term	1681

4. A right triangle has side lengths of 4 and 8.

Column A	Column B
The length of the hypotenuse	8

5. A square has a side length of 13.

Column A	Column B
The area of the square	52

6. The value of x quarters is equal to the value of x + 32 nickels.

Column A	Column B
5	x

Directions: For each problem, decide which answer is the best of the choices given.

7. If a Ψ b = $(1 + b)^{1/2}$ what is aΨ 15?

    a. 1/2
    b. 2
    c. 4
    d. 8
    e. 16

8. Find the number of sides of a polygon if the sum of the interior angles is 2,700 degrees?

    a.   14
    b.   16
    c.   17
    d.   18
    e.   19

9. What number, when squared, is equal to the cubic root of 15625?

    a.   1
    b.   5
    c.   15
    d.   25
    e.   125

10. Which of the following is the correct factorization of $k^2 - 6k + 9$?

    a. $(k - 3)(k + 3)$
    b. $(k - 3)^2$
    c. $(k + 3)^2$
    d. $3(1/k^2 + 1)$
    e. $1/9(k - 1)(k + 1)$

11. Which of the following are the solutions to the following equation? $2x^3 - 3x^2 - 5x = 0$

    a.   −1, -5/2, 2
    b.   0, 1, 2
    c.   1, 5/2, 6
    d.   0, 1, -5/2
    e.   0, -1, 5/2

12. Sara had to mail a package on the day that the Post Office increased its rates. The cost is 55 cents for the first ounce and 34 cents for each additional ounce. How much did Sara pay to mail a package that weighed three quarters of a pound?

    a. $3.74
    b. $3.95
    c. $4.08
    d. $4.29
    e. $4.63

13. An oven timer rings whenever the internal temperature reaches 425 °F. On a typical shift, the alarm rings five times every ten minutes. In a ten-hour shift, how many times will the alarm ring?

     a. 150
     b. 300
     c. 600
     d. 1500
     e. 3000

14. A number (x) is divisible by 2, 3, and 5. What is the smallest three-digit number that is divisible by 2, 3, 5, and 3x?

     a. 120
     b. 150
     c. 180
     d. 210
     e. 300

15. Three sisters took their mother for a nice dinner on Mother's Day. The total for four meals was $185.30. If the girls plan to leave a 20% tip and split the bill three ways, what dollar amount will each sister owe?

     a. $46.32
     b. $55.59
     c. $61.76
     d. $68.32
     e. $74.12

16. After careful negotiations, the Zippy Insurance Company agreed to pay 75% of Chad's accident expenses, after deducting $100 in non-covered items and a $325 administrative fee. If Chad's expenses totaled $14,625, how much did he receive from Zippy Insurance?

     a. $10,650
     b. $10,950
     c. $11,650
     d. $11,960
     e. $12,650

17. If Candy's age ten years from now minus her age eight years ago plus six times her age four years ago is equal to 120 years, how old will Candy be in eleven years?

     a. 20
     b. 21
     c. 30
     d. 32
     e. 41

18. Jack and Jill left home at the same time and traveled to the airport using the same route. Jack drove at an average speed of 75 miles per hour, while Jill drove an average speed of 45 miles per hour. In how many hours will Jack's car be 45 miles ahead of Jill's?

     a. ½
     b. 1
     c. 3/2
     d. 2
     e. 5/2

19. Olivia can transcribe three times as fast as Karen. If they both spend an equal amount of time transcribing 1200 pages of notes, how many pages will Olivia have transcribed?

    a. 300
    b. 450
    c. 800
    d. 900
    e. 1000

20. Connie has two investments, A and B. Her income from A, which pays 6%, is $10,000 more than her income from B, which pays 4%. If Connie has $750 more invested in A than B, what is the TOTAL amount of Connie's two investments?

    a. $497,750
    b. $498,500
    c. $996,250
    d. $1,006,250
    e. $1,026,160

21. If the population of Walnut Grove is 300,000 and grows by 5,000 people each year, in how many years will the population triple?

    a. 60
    b. 90
    c. 120
    d. 240
    e. 300

22. When a store owner compiled her weekly sales records, she had a stack of invoices numbered 014567 through 019876. Upon further examination, however, the store owner realized that invoice numbers 014876 and 018999 were missing. How many invoices did the store owner have available for her weekly calculations?

    a. 5307
    b. 5308
    c. 5309
    d. 5310
    e. 5311

23. For the following data set, what is the median minus the mode?
          7, 3, 15, 6, 7, 8, 9, 12, 5, 7, 6

    a. 0
    b. 0.7
    c. 1.0
    d. 1.7
    e. 2.0

24. X roommates agree to split the cost of utilities for their apartment, which usually cost Y per month. At the end of the year, the monthly cost of utilities increased by $250. How much did each roommate have to contribute each month for his/her total share?

    a. 250/X
    b. 250Y/X
    c. XY/250
    d. (Y + 250)/X
    e. X/Y + 250/X

25. Kelly wants to have her favorite picture enlarged to the size of a wall poster. The original picture measures 2 inches by 3 inches. If the shorter side of the poster will be 4 feet long, how long (in inches) will the longer side be?

    a. 6
    b. 36
    c. 64
    d. 72
    e. 78

26. Jake found a great deal on discontinued paint at Home Depot. When he brought the paint home, he discovered that the four cans he purchased were enough to paint three quarters of his bedroom. How many additional cans of paint will Jake need to buy to complete his bedroom and to paint three additional rooms that are the same size as his bedroom?

    a. 13.3
    b. 16.7
    c. 17.3
    d. 19.7
    e. 19.3

Refer to the following table for questions 27 and 28.

Caitlyn's Budget for August 2009 (in dollars)

Rent	700
Car Payment	350
Utilities	185
Cell Phone	80
Insurance	55
Food	100
Credit Card	240
Clothes	75
Miscellaneous	321
Savings	35

27. According to the table, what percentage of Caitlyn's budget is allocated for rent and utilities?

    a. 33%
    b. 41%
    c. 49%
    d. 55%
    e. 60%

28. According to experts, discretionary expenses include money spent for food, clothes, miscellaneous items and credit card debt. By this definition, what percentage of Caitlyn's budget is allocated to discretionary items?

    a. 23.1%
    b. 25.2%
    c. 34.4%
    d. 39.6%
    e. 54.4%

Answer Key for Quantitative Section 11

1. In this case, we have three distinct groups, which must add up to 100%. Since the original two groups are 10% and 20%, the remaining group must be 100 – 10 – 20 = **70**% of the total. Choice B is correct.

2. Probability = ½ x ½ x ½ x ½ = **1/16.** Choice B is correct.

3. The terms are squared, then increased by 5. The next term will be **1681**, which is the square of 41. Choice C is correct.

4. Use the Pythagorean theorem to find the length: $a^2 + b^2 = c^2$, or $16 + 64 = c^2$, which is the square root of 80, or **8.94**.   Choice A is correct.

5. Area = L x W = 13 x 13 = **169**. Choice A is correct.

6. This problem puts a new spin on the traditional coin problem. We must simply convert the information in the problem to a mathematical formula and solve. If we have x quarters, then their value is 25x. From the problem, we know that 25x is equal to that of (x + 32) nickels, which can be represented as 5(x + 32). Hence, 25x = 5(x + 32). Solving for x, we find **x = 8**. Choice B is correct.

7. If a Ψ b = $(1 + b)^{1/2}$ then aΨ 15 = $(1 + 15)^{1/2}$ = **4.** Choice C is correct.

8. To solve, we use the formula: 180 (X – 2) = 2,700. X = 17. Choice C is correct.

9. 5 x 5 = 25, which is the cubic root of 15,625. Choice B is correct.

10. $k^2 – 6k + 9 = (k – 3)^2$ Choice B is correct.

11. If $2x^3 – 3x^2 –5x = 0$, then x $(2x^2 – 3x –5)$ = 0, so x (2x - 5) (x+1) = 0. So, x = 0, -1, 5/2. Choice E is correct.

12. First, we must convert the weight of the package from pounds to ounces. In this case, 0.75 pounds X (16 ounces/1 pound) = 12 ounces. The total cost is $0.55 for the first ounce and $0.34 for the 11 additional ounces, or 55 + 11 (34) = $4.29 total cost to mail a 12-ounce package. Choice D is correct.

13. If the alarm rings five times every ten minutes, then it rings 5(6) times, or 30, times per hour. On a ten-hour shift, it will ring 5(6)(10) times, or 300 times. Choice B is correct.

14. The first step is to find the smallest number that is evenly divisible by 2, 3, and 5, which is 30. Thus 30 = x. Our second step is to find the smallest three-digit number that is divisible by 2, 3, 5, and 90, which is 3x. The fastest way is to check the answer choices in order. When we do, we discover that Choice C, 180, is correct.

15. First, we must add the amount of the tip to the bill: $185.30 x 0.2 = $37.06. Total cost = $222.36. Each share is 222.36 / 3 = **$74.12**. Choice E is correct.

16. First, we must subtract the deductions from the total: 14625 – 100 – 325 = 14,200. Chad received 75% of this amount, or **$10,650**. Choice A is correct.

17. For age problems with a single person, our chart is:

Candy Now	Candy plus 10	Candy minus 8	Candy minus 4

Now, let's fill in our values. As always, we will let Candy's current age = x.
Her age 10 years from now will be x + 10
Her age 8 years ago was x – 8
Her age 4 years ago was x - 4

Candy Now	Candy plus 10	Candy minus 8	Candy minus 4
X	x + 10	x – 8	x – 4

By definition, our equation is:

$(x + 10) - (x - 8) + 6(x - 4) = 120$
$x + 10 - x + 8 + 6x - 24 = 120$
$6x = 126$
$x = 21$ = Candy's current age. In 11 years, Candy will be **32**. Choice D correct

18. The first step is to draw a quick chart of what we know:

Driver	Distance	Rate	Time
Jack	75x	75	x
Jill	45x	45	x

In this case, Jack and Jill will drive the same amount of time at different speeds. We want to know the amount of time it will take for Jack to be 45 miles ahead of Jill, which can be represented by:

$75x - 45x = 45$
$30x = 45$
$X = 3/2$ hours. Choice C is correct.

Because this is a relatively simple scenario, it is easier for some students to think it through without the chart. If Jack drives 75 miles per hour while Jill drives 45 miles per hour, then he travels $75 - 45 = 30$ additional miles each hour. The time required for Jack to be 45 miles ahead of Jill is therefore 1.5 times 30 = **1.5** hours.

19. Let x = # of pages that Karen transcribes. 3x = # pages that Olivia transcribes. $x + 3x = 1200$, so $4x = 1200$, or $x = 300$. Olivia transcribed 3x, or **900** pages. Choice D is correct.

20. First, we must draw a table with the information that we know.

Investment	Amount	Interest Rate	Total Return
A	x + $750	6	6(x + 750)
B	x	4	4x

Here, we are asked to determine the total amount of money invested in A + B. First, we will solve for B. We will therefore let x = the amount of money invested in B, which means that the amount of money invested in A = x + 750. From the problem, we know that Connie's income from A is $10,000 more than her income from B. Therefore, our equation is:

Income from A – Income from B = 10,000
$0.06(x + 750) - 0.04x = 10,000$
$0.06x + 45 - 0.04x = 10,000$
$0.02x = 9955$
$x = \$497,750$ = amount of investment B
$x + 750 = \$498,500$ = amount of investment A
$A + B = \$497,750 + \$498,500 = \textbf{\$996,250.}$ Choice C is correct.

To check our answer, we can simply plug in the amount of interest that each investment earns to see if it matches the stipulations in the question stem.
The total return for A is 0.06($498,500) = $29,910.
The total return for B is 0.04($497,750) = $19,910.
Connie's income from A is indeed $10,000 more than her income from B.

21. This problem can easily be solved using an algebraic formula. First, let's define our variables.
We will let x = the # of years until the population triples. Mathematically, this can be expressed as:
$3(300,000) = 300,000 + 5,000x$
$900,000 = 300,000 + 5,000x$
$600,000 = 5,000x$
$x = \textbf{120}$ years. Choice C is correct.

22. To find the original number of invoices in the series, we must subtract the endpoints and add one:

019876 – 014567 + 1 = 5310. Next, we must subtract the two missing invoices: 5310 - 2 = **5308**. Choice B is correct.

23. First, we must arrange the numbers in ascending order: 3, 5, 6, 6, 7, 7, 7, 8, 9, 12, 15. Median = 7, Mode = 7. 7 – 7 = 0. Choice A is correct.

24. Let's assume that 2 roommates split the cost of utilities, which are usually $500 per month. Therefore, X = 2 and Y = 500. Every month, each roommate pays 500/2, or Y/X for his/her share of the utilities. If the cost of utilities increases by 250, then Y increases by 250. Each roommate's cost is (Y + 250)/X. Choice D is correct.

25. We can solve this by using a ratio: 2/48 = 3/x, so x = **72** inches. Choice D is correct.

26. We can solve this using a proportion. If 4 cans covered ¾ of one room, how many cans are needed to cover 3-1/4 rooms? 4 / 0.75 = x / 3.25. Solving for x = **17.3** additional cans. Choice C is correct.

27. 885/2141 = **41%**. Choice B is correct.

28. 100 + 240 + 75 + 321 = 736/2141= **34.4%**. Choice C is correct.

Quantitative Section 12: 28 questions   45 minutes

Each question has two quantities to be compared: one in Column A and one in Column B. Compare the quantities taking into consideration any other information given and choose
Answer A - if the quantity in Column A is greater
Answer B - if the quantity in Column B is greater
Answer C - if the two quantities are equal
Answer D - if the relationship cannot be determined without further information.

1. A restaurant received 112 cans of Coca-Cola for their busy rush hour. Waitress A served 18 cans of Coca-Cola, waitress B served 11 cans, and 5 cans were consumed by each of the three cooks.

Column A	Column B
The number of remaining cans	70

2.

Column A	Column B
The sum of the prime numbers between 20 and 30	52

3.

Column A	Column B
The number of 0.5 oz. chicken nuggets in a 2 lb. bag of chicken nuggets	64

4. A square has an area of 441.

Column A	Column B
The length of a side	19

5. A cube has a surface area of 96 square centimeters.

Column A	Column B
The volume of the cube (in cubic centimeters)	64

6. David has 20 pennies, 12 quarters and 27 dimes.

Column A	Column B
The number of nickels this money equals	118

Directions: **For each problem, decide which answer is the best of the choices given.**

7. $(15 - 11)^3 =$

    a. 4
    b. 16
    c. 64
    d. 121
    e. 225

8. Which of the following is the correct factorization of $12b^2 - 12$?

    a. $12b^2 - 144$
    b. $12 (b - 1)$
    c. $12(b - 1) (b + 1)$
    d. $12(b - 1)^2$
    e. $(4b - 3)(3b + 4)$

9. At which of the following points do the following lines intersect?
$$y = 5x + 4 \qquad y = 5x - 4$$

    a. (0, -4)
    b. (0, -4) (4, 0)
    c. (0, -5) (5, 0)
    d. (-4, 0)
    e. The two lines do not intersect

10. What is the diameter of a circle with area 81π?

    a. 3
    b. 9
    c. 18
    d. 36
    e. 54

11. If $f(a) = 1 + 1/3\,a$, what is $f(30)$?

    a. 11/3
    b. 10
    c. 11
    d. 31/3
    e. 31

12. A cattery has 85 Persian cats, 411 Siamese cats and 103 Calico cats. For a treat, the owner of the cattery purchases 88 lbs of catnip, to be distributed evenly among all of the cats. Assuming there are no other types of cats in the cattery, how much catnip (in ounces) would each cat receive?

    a. 2.35
    b. 5.80
    c. 6.80
    d. 11.60
    e. 23.50

13. Doris left her $600,000 in equal installments to her three sons. A week after Doris's death, one of her sons died before he could receive his inheritance. Instead, his portion of Doris's estate was divided equally among the man's four daughters. What fraction of Doris's original estate did each of the four granddaughters receive?

    a.   1/12
    b.   1/8
    c.   1/6
    d.   1/5
    e.   1/4

14. Barbie's salary is $720 per week after a 20% raise. Before Barbie's raise, her supervisor Connie's salary was 50% greater than Barbie's. If Barbie and Connie receive the same dollar amount raise, what is Connie's salary after the raise?

    a. $860
    b. $900
    c. $960
    d. $1020
    e. $1200

15. Maria put $4390 into a Platinum CD at her local bank, which she left untouched for six years and nine months, when she withdrew the entire amount, plus all of the simple annual interest she had earned. If the total balance in Maria's account was $6175, what simple rate of annual interest did she earn?

    a.   3.82%
    b.   4.62%
    c.   5.52%
    d.   6.02%
    e.   7.12%

16. If three less than eleven times a whole number is equal to 140, what is the number?

    a.   11
    b.   13
    c.   14
    d.   17
    e.   19

17. Rafe is four times as old as Monica. In ten years, Rafe will be 10 times as old as Monica was 5 years ago. How old will Rafe be in five years?

    a. 19
    b. 24
    c. 25
    d. 29
    e. 45

18. The distance between Annapolis and Charlotte is 150 miles. A car travels from Annapolis to Charlotte at 75 miles per hour and returns from Charlotte to Annapolis along the same route at 50 miles per hour. What is the average speed for the round trip?

    a.   60.0
    b.   62.5
    c.   65.0
    d.   67.5
    e.   70.0

19. A tank of sugar syrup can be filled in 3 hours and drained in 6 hours. How long will it take to fill the tank if an employee forgets to close the drain valve?

    a.   1.5
    b.   3.0
    c.   4.5
    d.   6.0
    e.   9.0

20. Fifty students in a local conservatory either studied voice, piano or both. 40% of the students studied voice, while 25% studied both voice and piano. What percentage of the students studied only piano?

    a.   20%
    b.   25%
    c.   30%
    d.   35%
    e.   40%

21. A candy dish contains only Snickers bars, Mars bars, and Hershey bars. The probability of choosing a Snickers bar at random is 1/5 and the probability of choosing a Mars bar at random is 3/10. If there are 200 candy bars in the dish, how many are Hershey bars?

    a.   50
    b.   75
    c.   100
    d.   125
    e.   150

22. For the repeating decimal 0.015689015689015689……, what is the 37th digit to the right of the decimal point?

    a.   0
    b.   1
    c.   5
    d.   6
    e.   8

23. What is the sum of the first 80 integers?

    a.   1,600
    b.   1,620
    c.   3,200
    d.   3,240
    e.   6,480

24. Jenny wants to blend a gourmet hot fudge sauce that costs 75 cents per pound with a caramel sauce that costs 95 cents per pound to make 500 pounds of a mixture that costs 80 cents per pound. How many pounds of the caramel sauce must Jenny use?

    a.   20
    b.   25
    c.   125
    d.   375
    e.   480

25. The ratio of professors to students at a private college is 1:12. If 36 new students are admitted, there will be 16 times as many students as professors. What is the new number of students at the college?

      a. 124
      b. 132
      c. 136
      d. 144
      e. 148

Use the following table to answer questions 26 – 28.

Percentage of Contact Lens Wearers (By Age)

	U.S.	U.K.	France	India
Under 10	2	5	1	0
10 – 18	21	30	15	3
19 – 30	38	35	29	19
31 – 50	29	25	40	66
Over 51	10	5	15	12

26. A leading economic journal recently estimated the number of contact lens wearers in France and India at 10 million and 20 million, respectively. If these numbers are accurate, what is the total number of people in both nations between 19 and 30 who wear contact lenses?

      a. 2.9 million
      b. 3.8 million
      c. 6.7 million
      d. 7.5 million
      e. Cannot be determined from the information given

27. If there are currently 5 million people who wear contact lenses in France, and the French government bans their use in people under 10 and over 51, how many *fewer* people will be allowed to wear them?

      a. 50,000
      b. 80,000
      c. 160,000
      d. 500,000
      e. 800,000

28. Optometrists in the U.K. recently estimated that 40% of contact lens wearers who are under 10 years old choose blue lenses, which are not available to older patients. If the total number of contact lens wearers in the U.K. is 1.8 million, how many of them wear blue lenses?

      a. 36,000
      b. 40,000
      c. 72,000
      d. 90,000
      e. 120,000

Answer Key for Quantitative Section 12

1. This problem includes a lot of unnecessary words to confuse you. The actual calculation is simple: $112 - 18 - 11 - 3(5) = \mathbf{68}$. Choice B is correct.

2. The prime numbers between 20 and 30 are 23 and 29. Their sum is **52**. Choice C is correct.

3. If each nugget weighs 0.5 oz, then 1 lb contains 32 nuggets; therefore, 2 lb = **64 nuggets**. Choice C is correct.

4. Area = L x W, so 441 = 21 x **21**. Choice A is correct.

5. Since a cube has 6 faces, its surface area of 96 can be divided by 6 to determine the area of a single face: 96/6 = 16 square centimeters. The length of each side is therefore the square root of 16, or 4 centimeters. Finally, the volume = s^3, where s is the length of a side. (4)(4)(4) = **64** cubic centimeters. Choice C is correct.

6. To solve, we must determine the number of nickels that each type of coins represented. Then, we must add the amounts together:

20 pennies = 4 nickels
12 quarters = 60 nickels
27 dimes = 54 nickels. Therefore, the total number of nickels = 4 + 60 + 54 = **118**. Choice C is correct.

7. 4 x 4 x 4 = **64**. Choice C is correct.

8. $12b^2 - 12 = 12(b^2 - 1)$ = **12(b – 1) (b + 1)**. Choice C is correct.

9. They do not intersect. Choice E is correct.

10. Area = πr^2 = π (9)(9). Diameter = 9 + 9 = **18**. Choice C is correct.

11. If (a) = 1 + 1/3 a, then f(30) = 1 + 1/ 3 (30) = 1 + 10 = **11**. Choice C is correct.

12. To solve, we must calculate the total number of cats in the cattery, which is 85 + 411 + 103 = 599 cats. Then, we must convert the amount of catnip to ounces, which is 88 lb x 16 oz/lb = 1408 oz. Finally, we must divide the total amount of catnip evenly among the total number of cats, which is 1408 / 599 = **2.35** ounces. Choice A is correct.

13. Doris's sons each inherited 1/3 of her $600,000 estate, or $200,000. One of the $200,000 shares was subsequently divided among one of the son's four daughters, who each received $200,000/4 or $50,000. The question asks us to determine what fraction of the *original estate* each girl received, which is $50,000/$600,000 = **1/12**. Choice A is correct.

14. First, we must find Barbie's original salary. 720 = 1.20x, x = 600. Thus, Barbie's raise was 720 – 600 = $120. Now, we must find Connie's original salary. $600 + 0.5(600) = 900. Now, we must add Connie's raise: 900 + 120 = **$1020**. Choice D is correct.

15. In this case, we know the beginning and ending amounts and are being asked to calculate the rate of simple annual interest that was earned over 6.75 years. To solve, we will use the basic equation:

Interest = Principal x Rate x Time. The trick is to work backwards from our final total to determine the rate of interest that was paid. In this case, our total of $6157 represents the initial deposit of $4390 PLUS the interest earned.

Mathematically, $6175 = $4390 + PRT = $4390 + ($4390)(X)(6.75), so 6175 = 4390 + 29632.50X, or X =1785/29632.5 = 0.0602 = **6.02**% Choice D is correct.

16. In this case, we will let x = the whole number we are trying to find. Once we define our variable, the problem easily converts to a simple equation: 11x – 3 = 140, so 11x = 143 and x= **13.** Choice B is correct.

17. Our first step will be to draw a quick chart for the information we are given. To avoid working with fractions, we will Let Monica's current age = x. Thus, we know that Rafe's current age = 4x. Ten years from now, Monica's age will be x + 10, while Rafe's age will be 4x + 10. Five years ago, Monica's age was x – 5, while Rafe's age was 4x – 5.

Name	Current Age	Age 10 years from now	Age 5 years ago
Rafe	4x	4x + 10	4x - 5
Monica	x	x + 10	x – 5

From the table, we know that Rafe's age ten years from now = 4x + 10. From the problem itself, we ALSO know that Rafe's age ten years from now is "ten times as old as Monica was 5 years ago," which can be written mathematically as 10 (x – 5). Our equation, therefore, is:

4x + 10 = 10(x – 5)
4x + 10 = 10x - 50
6x = 60 x =10 – Monica's current age.

Rafe's current age is 4(10) = 40. Five years from now, Rafe will be 40 + 5 = **45**. Choice E is correct.

18. The first step for this type of problem is to draw a quick chart of what we know:

Route	Distance	Rate	Time
To Charlotte	150	75	2
From Charlotte	150	50	3

A car traveling at 75 mph will cover 150 miles in 2 hours. A car traveling at 50 mph covers the same 150 miles in 3 hours. The total travel time is therefore 5 hours. Average speed = Total distance / Total time. For the entire round trip, the average speed = (150 + 150) / 5 = **60** mph. Choice A is correct.

19. In this case, the rate to fill the tank is x/3, while the rate to drain it is x/6. Since the drain is emptying the tank, our equation becomes x/3 – x/6 = 1. To solve, we must multiple both sides by the least common denominator, which is 6: 2x - 1x = 6, or x = **6** hours to fill the tank. Choice D is correct.

20. In this case, we have three distinct groups, which must add up to 100%. Since the original two groups are 40% and 25%, the remaining group must be 100% - 40% - 25% = **35%** of the total. Choice D is correct. In case you are wondering, it doesn't matter how many students are enrolled in the conservatory, because we are dealing with percentages. The number 50 is extraneous information that is included strictly to confuse you.

21. If the probability of choosing a Snickers bar is 1/5 (or 2/10) and the probability of choosing a Mars bar is 3/10, then the probability of choosing EITHER a Snickers bar or a Mars bar is 2/10 + 3/10 = 5/10.

Therefore, the probability of choosing a Hershey bar is 1 – 5/10 = 5/10 = 1/2.
If there are 200 candy bars in the dish, then there are 1/2 x 200 = **100** Hershey bars. Choice C is correct.

22. For repeating decimals, you must first determine the actual string of numbers that repeat. Then, you can simply count the number of decimal places to determine the identity of a specific digit in the string. In this case, the repeating pattern is 015689, which is a string of 6 digits. Hence, 37th digit to the right of the decimal point will be the *first* number in the series, which is 0. Choice A is correct.

23. The fastest way to solve this problem is to use the formula for the sum of the numbers in an arithmetic series: Sum = {(Number of Items) (First Item + Last or Desired Item)} / 2. In this case,

Sum = 80(1 + 80)/2 = (80)(81)/2 = **3,240**. Choice D is correct.

24. First, we must draw a table with the information that we know.

Ingredient	Quantity	Price/pound	Total Cost
Hot fudge	500 – x	75	75(500 – x)
Caramel	x	95	95x
Mixture	500	80	40,000

Since the problem asks us to calculate the amount of caramel that Jenny needs, we will let that value = x. Therefore, the amount of hot fudge = 500 – x. Once we label our variables, we can write the expression for the total cost of each ingredient. We can also calculate the cost of the final mixture.

Since the cost of the hot fudge plus the cost of the caramel equals the total cost of the blend, our equation becomes:

Cost of Caramel + Cost of Hot Fudge = Total Cost

95x + 75(500 − x) = 40,000
95x + 37,500 − 75x = 40,000
20x = 2500
X = **125** pounds of caramel needed. Choice C is correct.

25. The hardest part about this question is setting up the equation we need to solve it. First, it's important to acknowledge one key point: the # of professors (x) remains the same. We also know that the original number of students is 12 times this number, or 12x. Therefore, the number of new students is 12x + 36. Finally, we also know that 12x + 36 = 16x. Solving for x, we find that the number of professors (x) = 9. Therefore, the original number of students = (9)(12) = 108 and the new number of students = 108 + 36 = **144.** Choice D is correct.

26. France: 10 million wearers x (0.29) = 2,900,000 between 19 and 30
India: 20 million wearers x (0.19) = 3,800,000 between 19 and 30
Total number of people in both nations between 19 and 30 who wear contact lenses = **6.7** million. Choice C is correct.

27. 5 million (0.01) = 50,000 under age 10.   5 million (0.15) = 750,000 over age 51.
  750,000 + 50,000 = **800,000** people can no longer wear them. Choice E is correct.

28. 1.8 million (0.05) = 90,000 users under age 10 x (0.4) = **36,000** wear blue lenses. Choice A is correct.

Quantitative Section 13:   28 questions   45 minutes

Each question has two quantities to be compared: one in Column A and one in Column B. Compare the quantities taking into consideration any other information given and choose
Answer A - if the quantity in Column A is greater
Answer B - if the quantity in Column B is greater
Answer C - if the two quantities are equal
Answer D - if the relationship cannot be determined without further information.

1. A Laundromat emptied its vending machines at the end of the night and found 312 quarters, 234 dimes, 443 nickels and 444 pennies. The owner will retain $50.00 of this amount for petty cash and deposits the rest at the bank.

Column A	Column B
The amount of the bank deposit	$78.99

2. High school seniors in Pittsburgh must take science, history, or both. 18% of seniors take science, while 36% take both science and history.

Column A	Column B
The percentage of high school seniors that takes history	45%

3. A coin with one side heads and the other side tails is tossed six times.

Column A	Column B
1/64	The probability of getting six consecutive tails

4. The following series continues in the same pattern. 1, 1, 3, 9, 11.....

Column A	Column B
The next term	18

5. A right triangle has side lengths of 15 and 18.

Column A	Column B
The length of the hypotenuse	21

6. The value of P quarters is equal to the value of P + 45 dimes.

Column A	Column B
P	9

222

Directions: *For each problem, decide which answer is the best of the choices given.*

7. After a devastating fire, a city's population decreased by 38%. If the current population is 1.37 million, what was the original population?

   a. 931,600
   b. 1,890,600
   c. 2,209,677
   d. 2,876,900
   e. 3,605,263

8. If f (d) = (d + 6)(d − 4), what is f (9)?

   a. 36
   b. 45
   c. 54
   d. 60
   e. 75

9. Robin's wedding anniversary is 100 days after her birthday. If her birthday is on a Wednesday this year, on what day of the week will Robin's anniversary fall?

   a. Monday
   b. Tuesday
   c. Wednesday
   d. Thursday
   e. Friday

10. Simply $\sqrt{7}$ $\sqrt{8}$ $\sqrt{9}$

   a. 6.90
   b. 18.75
   c. 20.75
   d. 22.05
   e. 22.45

11. The mean of two numbers is 8x − 24. If one of the numbers is x, what is the other number?

   a. 8x + 24
   b. 3x + 8
   c. $(2x - 4)^2$
   d. 15x - 48
   e. it cannot be determined from the information given

12. What is 0.005% expressed as a fraction?

   a. 5/100
   b. 5/250
   c. 5/200
   d. 1/250
   e. 1/200

13. Arrange the following fractions in descending order: 11/13, 12/15, 21/27, 32/41, 48/63

    a.   11/13, 32/41, 21/27, 12/15, 48/63
    b.   48/63, 12/15, 11/13, 32/41, 21/17
    c.   11/13, 12/15, 21/27, 32/41, 48/63
    d.   11/13, 12/15, 32/41, 21/27, 48/63
    e.   11/13, 21/27, 12/15, 32/41, 48/63

14. For the following system of equations, what is the value of y? $2x + 6y = 10$, $2x + 10y = 6$

    a.   -3
    b.   -2
    c.   -1
    d. $-1/2$
    e. $-1/3$

15. Which of the following quantities is *greater than* 8.9×10^{-11}?

    a. 89×10^{-12}
    b. 0.89×10^{-12}
    c. 0.000000000089
    d. $0.0000000000445 \times 10^{-11} \times 2$
    e. 890000×10^{-6}

16. Grace and Edna own a small business that earned $48,000 in profits last year. If they agreed to split the profits in a 9:4 ratio, with Grace getting the larger share, how much did Edna earn from the business?

    a. $10,453.67
    b. $11,896.23
    c. $14,769.23
    d. $21,453.23
    e. $33,230.70

17. Theresa is 10 years older than Cindy. However, 5 years ago Theresa was twice as old as Cindy. How old is Cindy?

    a.   5
    b.   10
    c.   12
    d.   15
    e.   20

18. Julie drives to her grandmother's house every week at an average speed of 50 miles per hour. On the way home, she takes the same route, but averages 75 miles per hour. If Julie's total round trip is 10 hours, how far away is her grandmother's house?

    a.   30
    b.   60
    c.   150
    d.   300
    e.   600

19. Two dozen musicians auditioned for an orchestra. Fifteen played the piano, while nine played the harp. If one pianist and one harpist are chosen from the group of twenty-four, how many different pairs of musicians are possible?

    a. 24
    b. 48
    c. 96
    d. 112
    e. 135

20. Scientists recorded the daily temperature in a research aquarium. During a six-day period, the temperatures recorded (in °F) were 67, 73, 72, 56, 68, and 78. What was the median temperature (in °F)?

    a. 68.5
    b. 69
    c. 70
    d. 72.5
    e. 73

21. Jake is a wholesale dealer of foreign and vintage cars. If he can buy J cars for G dollars, how much will M cars cost (in dollars)?

    a. 1/MGJ
    b. (100/J)MG
    c. MG/J
    d. MJ/G
    e. MGJ

22. The sum of two numbers is 175 and their difference is 35. What is the smaller number?

    a. 65
    b. 70
    c. 75
    d. 100
    e. 105

23. The Boston Philharmonic charges $20 for adult tickets to their concerts and $5 for children's tickets. If they sold 1,000 tickets in a given weekend and received $11,000 in total ticket sales, how many adult tickets were sold?

    a. 300
    b. 400
    c. 600
    d. 750
    e. 800

24. The angles of a triangle are in the ratio of 3:4:5. What is the measurement (in degrees) of the smallest angle?

    a. 15
    b. 45
    c. 60
    d. 70
    e. 75

25. Jenny is making holiday decorations from a large piece of velvet fabric. How many circles, each with a 6-inch radius, can Jenny cut from a rectangular piece of the fabric, which measures 84 inches x 204 inches?

      a.   64
      b.   124
      c.   119
      d. 238
      e. 476

26. Joe will cover his bathroom floor with ceramic tiles that measure 6 inches by 12 inches. If the room is a rectangle that measures 12 feet by 14 feet, how many tiles will Joe need to cover the floor?

      a.   84
      b.   168
      c.   184
      d.   336
      e.   384

Refer to the following table for questions 27 – 28.

	2005	2006	2007	2008
Number of umbrellas sold (thousands)	A	B	C	D
Annual rainfall (inches)	E	F	G	H

27. In 2008, how many thousands of umbrellas were sold per foot of rainfall?

      a.   D/H
      b.   D/12H
      c.   12H/D
      d.   DH/12
      e.   12D/H

28. If the number of umbrellas sold in 2006 was overstated by 25% and the annual rainfall was understated by 50%, what is the correct number of umbrellas sold per inch of rainfall that year?

      a.   B/2F
      b.   F/2B
      c.   BF/2
      d.   0.75BF
      e.   0.75B/F

Answer Key for Quantitative Section 13

1. We must determine the total amount of money in the machines and subtract $50 to find the total bank deposit. 312 quarters = $78; 234 dimes = $23.40; 443 nickels = $22.15; 444 pennies = $4.44. 78 + 23.40 + 22.15 + 4.43 – 50.00 = **$77.99**. Choice B is correct.

2. In this case, we have three distinct groups, which must add up to 100%. Since the original two groups are 18% and 36%, the remaining group must be 100 – 18 – 36 = **46%** of the total. Choice A is correct.

3. Probability = ½ x ½ x ½ x ½ x ½ x ½ = **1/64.** Choice C is correct.

4. The terms are squared, then increased by 2. The next term will be **121**, which is the square of 11. Choice A is correct.

5. Use the Pythagorean theorem to find the length: $a^2 + b^2 = c^2$, or $225 + 324 = c^2$, which is the square root of 549, or **23.43**. Choice A is correct.

6. We can solve this problem by converting the words to an algebraic equation. If we have P quarters, their value is 25P. By definition, 25P = 10(P + 45). If we solve for P, we find 15P = 450, or P = **30.** Choice A is correct.

7. Let x = the original population. 0.62x = 1370000. Thus, x = **2,209,677**. Choice C is correct.

8. If f (d) = (d + 6)(d − 4), then f (9) = (9 + 6) (9 − 4) = (15)(5) = **75**. Choice E is correct.

9. 100/7 = 14 + 2 remainder. Her birthday will fall on a **Friday**. (Wednesday + 2). Choice E is correct.

10. (2.646)(2.828)(3) = **22.45**. Choice E is correct.

11. Let's assume the to numbers being averaged are x and y. From the problem, we know that (x + y)/2 = 8x − 24. If we "solve" this equation, we find that x + y = 16x − 48, or y = **15x − 48**, which is Choice D.

12. 0.005% = 0.5/100 = 5/1000 = **1/200**. Choice E is correct.

13. First, convert all of the fractions to decimal form. Then, arrange in descending order. The correct order is Choice D, **11/13, 12/15, 32/41, 21/27, 48/63**.

14. If 2x + 6y = 10 and 2x + 10y = 6, then we can subtract the equations to get −4y = 4, or **y =-1**. Choice C is correct.

15. Choice E is correct.

16. 9x + 4x = $48,000, or 13x = 48000, so x =3692.3. Edna's share = 4x = **$14,769.23.** Choice C is correct.

17. First, we must summarize our data in a table:

Name	Current Age	Age 5 years ago
Theresa	x + 10	(x + 10) − 5
Cindy	x	x - 5

Next, we must write our equation. Five years ago, Theresa was twice as old as Cindy, which gives us the following equation: x + 5 = 2 (x - 5), so x + 5 = 2x − 10 and x = **15.** Choice D is correct.

18. The first step for this type of problem is to draw a quick chart of what we know.

Route	Distance	Rate	Time
To Grandma's	50x	50	x
From Grandma's	75(10 − x)	75	10 - x

In this case, we will let the amount of time Julie travels to her grandmother's house = x. Her return time is therefore 10 − x. Once we have the expressions for the distance traveled to – and from – grandma's house, we can use them to write an equation to solve for the distance.

Distance to Grandma's = Distance from Grandma's
50x = 75(10 − x) or 50x = 750 − 75x. 125x = 750. x = 6. 50x = **300** miles. Choice D is correct.

19. The orchestra will fill two positions – one pianist and one harpist. The possible combinations are 15 X 9 = **135**. Choice E is correct.

20. To determine the median, we must first, arrange the numbers in ascending order: 56, 67, 68, 72, 73, 78. Since there is an even number of values, we must take the average of the middle two numbers as our median. Here, it is 68 + 72, which have an average of **70**. Choice C is correct.

21. To solve, let's plug in random numbers for each variable. In this case, let's assume that Jake bought 20 cars (J) for 100 dollars (G). The cost for a single car is therefore 100/20 or G/J or 5 dollars. The cost for any

value of M will simply be that number times 5, which, in symbols, is **MG/J**. Choice C is correct.

22. In this case, we can write one equation for the first condition and a second equation for the second condition. As always, we must first define our variables. We will let = x the smaller number and y = the larger number.

The first equation, which defines the first condition, is x + y = 175
The second equation, which defines the second condition, is y − x = 35
To solve the problem for x, we must combine the equations in a way that eliminates y.

The fastest way is to re-write equation 1 as y = 175 − x and substitute this value for y into equation 2. When we do, we get (175 − x) − x = 35, or 175 − 2x = 35. Therefore, 2x = 140. x = **70.** Choice B is correct. y = 175 − 70 = 105.

23. In this case, we can write two equations – one for the number of tickets and the other for their cost. As always, we must first define our variables. We will let = x the number of adult tickets and y = the number of children's tickets.

The first equation, which defines the *number* of tickets sold, is x + y = 1000
The second equation, which defines the *cost* of the tickets, is 20x + 5y = 11,000
To solve the problem for x, we must combine the equations in a way that eliminates y.

The fastest way is to re-write equation 1 as y = 1,000 − x and substitute this value for y into equation 2. When we do, we get: 20x + 5(1,000 − x) = 11,000
20x + 5,000 − 5x = 11,000
15x = 6000
x = **400** adult tickets sold. Choice B is correct.
y = 1,000 − 400 = 600 children's sold

24. 3x + 4x + 5x = 180, so 12x = 180, x = 15, 3x = **45**, 4x = 60, 5x = 75. Choice B is correct,

25. In this case, we are cutting a rectangular piece of fabric into smaller, circular pieces. If the circles have a 6-inch radius, then their diameter is 12 inches. For a piece of fabric measuring 84 inches by 204 inches, we can lay 204/12 - or 17 - circles across the *length* of the fabric. Since the width of the fabric is 84 inches, we can make 84/12, or 7 total rows of circles. Therefore, Jenny can make 17 x 7 = **119** total circles. Choice C is correct.

26. The area of the room is 12 x 14 = 168 square feet. The area of one tile is (0.50 foot) x (1.0 foot) = 0.50 square feet. Therefore, to cover the entire floor, Joe will need: 168 square feet (1 tile/0.50 square feet) = **336** tiles. Choice D is correct.

27. In 2008, D umbrellas were sold per H inches of rainfall. The number sold per foot of rainfall = D/(H/12) =**12D/H**. Choice E is correct.

28. The number of umbrellas sold per inch of rainfall in 2006 was B/F. If B was overstated by 25% and F was understated by 50%, then the corrected number of umbrellas sold per inch of rainfall would be 0.75B/1.5F = B/2F. Choice A is correct.

Alternatively, we can plug substitute numbers for the letters and see what we get. Let's let B = 100 and F = 10. Therefore, a 25% reduction in B = 75 and a 50% increase in F = 15. The corrected ratio is 75/15 = 5. Converting back to letters, 5 = 100/(2)(10), which is **B/2F**.

Quantitative Section 14:   28 questions   45 minutes

Each question has two quantities to be compared: one in Column A and one in Column B. Compare the quantities taking into consideration any other information given and choose
Answer A - if the quantity in Column A is greater
Answer B - if the quantity in Column B is greater
Answer C - if the two quantities are equal
Answer D - if the relationship cannot be determined without further information.

1. Rectangle ABCD has a length of 15 and a width of 9.

Column A	Column B
48	The perimeter of the rectangle

2. Greg splits his thousand dollar lottery prize evenly with his three brothers, after 30% is deducted from the winnings in taxes.

Column A	Column B
$175	The total dollar amount Greg gives away

3.

Column A	Column B
The largest integer less than 100 that leaves a remainder of 1 when divided by 17	85

4. A restaurant sold 150 chicken dinners, which used 3 cutlets per dinner. This quantity represents 5/6 of its stock of chicken cutlets.

Column A	Column B
The number of chicken cutlets remaining	96

5. A year ago, *The Sopranos* won 15 Emmy awards. This year, the show won only 3 Emmy awards.

Column A	Column B
500%	The % decrease this change represents

6. A cement truck can pour 600 gallons of concrete mix in 2.1 hours.

Column A	Column B
The number of minutes it will take the cement truck to pour 130,000 quarts of concrete mix	6600

Directions: *For each problem, decide which answer is the best of the choices given.*

7. What is the equation of the line that contains the points (4, 5) and (7, 11)?

    a. $y = 2x - 1$
    b. $y = 3x - 2$
    c. $y = 2x + 3$
    d. $y = -2x - 3$
    e. $y = 2x - 3$

8.   I. The diagonal of a parallelogram always bisects the other diagonal of the parallelogram.
    II. The diagonal of a parallelogram is perpendicular to the other diagonal of the parallelogram.
    III. The diagonal of a parallelogram bisects an angle of the parallelogram.

    Which of these statements is/are true?

    a. I
    b. II
    c. III
    d. I and II
    e. I and III

9. What is the average of the following numbers: 11/5, 33/42, 4/9, 8/7, 1/11?

    a. 0.567
    b. 0.786
    c. 0.932
    d. 1.091
    e. 1.140

10. $9^5 \times 9^3 =$

    a. 3^{11}
    b. 3^{12}
    c. 27^5
    d. 81^3
    e. 81^4

11. If $(x - 5)^2 / 8 = (5 - 3)^2 / 8$, what does x equal?

    a. 2
    b. 3
    c. 6
    d. 7
    e. 9

12. Which of the following expressions is equivalent to $(a + b - 1)(a - b)$?

    a. $a^2 - a - b^2 + b$
    b. $a^2 + a - b^2 + b$
    c. $a^2 + a + b^2 - b$
    d. $a^2 - 2a - b^2 + 2b$
    e. $a^2 - a - b^2 + b - 1$

13. What is the next term in the series? 5, 8, 7, 10, 9, 12.......

    a.   6
    b.   10
    c.   11
    d.   13
    e.   15

14. On spring break in Florida, Jennifer bought six shirts as souvenirs for her friends, which cost $14.50 each. If Jennifer works at a donut shop for $5.85 per hour, how many hours will she have to work to pay for the shirts (assuming no taxes or other deductions are withheld from her paycheck)?

    a.   5.85
    b.   6.00
    c.   8.70
    d.   14.50
    e.   14.87

15. After making preserves with her grandmother, Gayle had enough to fill 28.5 jars. If each full jar contained 23.1 oz, how many total pounds of preserves did Gayle have (to the nearest pound)?

    a.   32
    b.   41
    c.   46
    d.   56
    e.   65

16. A store sells both videos and DVDs. The average price of a video is $12.00, while the average price of a DVD is $15.00. If, last month, the store sold 40 more DVDs than videos, and the total receipts were $6000, how many DVDs did the store sell?

    a.   200
    b.   205
    c.   220
    d.   240
    e.   245

17. Three sisters, Hannah, Juliet and Patricia, have weights that are consecutive even numbers. Eighteen less than Juliet's weight equals 50 less than the sum of Hannah and Patricia's weights. What is Juliet's weight?

    a.   26
    b.   28
    c.   30
    d.   32
    e.   34

18. Wendy drove the 700 mile round trip between New York and Chicago in 12 hours. Before the 5 pm dinner rush, she averaged 70 miles per hour. Afterward 5 pm, Wendy averaged only 50 miles per hour. At what time did Wendy begin her trip?

    a.   9 am
    b.   11 am
    c.   12 noon
    d.   1 pm
    e.   It cannot be determined from the information given

19. You are arranging four brightly colored decorative tiles on the bathroom wall: they are red, green, pink and purple. How many possible ways are there to arrange them on the wall (assuming that no tile is repeated)?

    a.   4
    b.   8
    c.   16
    d.   24
    e.   64

20. For marketing purposes, Ace Hamburgers is recording the number of customers who order hot dogs during the lunch rush. For the first half of January, these are their daily values: 43, 56, 42, 56, 47, 28, 36, 65, 67, 89, 81, 45, 54, 44, 34. What is the mode?

    a.   47
    b.   52.5
    c.   54
    d.   56
    e.   65

21. There are P tenants in an apartment building, who agree to split the cost of utilities, N, in an equal manner. If the cost of utilities increases by $212 per month, how much must each tenant pay?

    a.   (P + 212)/N
    b.   (N + 212)/P
    c.   P(N − 212)/P
    d.   212/P
    e.   212P/N

22. The sum of two numbers is 24. Three times the larger number less two times the smaller number equals 17. What is the larger number?

    a.   9
    b.   11
    c.   13
    d.   15
    e.   17

23. If a triangle of base 16 has the same area as a circle of diameter 16, what is the altitude of the triangle (use $\pi = 3.1416$)?

    a.   4
    b.   8
    c.   12
    d.   16
    e.   25

24. A pizza is divided into slices of equal size, each with a side length of 7. Assuming that each slice meets at the center of the pizza, what is the pizza's circumference?

    a.   7
    b.   49
    c. 7π
    d. 14π
    e. 49π

25. If the base of a parallelogram increases by 12% and the height decreases by 18%, by what percent does the area change?

    a. 9% decrease
    b. 6% decrease
    c. 6% increase
    d. 10% increase
    e. 32% increase

26. A researcher pumps 100% nitrogen gas into an experimental chamber at a rate of 30 cubic inches per second. If the chamber's dimensions are 15 inches by 24 inches by 48 inches, how many minutes will it take the researcher to fill the chamber with nitrogen?

    a. 9.6
    b. 57.6
    c. 96
    d. 576
    e. 5,760

Refer to the following chart for questions 27 – 28.

Company Budget for September 2010 (in dollars)

Rent	1,500
Vehicle Lease	450
Utilities	200
Phone	50
Insurance	100
Advertising	300
Internet	50
Shipping	30
Computer	100
Taxes	200
Accounting	100
Attorney	150
Software	70
Miscellaneous	200

27. According to experts, the company can spend 5% of its monthly budget on technology expenses, such as internet, computer and software. By how many dollars did the company exceed this percentage in September of 2010?

    a. $30
    b. $35
    c. $40
    d. $45
    e. $50

28. In October of 2010, the company must eliminate 20% of its monthly expenses to purchase new machinery. Which of the following expenses, if eliminated, would allow the company to meet this goal?

    a. Advertising, Attorney, Internet, Computer
    b. Computer, Advertising, Accounting, Miscellaneous
    c. Vehicle Lease, Shipping, Miscellaneous
    d. Phone, Vehicle Lease, Software, and Shipping
    e. Taxes, Advertising, Insurance, and Internet

Answer Key for Quantitative Section 14

1. Perimeter = 2(15) + 2(9) = **48**. Choice C is correct.

2. The first step is to determine the actual amount that Greg won after taxes are deducted, which is 1000 – 300 = 700. Greg with give his brothers ¾ of this amount, which is ¾(700) = **$525**. Choice B is correct.

3. **86** (17 x 5 = 85; 85 + 1 = 86). Choice A is correct.

4. First, we must calculate the number of chicken cutlets the restaurant used, which is (150)(3) = 450. This number is equal to 5/6 of the total number of chicken cutlets in stock. Hence, 450/1 = 5/6. To determine the total number of cutlets, we simply cross multiply and divide: (450)(6) / 5 = 540. If the restaurant started with 540 cutlets and sold 450 of them, there were 540 – 450 = **90** left. Choice B is correct.

5. 15 - 3 = 12. 12/15 x 100 = **80% decrease**. Choice A is correct.

6. Although the original information is given in hours and gallons, the quantity in Column A is presented in terms of minutes and quarts. This means that both values must be converted:

2.1 hours/600 gallons = 126 min/600 gallons = 126 min / 2400 qt. 126 min / 2400 qt = **6825** min / 130,000 qt. Choice A is correct.

7. Slope = (11-5)/(7-4) = 6/3 = 2. y-intercept = -3. Therefore, the equation for the line is y = 2x – 3. Choice E is correct.

8. Choice A is correct.

9. The average is **0.932**, which is Choice C.

10. 9^5 x 9^3 = 9^8 = 4,304,672, which is **81^4**. Choice E is correct.

11. Just substitute each answer. **X = 7**. Choice D is correct.

12. (a + b –1) (a – b) = a^2 –ab + ab –b^2 –a +b = **a^2 – a – b^2 + b**. Choice A is correct.

13. The pattern in this series is to increase by 3, then decrease by 1. Hence, the next term will be **11**. Choice C is correct.

14. First, we must calculate the total amount that Jennifer spent on the shirts, which is $14.50 x 6 = $87.00 spent. Then, we divide this amount by her hourly pay to determine the number of hours she must work to pay for the shirts: 87/5.85 = **14.87** hours. Choice E is correct.

15. 28.5 x 23.1 = 658.35/16 = **41.14** pounds. Choice B is correct.

16. Let x be the number of videos sold and (x + 40) = the number of DVDs sold. Therefore, the value of the videos sold is 12x, while the value of the DVDs sold is 15(x + 40). Since the total sales figure is the sum of these two amounts, out equation becomes: 12x + 15(x+ 40) = 6000, or 27x + 600 = 6000. 27x = 5400. x = 200 = # of videos sold. x + 40 = **240** = number of DVDs sold. Choice D is correct.

17. We will use the information we have to build an equation to solve for Juliet's weight. Since the weights are consecutive even numbers, we can let Hannah's weight =x, Juliet's weight = (x + 2) and Patricia's weight = (x + 4). By definition, Juliet's weight less 18 equals the sum of Hannah and Patricia's weights minus 50. Mathematically, our equation becomes: (x+2) – 18 = {x + (x+4)} – 50, or x – 16 = 2x – 46 x = 30, x + 2 = 32, x + 4 = 34. Since Juliet's weight (x+2) = **32**, Choice D is correct.

18. The first step is to draw a quick chart of what we know:

Timeframe	Distance	Rate	Time
Before the dinner rush	70x	70	x
After the dinner rush	50(12 – x)	50	12 – x

Wendy's 12 hour trip is divided into two parts: before and after the dinner rush. If we let her time traveling before the dinner rush = x, then the time she traveled after dinner = 12 – x. We can now write an equation to solve for Wendy's time based on the total distance she traveled:

Distance Before Dinner + Distance After Dinner = Total Distance
70x + 50(12 – x) = 700
70x + 600 – 50x = 700
20x = 100
x = 5 hours = time Wendy travelled before 5 pm. Hence, Wendy left at **12 noon**. Choice C is correct.

19. For permutations, the correct formula is 4!/(4- 4)! = (4 x 3 x 2 x 1) / 1 = **24**. Choice D is correct.

20. The mode is the value that occurs most frequently in the set of data. To find it, we must first arrange the values in ascending order: 28, 34, 36, 42, 43, 44, 45, 47, 54, 56, 56, 65, 67, 81, 89. Here, the mode is **56**. Choice D is correct.

21. Since we are not given exact numbers for P and N, we can use the plug-in technique to determine the relationship. Let's randomly let P = 10 and N = 100. If the N increases by $212, then each tenant owes 1/10 (100 + 212), or 1/P (N+212) = **(N + 212)/P**. Choice B is correct.

22. In this case, we can write one equation for the first condition and a second equation for the second condition. As always, we must first define our variables. We will let = x the larger number and y = the smaller number.

The first equation, which defines the first condition, is x + y = 24
The second equation, which defines the second condition, is 3x – 2y = 17

To solve the problem for x, we must combine the equations in a way that eliminates y. The fastest way is to re-write equation 1 as y = 24 – x and substitute this value for y into equation 2. When we do, we get:
3x – (2)(24 – x) = 17, so 3x – 48 + 2x = 17. 5x = 65. x = **13** = larger number. Choice C is correct.
y = 24 – 14 = 11 = smaller number

23. The area of the circle is πr^2 = π(8)(8) = 64(3.1416) =201. In the triangle, the area = 1/2 (Base) (Height). We will let x = the height. Thus, for this triangle, 201 = 1/2 (16)x = 8x. Thus, x = **25**. Choice E is correct.

24. Circumference = π x Diameter   If the radius is 7, the circumference= **14π.** Choice D is correct.

25. The area of the original parallelogram = Base X Height. Let B = the length of the base and H = the height of the original parallelogram.   If the base increases by 12%, it becomes 1.12B. If the height decreases by 18%, it becomes 0.82H. The new area is therefore: (1.12)B (0.82)H = 0.9184BH, which is **9.18%** smaller than the original area. Choice A is correct.

26. Volume = (15)(24)(48) = 17,280 cubic inches /30 cubic inches per second = 576 seconds = **9.6** minutes. Choice A is correct.

27. 5% of 3,500 = $175. The company spent 50 + 100 + 70 = $220. The difference is **$45**. Choice D is correct.

28. 20% of $3,500 = $700. By eliminating miscellaneous ($200) + computer ($100) + advertising ($300) + accounting ($100), the company can reduce its expenses by $700. Choice B is correct.

Quantitative Section 15:   28 questions   45 minutes

Each question has two quantities to be compared: one in Column A and one in Column B. Compare the
quantities taking into consideration any other information given and choose
Answer A - if the quantity in Column A is greater
Answer B - if the quantity in Column B is greater
Answer C - if the two quantities are equal
Answer D - if the relationship cannot be determined without further information.

1. A dispenser contains 50 red M&Ms, 75 green M&Ms, 100 blue M&Ms and 75 white M&Ms.

Column A	Column B
The probability of getting a blue M&M	1/5

2. The following sequence continues indefinitely. 9,8,7,6,5,4,9,8,7,6,5,4,9,8,7,6,5,4,9,8,7,6,5,4 .....

Column A	Column B
8	The 300th term

3. A right triangle has two legs of length 8.

Column A	Column B
32	The area of the triangle

4. Jim's ticket won a lottery prize worth $433,890 after taxes. Jim decides to keep one-third of the amount
and to divide the remainder equally among his two parents and three sisters.

Column A	Column B
The amount of money Jim's two parents will receive	$115,704

5.

Column A	Column B
The sum of the prime numbers between 10 and 20	59

6. Two separate pipes are used to fill a 2000-gallon swimming pool. Pipe A fills the pool at a rate of 15
gallons of water per minute and Pipe B fills the pool at a rate of 45 gallons per minute.

Column A	Column B
The number of minutes will it take to fill the pool to the top, if it already has 500-gallons of water in it	25

Directions: For each problem, decide which answer is the best of the choices given.

236

7. (75% x 800) + (1/6 x 600) =

   a. 660
   b. 700
   c. 1060
   d. 1200
   e. 1400

8. If x = 10, what is the value of $x^2 + 1/x^2$?

   a. 100.001
   b. 100.010
   c. 100.100
   d. 101.010
   e. 110.010

9. What is the absolute value of twice the difference of the roots of the equation $5y^2 - 20y + 15 = 0$?

   a. 0
   b. 1
   c. 2
   d. 3
   e. 4

10. What is the set of all values of x for which $x^2 - x = 12$?

   a. (2, 6)
   b. (-3, 4)
   c. (3, -4)
   d. (-2, 6)
   e. (2, -6)

Use the following information to answer questions 11 –12.

F = {1, 2, 4, 5, 8}   G = {4, 5, 6, 9,}   H = {2, 6, 7, 10}

11. What is $(F \cup G) \cap H$?

   a. {2}
   b. {2, 6}
   c. {2, 4, 5}
   d. {2, 5}
   e. {9, 10}

12. What is $(F \cup G) \cup H$?

   a. {2}
   b. {2, 6}
   c. {1, 2, 4, 5, 6, 7, 10, 11, 12}
   d. {2, 3, 4, 5, 6, 7, 8, 9, 10, 12}
   e. {1, 2, 4, 5, 6, 7, 8, 9, 10}

13. Leslie added Y dolls to her large collection, which gave her a total of Z dolls. Then, Leslie sold Y – 96 of her dolls to a local collector. How many dolls did Leslie have left?

        a. Y - Z + 96
        b. Z + Y - 96
        c. Z - Y + 96
        d. Z - Y - 96
        e. (Y + Z – 96)/2

14. What is the circumference of a circle that has a radius of 4444 (use $\pi = 3.1416$)?

        a. 2.22×10^3
        b. 2.79×10^4
        c. 2.22×10^7
        d. 4.44×10^7
        e. 8.88×10^7

15. The Kline Corporation had to mail a package on the day that the Post Office increased its rates. The cost is 93 cents for the first ounce and 51 cents for each additional ounce. How much did the company pay to mail a package that weighed three pounds?

        a. $22.90
        b. $22.97
        c. $23.90
        d. $23.97
        e. $24.90

16. How many inches are there in X yards, Y feet and Z inches?

        a. 36X + 12Y + Z
        b. 3X + 12Y +12 Z
        c. 3X + 36Y +12 Z
        d. (X + Y + Z)/12
        e. (X +Y)/12 + Z

17. Beth's Bridal Shop sells two designer gowns online: Victorian Lady and Summer Delight. Selling just these two products, the company makes $44,995 in profits each year on the sale of 450 gowns. If the profit per gown is $75 and $140 for Victorian Lady and Summer Delight, respectively, how many Victorian Lace gowns does the shop sell per year?

        a.   173
        b.   177
        c.   273
        d.   277
        e.   303

18. How much greater than 10 – 8y is 5y - 3?

        a. 3y - 11
        b. 13y - 5
        c. 13y - 13
        d. -3y - 11
        e. 13y + 11

19. The Boston Philharmonic invited the top five student violinists to perform on their national tour. Only the top three would be offered a chance to play solos. How many possible ways are there to order the top three finalists?

  a. 3
  b. 9
  c. 15
  d. 27
  e. 60

20. If y is g less than h times x, what is the value of x?

  a. $(y - g)/h$
  b. $(y + g)/h$
  c. $hy + 20$
  d. $hy - 20$
  e. $h/g \, y$

21. How many positive integers less than 50 are evenly divisible by 3, 6 and 9?

  a. 1
  b. 2
  c. 3
  d. 4
  e. 5

22. A chef must blend a type of oregano that costs $25 per pound with one that costs $10 per pound to make 2000 pounds that cost $20 per pound. How many pounds of the $25 oregano can the chef use?

  a. 668
  b. 998
  c. 1002
  d. 1332
  e. 1667

23. A base angle of an isosceles triangle is 30 degrees. How many degrees are in the vertex angle?

  a. 100
  b. 110
  c. 120
  d. 140
  e. 150

24. A rectangle that measures 9 inches by 16 inches is completely inscribed in a circle. If all four corners of the rectangle touch the circumference of the circle, what is the area of the circle?

  a. 12π
  b. 36π
  c. 84π
  d. 144π
  e. 720π

25. The sides of a hexagonal shaped lot are 24.5 ft, 12.0 ft, 9.75 ft, 11.9 ft, 34.0 ft and 21.6 ft. If the cost of chain link fencing is $36.00 per linear yard, how much will it cost the owner of the lot to buy a fence to secure the entire lot?

    a. $1,222
    b. $1,365
    c. $1,643
    d. $4,086
    e. $4,104

26. A Brinks truck is making a special delivery of 24 gold bars to the U.S. Treasury. Each bar is 3 feet long, 6 inches wide and 12 inches deep. If the gold is certified to weigh 3 ounces per cubic inch, how many pounds does each bar weigh?

    a. 54
    b. 486
    c. 864
    d. 1,296
    e. 7,776

Refer to the following chart for questions 27 and 28.

	1960's	1970's	1980's	1990's
Percentage of mothers in the workforce	10	30	50	120
Number of women in the workforce (millions)	15	20	30	45

27. In which decade did the number of mothers in the workforce increase the most?

    a. 1960s to 1970s
    b. 1970s to 1980s
    c. 1980s to 1990s
    d. The increase was the same for each decade
    e. It cannot be determined from the information given

28. In which decade was the percentage of women in the workplace the highest?

    a. 1960s
    b. 1970s
    c. 1980s
    d. 1990's
    e. It cannot be determined from the information given

Answer Key for Quantitative Section 15

1. First, we must find the total: 50 + 75 + 100 + 75 = 300. Then, we can determine the fraction: 100/300 = **1/3**. Choice A is correct.

2. The series includes 6 digits that repeat indefinitely in the order: 9,8,7,6,5,4. 300/6 = 50 + a remainder of 0. The 300st digit will be **4**. Choice A is correct.

3. Area = ½ (8)(8) =**32**. Choice C is correct.

4. If Jim keeps one third of the lottery money, then the portion he gives to his family must equal 2/3 of $433,890, or $289,260. This amount will later be split among five people, two of whom are Jim's parents. Their portion is therefore 2/5 of $289,260, or $115,704. Choice C is correct.

5. The prime numbers between 10 and 20 are 11, 13, 17, and 19. Their sum is **60**. Choice A is correct.

6. Here, we must use the basic work equation to solve for the total time. The trick is to use the correct amount of water needed, considering that the 2000-gallon pool already contains 500 gallons of water. Hence, our equation becomes: 1/Time A + 1/Time B = 1/ Total Time. 15/1500 + 45/1500 = 1/X. 60/1500 = 1/X. Thus, X = **25 minutes**. Choice C is correct.

7. (3/4 x 800) + (1/6 x 600) = 600 + 100 = **700**. Choice B is correct.

8. If x = 10, then $x^2 + 1/x^2$ = 100.+ 0.01 = **100.01**. Choice B is correct.

9. Choice E is correct. First, factor the 5 out of the original equation which yields $5(y^2 - 4y + 3)$. The trinomial factors into (y - 3)(y - 1) = 0. Setting each term to 0 yields y = 3 and y = 1. The difference is 2. Two times two equals **4.**

10. $x^2 - x = 12$, or $x^2 - x - 12 = 0$, or (x+3)(x-4) = 0. x = **(-3, 4).** Choice B is correct.

11. F ∪ G = {1, 2, 4, 5, 6, 8, 9}. {1, 2, 4, 5, 6, 8, 9} ∩ {2, 6, 7, 10} = **{2, 6}**. Choice B is correct.

12. (F ∪ G) ∪ H = {1, 2, 4, 5, 6, 7, 8, 9, 10}. Choice E is correct.

13. The fastest way to solve this problem is to substitute numbers for the variables. Then, we can convert the relationship back to letters. Let's say Y = 100 and Z = 200. Therefore, (Y – 96) = 4. When Leslie sold the dolls, she reduced her collection by the following amount: 200 – (Y – 96) = 200 – Y + 96. Converting this back to letters, she had **Z – Y + 96** dolls left. Choice C is correct.

14. Circumference of a circle = 2πr. In this case, C = 2(3.1416)(4444) = **2.79 x 10^4**. Choice B is correct.

15. First, we must convert the weight of the package from pounds to ounces. In this case, 3.00 pounds X (16 ounces/1 pound) = 48 ounces. The total cost is $0.93 for the first ounce and $0.51 for the 47 additional ounces, or 0.93 + 47 (0.51) = 0.93 + 23.97 = **$24.90** total cost to mail a 3-pound package. Choice E is correct.

16. To solve, we must convert all of the terms to inches and add them together. Let's start with what we know. The term for inches is represented by Z. There are 12 inches in 1 foot. Hence, our coefficient for Y is 12. There are 3 feet in one yard and 12 inches in one foot. Hence, our coefficient for X is 3 x 12 = 36. The number of inches in a distance of X yards, Y feet and Z inches is therefore **36X + 12Y + Z.** Choice A is correct.

17., Let x = the # of Victorian Lady gowns sold and 450 – x = the # of Summer Delight gowns sold. The total profit ($44,995) is the sum of the two gowns, which makes our equation: 75x + 140 (450 –x) = 44,995. 75x + 63,000 – 140x = 44,995. - 65x = -18005. x = **277** Victorian Lady Gowns; 450 –277 = 173 Summer Delight Gowns. Choice D is correct.

18. Here, we are simply being asked to find the difference between the two quantities: 5y – 3 - (10 - 8y) = 5y - 3 – 10 + 8y = **13y – 13**. Choice C is correct.

19. For situations in which the *order matters*, the correct formula is 5!/(5- 3)! = 5! / 2! = (5 x 4 x 3 x 2 x 1) / (2 x 1) = **60**. Choice E is correct.

20. According to the problem, y = hx – g. If we solve for x, we find x = **(y + g)/h**. Choice B is correct.

21. Choice B is correct. The **two** integers are 18 and 36.

22. In this case, we can write two equations – one for the amount of each type of oregano and the other for their cost. As always, we must first define our variables. We will let = x the amount of $25 oregano and y = the amount of $10 oregano.

The first equation, which defines the *amount* of oregano, is simply x + y = 2000
The second equation, which defines their *cost*, is 25x + 10y = 20
To solve the problem for x, we must combine the equations in a way that eliminates y.

We can re-write equation 1 as y = 2000 – x and substitute this value for y into equation 2. When we do, we get: 25x + 10(2000 – x) = 20
25x + 20,000 – 10x = 20
15x = -19980
x = **1,332** pounds of $25 oregano. Choice D is correct.

23. By definition, an isosceles triangle has two equal sides. Additionally, the two opposite angles, which are called base angles, are also equal. If one of the base angles = 30 degrees, then the second base angle also equals 30 degrees. The vertex angle is therefore 180 – 60 = **120** degrees. Choice C is correct.

24. In this situation, the diagonal of the rectangle is equal to the diameter of the circle. Because the rectangle can also be viewed as two triangles that share the diagonal as a common side, we can use the Pythagorean theorem to calculate its length. Accordingly, the square of the diagonal is equal to (9)(9) + (16)(16) = 81 + 256 = 337. This means that the diameter of the circle is the square root of 337, or 18.36; the radius is therefore 9.18. Now, we can calculate the area of the circle, which is (9.18)(9.18)(π), = **84π**. Choice C is correct.

25. The perimeter of the lot is the sum of its six sides, or 24.5 + 12 + 9.75 + 11.9 + 34 + 21.6 = 113.75 feet / 3 = 37.9 yards. 37.9 x $36 = **$1,365**. Choice B is correct.

26. Volume = (36)(6)(12) = 2,592 cubic inches x 3 oz/ inch = 7,776 oz./16 oz. per pound = **486** lbs. Choice B is correct.

27. Choice E is correct. The table only gives us the *% increase* in working mothers – it does not given us the *number* of working mothers. Without this information, it is impossible to answer the question.

28. Choice E is correct. The table only gives us the *number* of women in the workforce, not the percentage. Consequently, it is impossible to answer the question.

Quantitative Section 16:   28 questions   45 minutes

Each question has two quantities to be compared: one in Column A and one in Column B. Compare the quantities taking into consideration any other information given and choose
Answer A - if the quantity in Column A is greater
Answer B - if the quantity in Column B is greater
Answer C - if the two quantities are equal
Answer D - if the relationship cannot be determined without further information.

1. A cattery has 90 Persian cats, 400 Siamese cats and 110 Calico cats.   For a treat, the owner of the cattery purchases 150 lbs of catnip, to be distributed evenly among all of the cats. There are no other types of cats in the cattery.

Column A	Column B
4	The amount of catnip (in ounces) each cat receives

2. **Column A**

	Column B
The number of positive integers less than 50 that are evenly divisible by 6, 8 and 12?	3

3. At the beginning of her shift, Kate had 60-½ dozen cans of Pepsi. At the end of her shift, 54-1/3 dozen cans remained.

Column A	Column B
72	The # cans Kate sold during her shift

4. Every time Wendy travels west on highway B, she must pay a $5.00 toll. Every time she travels east on the same road, she receives a $4.00 credit. Wendy travels west on highway B nineteen times during April and she travels east on highway B fifteen times during the same period.

Column A	Column B
The amount of money Wendy lost from traveling on highway B	$34

5.   y is 3 less than 5 times x.

Column A	Column B
x	$(y +3)/5$

6. If Kyle works alone, he can wash the night shift dishes in 55 minutes. It will only take him 40 minutes if he works together with Harry.

Column A	Column B
The number of minutes it will take Harry to wash the night shift dishes by himself	120

7. The perimeter of triangle LMN is 111. If LM = 22 and MN = 33, what is the length of LN?

    a. 55
    b. 56
    c. 65
    d. 66
    e. 77

8. If a Ψ b = $(1 + b)^{1/2}$ what is aΨ 3024?

    a. 24
    b. 30
    c. 55
    d. 64
    e. 72

9. If the average of nine consecutive odd integers is 999, what is the smallest of the nine integers?

    a. 987
    b. 989
    c. 991
    d. 993
    e. 997

10.   2.05 x 8.99 x 54.22 =

    a. 99.25
    b. 487.43
    c. 974.87
    d. 999.25
    e. 1949.75

11. What is the sum of the following fractions: 1/5, 2/20, 3/5, 3/10, 3/20

    a. 23/20
    b. 12/10
    c. 27/20
    d. 27/10
    e. 29/20

12. The sum of two numbers is 12. When four times the larger number is subtracted from 6 times the smaller number, the difference is 2. What is the larger number?

    a. 4
    b. 5
    c. 6
    d. 7
    e. 9

13. If x = 2, y = 1 and z = 3, what is the value of $3x^3 - 5y^4 + 2z^2$?

    a.   1
    b.   6
    c.   23
    d.   37
    e.   42

14. Which of the following is equal to 0.0000543?

    a. 54.3×10^5
    b. $54.3 \ 10^{-7}$
    c. 543×10^{-8}
    d. 5.43×10^{-6}
    e. 5.43×10^{-5}

15. What is the largest integer that will divide evenly into 64 and 118?

    a.   2
    b.   4
    c.   6
    d.   8
    e.   12

16. If x + 5 is an even integer, the sum of the next two even integers is:

    a.   x + 9
    b.   2(x +5)
    c.   2x + 16
    d.   2x + 27
    e.   It is impossible to determine from the information given.

17. In Triangle D, the length of one side is 21 and the other side is 36. Which of the following could possibly be the length of the third side?

    a.   13
    b.   14
    c.   16
    d.   60
    e.   63

18. A parallelogram has an interior angle of 75 degrees. What is the measure of the adjacent angle (in degrees)?

    a.   75
    b.   90
    c.   105
    d.   115
    e.   285

19. How many 6 ounce rib eye steaks are in a carton of steaks that weighs 48 pounds? (Assume that all of the steaks are rib eye and that they account for the total weight of the box)

    a.   96
    b.   108
    c.   128
    d.   146
    e.   196

20. At the company picnic, each of the firm's 20 employees placed a raffle ticket into a bowl. At the end of the night, the company president picked one ticket randomly from the bowl and awarded the first prize to Greg. He then picked another ticket randomly from the bowl and awarded the second prize to Pete. Finally, after awarding two more prizes in the same manner, the president picked a fifth random ticket from the bowl and awarded the fifth prize to Jim. Assuming that the first four tickets were not placed back into the bowl after the first four prizes were awarded, what was the probability of Jim winning the fifth prize?

    a.   1.25%
    b.   2.50%
    c.   5.00%
    d.   5.25%
    e.   6.25%

21. If the following series continues in the same pattern, what will the next term be?
        3, 5, 4, 7, 5, 9, 6, 11.........

    a.   3
    b.   5
    c.   6
    d.   7
    e.   13

22. The final exam for English Literature class is worth 1/3 of the overall grade. The average of 4 monthly exams counts for another third, while an oral presentation on sonnets is worth the final third. So far, Becky's exam scores are 68, 73, 80 and 95. She only scored a 70 on her oral presentation. What will Becky have to earn on the final exam to raise her average to 80?

    a.   87
    b.   88
    c.   89
    d.   91
    e.   92

23. Two airplanes leave the Orlando Airport at the same time and head in opposite directions. Plane A flies four times as fast as Plane B. Three hours later, they are 5,000 miles apart. How fast is Plane B flying (in miles per hour)?

    a.   300
    b.   333
    c.   500
    d.   667
    e.   900

24. The perimeter of right triangle DEF is 144 inches. If we connect the midpoints of the three sides of DEF, we can form a smaller triangle. What will its perimeter be?

    a.   12
    b.   36
    c.   48
    d.   64
    e.   72

Use the following table to answer questions 25 – 28.

Percentage of Diabetics (By Age)

	China	Italy	France	Germany
Under 10	5	5	2	0
10 – 18	20	30	15	13
19 – 30	35	30	28	29
31 – 50	30	30	40	48
Over 51	10	5	15	10

25. If there are 10 million diabetics in Italy, how many of them are over 31 years old?

    a.   1.5 million
    b.   3 million
    c.   3.5 million
    d.   6 million
    e.   6.5 million

26. If there are 20 million diabetics in Germany, and they each purchase two insulin pumps per year, how many pumps are needed by the diabetics who are under 30?

    a.   4.2 million
    b.   8.4 million
    c.   11.6 million
    d.   16 million
    e.   16.8 million

27. Which country has the smallest percentage of diabetics under age 19?

    a.   China
    b.   Italy
    c.   France
    d.   Germany
    e.   Cannot be determined from the information provided

28. Which country has the largest number of diabetics between 31 and 50?

    a.   China
    b.   Italy
    c.   France
    d.   Germany
    e.   Cannot be determined from the information given

Answer Key for Quantitative Section 16

1. To solve, we must calculate the total number of cats in the cattery, which is 90 + 400 + 110 = 600 cats.

Then, we must convert the amount of catnip to ounces, which is 150 lb x 16 oz/lb = 2400 oz. Finally, we must divide the total amount of catnip evenly among the total number of cats, which is 2400 / 600 = **4** ounces. Choice C is correct.

2. The question asks us to determine how positive integers less than 50 are evenly divisible by 6, 8, and 12. First, we will list the integers that are evenly divisible by our largest number, which is 12: 12, 24, 36, and 48. (Note: Because they are all multiples of 12, these numbers are also evenly divisible by 6.)

Next, we eliminate numbers from this group that are NOT evenly divisible by 8, which leaves us with 24 and 48. Thus, there are **2** positive integers that meet the criterion: they are 24 and 48. Choice B is correct.

3. To solve this problem, we simply need to subtract the number of remaining cans of Pepsi (54-1/3 dozen) from the original number of cans (60-1/2 dozen). First, we must convert each value from "dozens" to single cans. 60-1/2 dozen = (60)(12) + (1/2)(12) = 720 + 6 = 726. 54-1/3 dozen = (54)(12) + (1/3)(12) = 648 + 4 = 652. Finally, we must subtract the remaining cans from the original number to determine the number of cans sold: 726 − 652 = **74 cans sold**. Choice B is correct.

4. To solve, we must calculate the amount of money that Wendy pays in tolls to the amount that she receives in credits. Her tolls = 19 (5) = $95. During the same period, Wendy gets back 15 (4) = $60. The difference is $95 - $60 = **$35**. Choice A is correct.

5. According to the problem, $y = 5x - 3$. If we solve for x, we find **x = (y +3)/5**. Choice C is correct.

6. In this case, our variable x is the amount of time that Harry needs to complete the dishes alone. Thus, our equation becomes $40/55 + 40/x = 1$. To solve, we must multiply both sides of the equation by 55x, which is our least common denominator: $40x + 2200 = 55x$, which simplifies to $2200 = 15x$ or $x = 146.67 =$ **147 minutes**. Choice A is correct.

7. The perimeter is simply the sum of the three side lengths, Therefore, we can solve the problem using the following equation: 22 + 33 + LN = 111. LN = **56.** Choice B is correct.

8. If $a \Psi b = (1 + b)^{1/2}$ then $a\Psi 3024 = (1 + 3024)^{\frac{1}{2}} =$ **55**. Choice C is correct.

9. If 999 is the mean, then it is the fifth in the series of nine consecutive odd numbers. We can simply count back to get the first in the series, which will be **991** (999 –997- 995 – 993 - 991). Choice C is correct.

10. 2.05 x 8.99 x 54.22 = **999.35**. Choice D is correct.

11. Convert all fractions to the form with an LCD of 20. The sum is:
1/5 + 2/20 + 3/5 + 3/10 + 3/20 = 4/20 + 2/20 + 12/20 + 6/20 + 3/20 = **27/20**. Choice C is correct.

12. First, we must define our variables. For convenience, we will let the smaller number = x and the larger number = (12 – x). We also know that $6x - 4(12 – x) = 2$. When we solve this equation, we find that $6x – 48 + 4x = 2$, or $10x = 50$, so $x = 5$ and $12 – 5 = $ **7**. Choice D is correct.

13. If $x = 2$, $y = 1$ and $z = 3$, then $3x^3 - 5y^4 + 2z^2 = (3)(2)(2)(2) - (5)(1)(1)(1)(1) + (2)(3)(3) = 24 - 5 + 18 = $ **37**. Choice D is correct.

14. **5.43 x 10$^{-5.}$** Choice E is correct.

15. The fastest way to solve this problem is to try each answer choice. Choice A is correct.

16. $(x + 7) + (x + 9) = $ **2x + 16**. Choice C is correct.

17. According to the triangle inequality theorem, the length of one side of a triangle must be greater than the difference and less than the sum of the lengths of the other two sides. Therefore, in Triangle D, the length of the third side must be greater than 36 – 21 = 15 and less than 36 + 21 = 57. The only answer choice between 15 and 57 is Choice C.

18. The adjacent angle = 180 –75 = **105** degrees. Choice C is correct.

19. We can solve this using a proportion. 1 steak / 6 oz = x steaks / 768 oz, so x = **128**. Choice C is correct.

20. Jim's ticket was one of 16 tickets left in the bowl during the fifth drawing. His probability of winning the prize was 1/16, or 0.0625, which is **6.25%**. Choice E is correct.

21. This problem is a combination of two sub-series. In the first one, each number increase by 1 (3,4,5,6); in the second, each number increases by 2 (5,7,9,11). The next number would be 6 + 1, or **7.** Choice D is correct.

22. Let's let x = the final exam grade. The average of Becky's four exams is (68 + 73 + 80 + 95)/4 = 79. Finally, her score for the oral presentation is 70. Since the final exam grade, oral presentation score and the average of her four exam grades all equal one-third of Becky's final grade, we simply need to solve the following equation for x: 1/3 (79) + 1/3 (70) + 1/3 (x) = 80. Hence, x = **91**. Choice D is correct.

23. In this case, we can write two equations – one for the speed of the planes and the other for the distance they travel. As always, we must first define our variables. We will let x = Plane B's speed and y = Plane A's speed.

The first equation, which defines the *speed* of the planes, is simply y = 4x
The second equation, which defines the *distance* they travel, is 3x + 3y = 5,000
To solve the problem for x, we must combine the equations in a way that eliminates y.

The fastest way is to substitute equation 1 into equation 2. When we do, we get
3x + 3(4x) = 5,000
15x = 5,000
x = **333.33** = Plane B's speed. Choice B is correct.
4x = 1333.33 = Plane A's speed

24. The new triangle will have sides that are one-half the length of those in triangle DEF. Hence, its perimeter will be one-half of DEF, which is **72**. Choice E is correct.

25. (10 million)(0.35) = **3.5** million. Choice C is correct.

26. If Germany has a total of 20 million diabetics, then the number of them who are under 30 is (20 million) (0.42) = 8.4 million. If all of these patients purchase 2 insulin pumps per year, they will require a total of **16.8** million. Choice E is correct.

27. Choice D is correct. Germany has the smallest percentage, which is **13%**.

28. Choice E is correct. The chart only gives the % of diabetics in each nation; it does not reveal the actual numbers. Without them, we cannot answer this question.

Quantitative Section 17: 28 questions   45 minutes

Each question has two quantities to be compared: one in Column A and one in Column B. Compare the quantities taking into consideration any other information given and choose
Answer A - if the quantity in Column A is greater
Answer B - if the quantity in Column B is greater
Answer C - if the two quantities are equal
Answer D - if the relationship cannot be determined without further information.

1.   Diane has 18 errands to run, which take 14 minutes each.

Column A	Column B
The number of seconds Diane needs to complete the errands	25,500

2. **Column A**

Column A	Column B
The sum of the prime numbers between 45 and 65	220

3. Brad decided to fill the gas cans for three of his elderly neighbors: Jim, Bill and Marge. Jim needed 4 ½ gallons of gas, Bill needed 6 -2/5 gallons, and Marge needed 3 gallons.

Column A	Column B
The amount that Brad spent to fill all three gas cans, assuming that gas costs $3.95 per gallon	$55.91

4. It takes 12 people to serve 500 meals at the soup kitchen.

Column A	Column B
The number of people needed to serve 14,280 meals	343

5. **Column A**

Column A	Column B
The ratio of 12 ounces to 12 pounds	1/12

6. A faucet can fill a tank in 60 minutes, while the drain takes 80 minutes to empty it.

Column A	Column B
The number of minutes it will take to fill the tank if the drain is left open when the faucet is turned on	480

**Directions**: _For each problem, decide which answer is the best of the choices given._

7. How many divisors of 60 are prime numbers?

    a. 2
    b. 3
    c. 4
    d. 5
    e. 6

8. For the following fractions, what is the least common denominator?
        2/3, 3/5, 4/6, 9/10, 1/3

    a. 10
    b. 15
    c. 30
    d. 36
    e. 60

9. If the 8% hotel tax on a room is $16.20, what was the total price of the room (including tax)?

    a. $186.30
    b. $202.50
    c. $218.70
    d. $222.50
    e. $228.70

10. If you roll a 6-sided die, which sides are numbered 1 through 6, what is the probability that you will roll two consecutive 5s?

    a. 1/36
    b. 1/12
    c. 1/6
    d. 1/5
    e. 2/5

11. If $x = 0.1$, what is the value of $(10x)^2 + 100x^2$?

    a. 0.1
    b. 1
    c. 2
    d. 10
    e. 11

12. What is the area (in cubic centimeters) of a trapezoid with a height of 12 cm and parallel side lengths of 16 cm and 18 cm?

    a. 84
    b. 96
    c. 192
    d. 204
    e. 216

13. What is the product of (8/3)(5/4)(9/3)?

    a.   4.4
    b.   40/9
    c.   10
    d.   180/9
    e.   100

14. Two individual price reductions of 20% and 30% are equal to a single price reduction of:

    a.   25%
    b.   27%
    c.   37%
    d.   44%
    e.   47%

15. $1/18 \, (22 + 33)^2 =$

    a.   9
    b.   168
    c.   336
    d.   5,450
    e.   54,450

16. W, which is a positive integer, is the first term in a sequence. After W, each term in the sequence is 2 greater than one-half the preceding term. What is the ratio of the second term to W?

    a. 1/2W/(W + 2)
    b. (W + 4)2W
    c. (W + 2)/2
    d. W/2
    e. 4(W + 1)/2

17. Square X has a side of 17 inches, while square Y has a side of 27 inches. How much greater is the area of square Y than square X (in square inches)?

    a.   100
    b.   270
    c.   289
    d.   440
    e.   729

18. What is the next term in the following series? 1, 7, 13, 19…….

    a.   13
    b.   21
    c.   25
    d.   27
    e.   29

19. In a family of eight children, half are girls and half are boys. If the average height of the girls is 56 inches and the average height of the boys is 42 inches, what is the average height of all eight children?

    a. 48
    b. 49
    c. 50
    d. 51
    e. 52

20. At the end of the day, the clerk in a Laundromat has 3,500 coins that are a combination of nickels and quarters. If the coins are worth $750, how many of them are nickels?

    a. 625
    b. 750
    c. 1,350
    d. 2,750
    e. 2,875

21. A parallelogram with an area of 36 has a base of $(x + 8)$ and a height of $(x - 8)$. What is the exact measure of its height?

    a. 2
    b. 4
    c. 8
    d. 10
    e. 18

22. A mechanic must store his leftover antifreeze in a tank in his garage. His largest tank is a cylinder with a radius of 14 and a height of 16 inches. If the antifreeze has a density of 12 cubic inches per gallon, how many gallons of it will fit in the bucket? (Use $\pi = 3.1416$)

    a. 205
    b. 261
    c. 421
    d. 704
    e. 821

23. If the area of a rectangle is 144, what is its perimeter?

    a. 12
    b. 48
    c. 96
    d. 288
    e. It cannot be determined from the information given

Refer to the following table for questions 24 – 28

	2006	2007	2008	2009
Number of Books Sold (thousands)	54	106	189	312
Profit from Books Sold (millions)	3	11	24	21

24. What is the percentage increase in the number of books sold between 2006 and 2008?

    a.   150%
    b.   175%
    c.   250%
    d.   300%
    e.   350%

25. What is the percentage increase in profit from books sold between 2007 and 2009?

    a.   50%
    b.   91%
    c.   150%
    d.   191%
    e.   218%

26. In what year was the profit per book the lowest?

    a. 2006
    b. 2007
    c. 2008
    d. 2009
    e. It cannot be determined from the information given

27. In 2010, the company sold 20% fewer books than in 2009, but the profit increased by 20%. What was the average profit per book?

    a.   67.30
    b.   87.96
    c. 100.96
    d. 107.30
    e. 167.30

28. The company accountants discovered an error in the data that was presented for 2007 and 2008. The number of books sold in 2007 was understated by 50,000, while the number of books sold in 2008 was overstated by 19,000. When the data is corrected, what impact will it have on the change in the profit per book between 2007 and 2008?

    a.   It will double
    b.   It will increase by 50%
    c.   It will decrease by 50%
    d.   It will remain unchanged
    e.   It is impossible to determine from the information given

Answer Key for Quantitative Section 17

1. First, we must calculate the total number of minutes that Diane needs to complete her errands, which is 18 x 14 = 252 minutes. Next, we must multiply this number by 60 to get the number of seconds: 252(60) = **15,120**. Choice B is correct.

2. The prime numbers between 45 and 65 are 47, 53, 59, and 61. Their sum is **220**. Choice C is correct.

3. To solve, we must first add the individual gallons of gas that each person needs: 4-1/2 + 6-2/5 + 3-0/2. To do so, we will convert the mixed number to fractions, which become 9/2 + 32/5 + 6/2. Second, we must add these fractions together, which requires them to have the same denominator. In this case, the least common denominator (which is evenly divisible by 2 and 5) is 10, which makes our equation: 45/10 + 64/10 + 30/10 = 139/10 = 13.90 gallons. Finally, we must multiply the number of gallons Brad needs by the price

per gallon of gas: (13.90 gallons)($3.95 per gallon) = **$54.91**. Choice B is correct.

4. We can solve this problem by using a proportion. 12/500 = x /14,280.   x= 342.7 = **343**. Choice C is correct.

5. 12 pounds = 192 oz. 12/192 = **1/16**. Choice B is correct.

6. In this case, our variable x is the amount of time it will take to fill the tank. Thus, our equation becomes x/60 - x/80 = 1. To solve, we must multiply both sides of the equation by 240, which is our least common denominator: 4x – 3x = 240, or x = **240 minutes** to fill the tank. Choice B is correct.

7. Choice B is correct. The divisors of 60 that are prime numbers are **2, 3 and 5**. By definition, 1 is NOT prime.

8. Choice C is correct, **30.**

9. If 0.08x = $16.20, then x = $202.50 Total price = **$218.70**. Choice C is correct.

10. The probability is 1/6 x 1/6 = **1/36,** or Choice A.

11. For x = 0.1, $(1)^2$ + 100(0.01) = **2**. Choice C is correct.

12. Area of Trapezoid = (Average of parallel sides) x Height. In this case, the area = {(16 + 18)/2} x (12) = (17)(12) = 204 cubic centimeters. Choice D is correct.

Alternatively, we calculate the areas of the respective parts of the trapezoid (a triangle and a rectangle) and add them together. The area of the rectangle = (12)(16) = 192. The area of the triangle is ½ (2)(12) = 12. The total area is 192 + 12 = **204** cubic inches.

13. Choice C is correct,   360/36 = **10**.

14. Two price reductions = 0.80 x 0.70 = 0.56, which is a **44%** reduction. Choice D is correct.

15. 1/18 $(22 + 33)^2$ = (55)(55)/18 = 168.05 = **168**. Choice B is correct.

16. If W is the first term, then the second term is W/2 + 2. The ratio of these two values is (second term)/(first term) = (W/2 + 2)/W, which simplifies to (W + 4)/2W. To check our work, let's assume that the first term W = 100. The second term would be 2 greater than one-half of one hundred, or 52. The ratio of 52/100 = 26/50= 13/25. **(W + 4)/2W** = 104/200 = 52/100 = 26/50 = 13/25. Choice B is correct.

17. Area of Y = 27 x 27 = 729 square inches. Area of X = 17 x 17 = 289 square inches. 729 – 289 = **440** square inches. Choice D is correct.

18. Each term in the series increases by 6. Hence, the next term will be 19 + 6 = **25**. Choice C is correct.

19. In this case, the number of girls (4) is equal to the number of boys (also 4), which means that we can simply take the average of 56 + 42 and apply it to the entire group of siblings.   The result is (56 + 42)/2 = **49** inches. Choice B is correct.

20. In this case, we can write two equations – one for the number of coins and the other for their value. As always, we must first define our variables. We will let = x the number of nickels and y = the number of quarters.

The first equation, which defines the *number* of coins, is simply x + y = 3,500
The second equation, which defines their *monetary worth*, is 0.05x + 0.25y = 750.00
To solve the problem for x, we must combine the equations in a way that eliminates y.

First, we will multiply equation 2 by 100 to eliminate the decimals. When we do, we get:
x + y = 3,500
5x + 25y = 75000

Then, we can re-write equation 1 as y = 3,500 – x and substitute this value for y into equation 2. When we

do, we get 5x + 25(3500 − x) = 75000
5x + 87,500 − 25x = 75000
−20x = −12,500
x = **625** nickels. Choice A is correct.
y = 3,500 − 625 = 2,875 quarters.

21. The area of a parallelogram is equal to its base times its height. Therefore, $(x + 8)(x − 8) = 36$.
$x^2 − 64 = 36$
$x^2 = 100$
$x = 10$
The base of the parallelogram = 10 + 8 = 18 and its height is 10 − 8 = **2**. Choice A is correct.

22. The problem is asking us to determine the capacity, or volume, of a cylinder. To do so, we can simply use the formula: Volume = $\pi r^2 h$ = (3.1416)(14)(14)(16) = 9,852.06 cubic inches. To convert this to gallons, we must divide by 12: 19,852.06/ cubic inches/12 cubic inches per gallon = **821** gallons. Choice E is correct.

23. Choice E is correct. The area of a rectangle does not give us enough information to calculate the perimeter.

24. 189,000 − 54,000 = 135,000/54,000 = 2.5 x 100 = **250%** increase. Choice C is correct.

25. 21,000,000 − 11,000,000 = 10,000,000/11,000,000 = 0.90 x 100 = **91%** increase. Choice B is correct.

26. To find the average profit per book, we must divide the profit by the number of books sold each year. When we do, we find that the lowest average profit was in 2006. ($3 million in profits / 54,000 books = **55.5** profit per book). Choice A is correct.

27. In 2010, the number of books sold = 312,000 (0.80) = 249,600, while the profit was (21 million)(1.2) = 25.2 million). Thus, the average profit per book = 25.2million/249,600 = **100.96**. Choice C is correct.

28. In 2007, the revised profit per book = 11 million/156,000 = 70.5, while the revised profit per book for 2008 = 24 million/170,000 = 141.2. The profit per book **doubled**. Choice A is correct.

Quantitative Section 18: 28 questions   45 minutes

Each question has two quantities to be compared: one in Column A and one in Column B. Compare the quantities taking into consideration any other information given and choose
Answer A - if the quantity in Column A is greater
Answer B - if the quantity in Column B is greater
Answer C - if the two quantities are equal
Answer D - if the relationship cannot be determined without further information.

1. Liza can wear her leather coat nine times before she needs to have it drycleaned. She wears the coat to church every Sunday and to the annual Christmas and Easter pageants. It costs $13.00 for each individual cleaning, and Liza does not wear the coat on any other occasions.

Column A	Column B
The annual cost of dry cleaning Liza's coat	$96.00

2. **Column A**

Column A	Column B
The sum of the prime numbers between 3 and 11, inclusive	23

3. A seamstress bought a beautiful bolt of silk material to use to make wedding dresses. The bolt contained 65 yards of material and each dress required 8-1/5 yards.

Column A	Column B
The number of dresses the seamstress could make from a single bolt of the material	8

4. The asking prices of two cars, which together cost $100,000, are in the ratio of 8:10.

Column A	Column B
$45,000	The cost of the cheaper car

5. The results of a beauty pageant are determined by a personal interview, a swimsuit competition, an evening gown competition, a talent show and a quiz about current events. The personal interview counts twice as much as each of the other selection criteria.

Column A	Column B
The fraction of each contestant's final score that is determined by the talent show	1/5

6. A chef must blend a gourmet cheese that costs $50 per pound with processed cheese spread that costs $10 per pound to make a 500-pound batch that costs $25 per pound.

Column A	Column B
The # pounds of gourmet cheese the chef can use	195

7. For what value of m does $12 - m = m - 12$?

    a. -12
    b. 0
    c. 12
    d. 36
    e. 144

8. If $x + 2 = 11$, then what is $(x - 7)^3$?

    a. 1
    b. 8
    c. 9
    d. 16
    e. 81

9. Rectangle ABCD has a length of 10 and a diagonal of 26. What is its area?

    a. 72
    b. 240
    c. 260
    d. 420
    e. 480

10. If $f(v) = 5v^2 - 1/8v - 3$, what is $f(v^3)$?

    a. $5v^5 - 1/8v^4 - 3v^3$
    b. $5v^5 - 1/8v^4 - 3$
    c. $15v^5 - 3/8v^4 - 9$
    d. $(5v^2 - 1/8v - 3)^3$
    e. $(5v^5 - 1/8v^4 - 3)^{-3}$

11. What is the slope of the line that contains points (2,3) and (8, 10)?

    a. 5/4
    b. 6/7
    c. 7/6
    d. 4/5
    e. 1

12. What positive integer is 30% less than 1,540?

    a. 308
    b. 462
    c. 972
    d. 1,078
    e. 1,386

13. The line represented by 2x −4y = 6 is parallel to which of the following lines?

    a.   y = 1/2x + 3
    b.   y = x + 3/2
    c.   y = 3/2x - 8
    d.   y = 2 x - 6
    e.   y = 3x + 4/3

14. Which of the following are the solutions to the following equation? x^2 + 9x + 20= 0

    a.   4, 5
    b.   4, -5
    c.   −4, -5
    d.   −4, 5
    e.   2, 10

15. If Jake walks south for 50 yards, then west for 120 yards, then walked directly back to his starting point on a diagonal, how many yards did he walk altogether?

    a.   170
    b.   255
    c.   270
    d.   290
    e.   300

16. Karen inherited a valuable oil painting that she wants to have framed. If the painting is a rectangle, with a width of 48 inches and a length of 64 inches, how much framing, in linear feet, does Karen need to buy?

    a.   19
    b.   32
    c.   112
    d.   224
    e.   448

17. Eighteen seconds is what fraction of eighteen minutes?

    a.   1/6
    b.   1/10
    c.   1/18
    d.   1/30
    e.   1/60

18. What is the probability of getting a red jelly bean from a dispenser that contains 80 red jelly beans, 48 green ones, 36 purple ones, 26 pink ones and 210 white ones?

    a.   1/8
    b.   1/6
    c.   1/5
    d.   1/4
    e.   1/3

19. What is the next term in the following series: 11, 12, 13, 24, 15, 48.......

      a.   14
      b.   17
      c.   36
      d.   96
      e.   None of the above.

20. In a class of 55 students, the average waistline of the 30 girls was 24, while the average waistline of the 25 boys was 36. What was the average waistline for the entire class?

      a.   27.45
      b.   28.00
      c.   29.45
      d.   30.00
      e.   31.45

21. A teenage actress set up a trust fund for her younger brother and sister. If she gave her sister $10,000 less than three times what she gave her brother, and the total amount in the trust fund was $500,000, how much did the actress give her brother?

      a. $125,000
      b. $127,500
      c. $170,000
      d. $375,000
      e. $372,500

22. In Triangle DOG, angle D is six times as large as angle O. The exterior angle at G is 140 degrees. How many degrees are in angle D?

      a.   20
      b.   40
      c.   100
      d.   120
      e.   140

23. If the radius of a circle increases by 8, how much will its circumference increase?

      a. 4π
      b. 8π
      c. 16π
      d. 32π
      e. 64π

24. Find the edge (in inches) of a cube whose volume is equal to the volume of a rectangular solid that is 2 in by 36 in by 81 in.

      a.   9
      b.   18
      c.   27
      d.   36
      e.   54

25. Integer X is equal to Integer Y + 8. If the product of Integer X and Integer Y is 20, what is Integer X?

    a.   -10
    b.   -5
    c.   -2
    d.   2
    e.   5

Refer to the following table for questions 26 – 28.

	2005	2006	2007	2008
Number of snow plows sold (thousands)	50	70	75	80
Annual snowfall (inches)	110	150	140	175

26. In what year was the number of snow plows sold per foot of snow 5600?

    a.   2005
    b.   2006
    c.   2007
    d.   2008
    e.   It cannot be determined from the information given

27. In which year was the number of snowplows sold per inch of snow the highest?

    a.   2005
    b.   2006
    c.   2007
    d.   2008
    e.   It cannot be determined from the information given

28. In which two years were the number of snowplows sold per foot of snowfall nearly identical?

    a.   2005 and 2006
    b.   2006 and 2007
    c.   2007 and 2008
    d.   2005 and 2008
    e.   2005 and 2007

Answer Key for Quantitative Section 18

1. To solve, we must first calculate the total number of times that Liza wears the coat each year, which is 52 + 2 = 54. Then, we must calculate the total number of times that she needs to have it cleaned per year, which is 54/9 = 6. If the cost per cleaning is $13.00, then Brenda's annual cost of dry cleaning it will be (6)($13.00) = **$78**. Choice B is correct.

2. The prime numbers between 3 and 11, inclusive, are 3, 5, 7, and 11. Their sum is 26. Choice A is correct.

3. To answer this question, we must divide the total amount of material (65 yards) by the quantity needed to make a single dress (8-1/5 yards). When we do, we find that the seamstress has enough material to make 7.92 dresses. Since she cannot sell a fraction of a dress, we must round our answer down to **7 dresses**. Choice B is correct.

4. An 8/10 ratio means the total is 18. 8/18 x 100,000 = **$44,444**. Choice A is correct.

5. The contest is judged on the results of 5 events. One of them, the personal interview, counts as two of the other events. Hence, it is worth 2/6 of the overall score, with each of the other 4 events being worth an

additional 1/6. Therefore, on its own, the talent show is worth **1/6** of the total score. Choice B is correct.

6. First, we must draw a table with the information that we know.

Ingredient	Quantity	Price/pound	Total Cost
Gourmet cheese	x	$50	$50x
Processed cheese	500 – x	$10	$10(500 – x)
Blend	500	$25	$12,500

Since the problem asks us to calculate the amount of gourmet cheese the chef can use, we will let that value = x. Therefore, the amount of processed cheese = 500 – x. Once we label our variables, we can write the expression for the total cost of each ingredient. From the problem, we can also calculate the cost of the final blend.

Since the cost of the gourmet cheese plus the cost of the processed cheese equals the total cost of the blend, then our equation becomes: Cost of Gourmet Cheese + Cost of Processed Cheese = Total Cost
$50x + 10(500 – x) = 12,500$
$50x + 5,000 – 10x = 12,500$
$40x = 7,500$
$x =$ **187.50** pounds of gourmet cheese. Choice B is correct.

7. The easiest way to solve is to test each answer choice. When we do, we find that Choice C is correct.
$m =$ **12**.

8. $(9-7)^3 =$ **8**. Choice B is correct.

9. This rectangle is actually two 5-12-13 (10-24-26) triangles, in which the hypotenuse is the diagonal. The area is L x W, or 10 x 24 = **240**. Choice B is correct.

10. If $f(v) = 5v^2 - 1/8v – 3$, then $f(v^3) =$ **$5v^5$ - $1/8v^4$ – 3**. Choice B is correct.

11. Slope = $(10 – 3)/ (8 – 2) =$ **7/6**. Choice C is correct.

12. $(1,540)(0.7) =$ **1,078**. Choice D is correct.

13. Parallel lines have the same slope. In this case, the slope of $2x – 4y = 6$ is 1/2, because the equation simplifies to $4y = 2x – 6$, or $y = 1/2x – 3/2$.   Choice A also has a slope of **1/2.**

14. If $x^2 + 9x + 20 = 0$, then $(x + 4)(x + 5) = 0$. So, **x = -4 or -5.** Choice C is correct.

15. The area that Jake walked is a "special" right triangle with sides equal to 50, 120 and 130. Therefore, the total distance Jake walked is the perimeter of that triangle, which is 50 + 120 + 130 = **300** yards. Choice E is correct.

16. The perimeter of a rectangle is 2L + 2W = 2(48) + 2 (64) = 224 inches. But this is not our answer – we must first convert the units from inches to feet by dividing by 12. 224/12 = 18.7 = **19** linear feet. Choice A is correct.

17. Eighteen minutes = (60)(18) = 1080 seconds. 18 /1080 **= 1/60.** Choice E is correct.

18. First, we must determine the total number of jelly beans in the dispenser, which is 80 + 48 + 36 + 26 + 210 = 400.   Then, we must calculate the probability of getting a red jelly bean, which is 80/400 = **1/5.** Choice C is correct.

19. If you look carefully, you will see that this example is actually a combination of TWO sub-series. The odd numbers (11, 13, 15 ….) form an arithmetic series, in which each number increases by two. The even numbers (12, 24, 48, ….) form an arithmetic sequence, in which each number is twice the previous one. The next number in the series will be part of the arithmetic sequence. According to the design, it is 15 + 2, or **17.** Choice B is correct.

20. Because the number of boys and girls is not the same, we must take a *weighted average* for each of the two groups. Average for entire class =(Sum of Girls' Waistlines + Sum of Boys' Waistlines) / Total #

Students. Average = {(30)(24) + (25)(36)} / 55 = (720 + 900)/55 = 1620/55 = **29.45**. Choice C is correct.

21. In this case, we can write two equations – one for the total amount of funds and the other for the respective shares that were given to each sibling. As always, we must first define our variables. We will let = x the brother's share and y = the sister's share.

The first equation, which defines the amount of money invested, is simply x + y = 500,000
The second equation, which defines how the shares are divided, is y = 3x – 10,000
To solve the problem for x, we must combine the equations in a way that eliminates y. When we do, we get:
x + (3x – 10,000) = 500,000
4x – 10,000 = 500,000
4x = 510,000
x = **$127,500** = the brother's share. Choice B is correct.
y = 3($127,500) - $10,000 = $372,500 = the sister's share

22. By definition, the exterior angle is equal to the sum of the two remote interior angles. If angle D is six times as large as angle O, then their sum is 6x + 1x = 7x. Hence,
7x =140
x = 20 = angle O
6x = **120** = angle D. Choice A is correct.

23. The circumference of the circle =$2\pi r$. Hence, the question is asking us to determine the difference between the first circumference and the second.
First circumference = $2\pi r$
Second circumference = $2\pi(r + 8) = 2\pi r + 2\pi(8) = 2\pi r + 16\pi$
The difference between the two circumferences – which is the amount that it increases – is equal to **16π**. Choice C is correct.

24. The volume of the rectangular solid is Length x Width x Height = 2 x 36 x 81 = 5,832 cubic inches.
The volume of the cube = 5,832 = (Side length)^3
Side length = **18** inches. Choice B is correct.

25. First, let's define our variables. We will let x = Integer X and x – 8 = Integer Y. Since their product is 152, our equation becomes:
x(x – 8) = 20
x^2 – 8x – 20 = 0
(x – 10)(x + 2) = 0
Therefore, x = 10 and -2. Since the problem does not specify that the integers must be positive, we must test both roots in our original equation to confirm that they both hold.

If Integer X = 10, then Integer Y = 10 – 8 = 2. (10)(2) = 20
If Integer X = -2, then Integer Y = -2 – 8 = -10. (-10)(-2) = 20
Hence, both roots are correct. The only answer choice that includes one of them is Choice C, **-2**.

26. In 2006, the number of snowplows sold per foot of snow = 5600. 70,000/12.5 feet = 5,600. Choice B is correct.

27. In 2007, the number of snowplows sold per inch of snow was 75,000/140 inches = 535.71. Choice C is correct.

28. In 2005, the number of snowplows sold per foot of snow = 50,000/9.17 feet = 5,454. In 2008, the number of snowplows sold per foot of snow = 80,000/14.58 feet = 5,486. Choice D is correct.

Quantitative Section 19:   28 questions   45 minutes

Each question has two quantities to be compared: one in Column A and one in Column B. Compare the quantities taking into consideration any other information given and choose
Answer A - if the quantity in Column A is greater
Answer B - if the quantity in Column B is greater
Answer C - if the two quantities are equal
Answer D - if the relationship cannot be determined without further information.

1. Eve's boyfriend asked her to buy five items at the grocery store, which only accepts cash. They include a frozen pizza that costs $3.25, a bottle of juice that costs $4.89, a pound of butter that costs $2.89, a six-pack of root beer that is marked down from $3.59 to $3.19 and two packs of gum that cost 89 cents each.   Eve also wants to buy a magazine for herself that costs $3.50.

Column A	Column B
The amount of money Eve needs to purchase these items	$19.50

2. **Column A**

Column A	Column B
The smallest three-digit integer that leaves a remainder of 1 when divided by 8	137

3. Gayle arranged four types of stones in a decorative rock garden. She used 5- ¼ pounds of gray stones, 12 -1/4 pounds of red stones, 25- 1/5 pounds of white stones and 44-1/2 pounds of blue stones.

Column A	Column B
The total weight (in pounds) of the stones in the rock garden	88-1/2

4. **Column A**

Column A	Column B
The number of quarters of a yard in 75/5 yards	60

5. Caitlyn had $38 dollars left after she spent 4/9 of her birthday money.

Column A	Column B
The amount that Caitlyn received for her birthday	$78.40

6. At the end of a shift, a cosmetics factory salvages its leftover shampoo by evaporating the extra water and using the resulting solution in a different formulation. On Monday, they ended the shift with 1,000 pounds of shampoo that was 20% alcohol.

Column A	Column B
The number of pounds of water the factory needed to evaporate from the batch to increase the alcohol concentration to 30%	100

264

Directions: For each problem, decide which answer is the best of the choices given.

7. If $x^2 - y^2 = 16$ and $x - y = 2$, what is the value of $x + y$?

    a. 1
    b. 2
    c. 4
    d. 8
    e. 12

8. For the following systems of equations, what is the value of x? $y = 10 + 2x$, $y = 5x$

    a. 1/3
    b. 1/2
    c. 10/3
    d. 11/3
    e. 50/3

9. Simplify the following expression: $(x^4y^7/x^5y^6)^4$

    a. y^3x^2
    b. y^4/x^4
    c. $(y/x)^{12}$
    d. y^{28}/x^{20}
    e. none of the above

10. What is the sum of the integers between 11 and 39, inclusive?

    a. 525
    b. 625
    c. 725
    d. 1,400
    e. 1,500

11. A business executive and his client are charging their dinner tab on the executive's expense account. The company will only allow them to spend a total of $50 for the meal. Assuming that they will pay 7% in sales tax for the meal and leave a 15% tip, what is the most that their food can cost?

    a. $39.55
    b. $40.03
    c. $40.63
    d. $41.15
    e. $43.15

12. The graph of $y = 4x^2 - 12$ is:

    a. A straight line
    b. A parabola opening upward
    c. A parabola opening downward
    d. A circle
    e. None of the above

13. Which of the following is not a factor of 680?

    a.   10
    b.   30
    c.   34
    d.   40
    e.   68

14. Roxie inherited $3 million from her maternal grandfather and placed the entire amount in account that earns 7 1/2% simple annual interest. Assuming that Roxie leaves the money in the account and does not withdraw any of the interest, how much will she have (principal + interest) exactly one year from today?

    a. $3,000,225
    b. $3,002,250
    c. $3,072,500
    d. $3,225,000
    e. $3,725,000

15. A city park is frequently used as an exercise path. If the park is a square, with each side 2,400 feet long, how many minutes would it take someone walking 600 feet per minute to walk the entire perimeter of the park?

    a.   8
    b.   12
    c.   16
    d.   20
    e.   40

16. There are five possible electives for Julie to take at her local community college this summer: English, Math, Statistics, History and Social Studies. Her counselor has advised Julie to choose two of them. How many possible combinations of the two courses are there?

    a.   30
    b.   25
    c.   15
    d.   12
    e.   10

17. When a store owner compiled her weekly sales records, she had a stack of invoices numbered 014567 through 019876. Upon further examination, however, the store owner realized that invoice numbers 014876 and 018999 were missing. How many invoices did the store owner have available for her weekly calculations?

    a.   5307
    b.   5308
    c.   5309
    d.   5310
    e.   5311

18. To get a grade of A in Spanish, Sara must achieve an average of 90 or above on six exams. Thus far, Sara's scores on the first five exams are 96, 81, 79, 87 and 100. What is the lowest possible score that Sara can get on the final exam to get an A grade in Spanish?

    a.   95
    b.   96
    c.   97
    d.   98
    e.   99

19. In Triangle CAT, CA = AT. If angle A = 3x – 20 and angle C = 1.5x + 115, how many degrees are in angle T?

    a.   30
    b.   45
    c.   60
    d.   75
    e.   90

20. A circle is inscribed in a square whose side is 48. What is the area of the circle?

    a. 24π
    b. 48π
    c. 576π
    d. $2,304\pi$
    e.   It cannot be determined from the information given.

21. A wholesale dairy sells blocks of butter in cubic containers that have an edge of 20 inches. If the butter weighs 32 pounds per cubic foot, what is the weight of a single cube of butter (to the nearest tenth of a pound)?

    a.   2.75
    b.   4.60
    c.   53.33
    d.   106.65
    e.   148.15

22. A + B = 50. $A^2 – B^2 = 500$. What is the larger number?

    a.   15
    b.   20
    c.   25
    d.   30
    e.   40

Refer to the following table for questions 23 – 28.

Number of Items Sold (in thousands)

	Wal-Mart	K-Mart
Dresses	325	650
Jeans	475	425
Shoes	750	500

Total Sales (in millions)

	Dresses	Jeans	Shoes
Wal-Mart	8.125	14.250	26.250
K-Mart	13.000	8.500	8.750

23. If Wal-Mart and K-Mart both earn 30% profit on jeans that they sell, what is the total profit (in millions) from jean sales at both stores for the period of time that this table represents (assuming the sales price of jeans at both stores remain the same)?

    a. $3,275,000
    b. $4,275,000
    c. $6,825,000
    d. $31,187,000
    e. $93,750,000

24. If K-Mart sells 25% more shoes next year and earns 15% profit on those sales, what would be their total profit from shoes (assuming the price per pair remains the same)?

    a. $1,181,250
    b. $1,312,500
    c. $1,575,000
    d. $1,640,625
    e. $1,968,750

25. If Wal-Mart and K-Mart both earn 20% profit on all dress sales, what is the total profit (in millions) from dress sales at both stores for the period of time that this table represents (assuming the sales price of dresses at both stores remain the same)?

    a. $1,625,000
    b. $2,600,000
    c. $3,250,000
    d. $4,225,000
    e. $6,500,000

26. Of the three items – dresses, jeans, and shoes – which commands the highest price per unit at Wal-Mart?

    a.   Dresses
    b.   Jeans
    c.   Shoes
    d.   All three items sell for the same price per unit
    e.   It cannot be determined from the information given

27. Of the three items – dresses, jeans, and shoes – which two sell for the same price per unit at K-Mart?

    a.   Dresses and Jeans
    b.   Jeans and Shoes
    c.   Shoes and Dresses
    d.   All sell for the same price per unit
    e.   It cannot be determined from the information given

28. Which item sells for the same price per unit at both Wal-Mart and K-Mart?

    a.   Dresses
    b.   Jeans
    c.   Shoes
    d.   None
    e.   It cannot be determined from the information given

Answer Key for Quantitative Section 19

1. To solve, we must add the amounts that Eve will spend at the store, which are $3.25 + 4.89 + 2.89 + 3.19 + 2(0.89) + 3. 50 = **$19.50**. Choice C is correct.

2. The smallest three digit integer that leaves a remainder of 1 when divided by 8 is **105**. Choice B is correct. (104/8 = 13; 105 = 104 + 1)

3. To solve, we must add the total weights of the stones: 5-1/4 + 12-1/4 + 25-1/5 + 44-1/2. First, we will convert the mixed number to fractions, which become 21/4 + 49/4 + 126/5 + 89/2. Second, we must add these fractions together, which requires them to have the same denominator. In this case, the least common denominator (which is evenly divisible by 2, 4, and 5) is 60, which makes our equation: 315/60 + 735/60 + 1512/60 + 2670/60 = 5232/60 = 87-12/60 = **87-1/5 pounds**. Choice B is correct. Alternatively, you can convert the numbers to decimals and add. (5.25 + 12.25 + 25.2 + 44.5 = 87.2 = 87-1/5)

4. 75/5 yards is equal to 15 yards. Each yard is equal to 4 quarters of a yard. Therefore, the number of quarter yards in 75/5 yards is (15)(4) = **60.** Choice C is correct.

5. 5/9 of the birthday money = $38. Thus, we can set up a ratio to determine the original whole: 5/9 = 38/X. Hence, X = **$68.40**. Choice B is correct.

6. First, we must draw a table with the information that we know.

Weight of Solution (lbs)	% Alcohol	Amount of Alcohol (lbs)
1000	20	0.20(1,000) = 200
X	0	0
1000 – x	30	0.30(1000 – x) = 300 – 0.30x

In this case, we will let x = the amount of water to be removed. Therefore, the weight of the final solution (in which the water has been evaporated off) will equal 1000 – x. Once we have these variables, we can complete the rest of the chart, and derive our expressions for the AMOUNT of alcohol in each solution. We can then use the information to write an equation to solve for our unknown. Since our only change is to remove water – and to concentrate the amount of alcohol – our equation is: 200 = 300 – x. 200 = 300 – 0.30x. 0.330x = 100. x = **333.33** pounds of water must be removed. Choice A is correct.

7. If $x^2 - y^2 = 16$, then (x +y)(x - y) = 16. If (x - y) = 2, then (x + y) = 16/2 = **8**. Choice D is correct.

8. If y = 10 + 2x and y = 5x, then 5x = 10 + 2x, and 3x = 10. So, x = **10/3**. Choice C is correct.

9. $(x^4y^7/x^5y^6)^4 = (y/x)^4 = $ **y^4/x^4** . Choice B is correct.

10. The find the sum of the integers between 11 and 39, inclusive, we must use the formula, Sum = Average x Number of terms. The Average = 11 + 39 / 2 = 25. Number of terms = 39 – 11 + 1 = 29. The Sum = 25 x 29 = **725**. Choice C is correct.

11. The total bill, which can be no more than $50, includes the cost of the meal, 7% sales tax and a 15% tip. If we let x = the cost of the food, then the tax = 0.07x. The tip is 15% of the total cost of the food and the 7% tip. Algebraically, we can represent the tip as 0.15 (x + 0.07x) = 0.1605x. Since the total bill can be no more than $50, our final equation for the meal is: Meal + Tax + Tip = 50, or x + 0.07x + 0.1605x = 50. Solving for x, the cost of the meal must be less than **$40.63**. Answer Choice C is correct.

12. A parabola opening upward. Choice B is correct.

13. Choice B, **30.**

14. $3,000,000 x 0.075 = $225,000 interest. Total = **$3,225,000**. Choice D is correct.

15. If the park is a square with a side length of 2,400 feet, the perimeter is 2,400 (4), or 9,600 feet. Someone walking 600 feet per minute would take 9,600/600, or **16** minutes to walk the perimeter of the park. Choice C is correct.

16. For 5 items, there are **10** possible combinations of any 2 of them (5 x 2 = 10). In this case, they are: English/Math, English/Statistics, English/History, English/Social Studies, Math/Statistics, Math/History, Math/Social Studies, Statistics/History, Statistics/Social Studies, and History/Social Studies. Choice E is correct.

17. To find the original number of invoices in the series, we must subtract the endpoints and add one: 019876 – 014567 + 1 = 5310. Next, we must subtract the two missing invoices: 5310 - 2 = **5308**. Choice B is correct.

18. To solve, we can use the following equation: 90 = (x + 96 + 81 + 79 + 87 + 100) / 6. When we solve the equation for x, we find that it is **97**, which is Choice C.

19. If sides CA and AT are equal, then their angles are also equal. Hence,
3x – 20 = 1.5x + 115 or 1.5x = 135. Therefore, x = **90** degrees. Choice E is correct.

20. If the square has a side of 48, then the diameter of the circle is also 48. The radius is therefore 24, which makes the area of the circle π (24)(24) = **576π**. Choice C is correct.

21. The side length is 20 inches = 5/3 feet. Therefore, the volume of the cube = $(5/3)^3$ = 4.63 cubic feet x 32 pounds/cubic foot = **148.15** pounds. Choice E is correct.

22. First, let's define our variables. We will let x = A. Therefore, B = 50 – x. If the difference between their squares is 500, our equation becomes: $(50 – x)^2 – x^2$ = 500. $(50 – x)(50 – x) – x^2$ = 500.
$2,500 – 50x – 50x + x^2 - x^2$ = 500. 2,500 – 100x = 500. 2,000 = 100x. X = 20. 50 – X = **30**. Choice D is correct.

23. The profit from jeans at Wal-Mart is ($14,250,000 sales)(0.30) = $4,275,000
The profit from jeans at K-Mart is ($8,500,000 sales)(0.30) = $2,550,000
The total profit is therefore $4,275,000 + $2,550,000 = **$6,825,000**. Choice C is correct.

24. K-Mart's current shoe sales = $8,750,000. Projected sales = ($8,750,000)(1.25) = $10,937,500. 15% of this value is **$1,640,625**. Choice D is correct.

25. The profit from dress sales at Wal-Mart is ($8,125,000 sales)(0.20) = $1,625,000
The profit from dress sales at K-Mart is ($13,000,000 sales)(0.20) = $2,600,000
The total profit is therefore $1,625,000 + $2,600,000 = **$4,225,000**. Choice D is correct.

26. The item with the highest price per unit at Wal-Mart are shoes, which are **$35** per pair ($26,250,000/750,000). Choice C is correct.

27. At K-Mart, dresses and jeans both sell for **$20**. Choice A is correct.
Dresses: ($13,000,000/650,000 sold) = $20 per unit; Jeans: ($8,500,000/425,000 sold) = $20 per unit.

28. Choice D is correct. None of the items sells for the same price at both stores.

Quantitative Section 20: 28 questions   45 minutes

Each question has two quantities to be compared: one in Column A and one in Column B. Compare the
quantities taking into consideration any other information given and choose
Answer A - if the quantity in Column A is greater
Answer B - if the quantity in Column B is greater
Answer C - if the two quantities are equal
Answer D - if the relationship cannot be determined without further information.

1. **Column A**

The number of two-digit positive integers
that are multiples of both 7 and 11?

Column B

1

2. Jed bought 8 cartons of plants from a local nursery that offers a 5% discount for paying cash.   Each plant
cost $5.00 and there were 12 plants per carton

Column A

The total cost for 8 cartons, assuming that
Jed pays cash

Column B

$466

3. Two Fed Ex trucks are 300 miles apart. At noon, they start to travel toward each other at rates of 30 and
20 miles per hour.

Column A

The number of hours before they pass each other

Column B

8

4. A bartender is mixing Liquor A, which is 5% alcohol, with Liquor B, which is 20% alcohol, to yield a 3,000
batch of Liquor C, which is 15% alcohol.

Column A

2000

Column B

The ounces of Liquor B he must use

5. **Column A**

The # seconds in five hours

Column B

The # minutes in twelve days

6. The sum of two numbers is 48. Their difference is 12.

Column A

30

Column B

The smaller number

Directions: *For each problem, decide which answer is the best of the choices given.*

271

7. What is the mean of the following set of numbers? 112, 89, 145, 88, 117

        a.   101.0
        b.   101.2
        c.   110.2
        d.   111.2
        e.   112.0

8. 46/98 – 23/196 =

        a.   23/196
        b.   69/196
        c.   23/98
        d.   23/66
        e.   69/98

9. For the repeating decimal 0.23896238962389623896….., what is the 43rd digit to the right of the decimal point?

        a.   2
        b.   3
        c.   6
        d.   8
        e.   9

10. 8.75 =

        a.   35/5
        b.   70/7
        c.   45/5
        d.   85/8
        e.   35/4

11. Which of the following expresses the ratio of 8 ounces to 10 pounds?

        a.   1/20
        b.   1/16
        c.   1/12
        d.   1/10
        e.   1/8

12. If $f(j) = j^2 + 0.002j$, what is $f(0.5)$?

        a.   0.2550
        b.   0.2510
        c.   0.0252
        d.   0.0250
        e.   0.0251

13. Reduce the following fraction to its simplest form: 2,000 / 2 million

        a.   1/1000
        b.   2/1000
        c.   1/100
        d.   2/100
        e.   1/10

14. $(5y^2)^3(2y^3)^2 =$

    a. $10y^6$
    b. $250y^6$
    c. $500y^6$
    d. $250y^{12}$
    e. $500y^{12}$

15. If the following series continues in the same pattern, what will the next term be?
        3, 5, 4, 7, 5, 9, 6, 11.........

    a. 3
    b. 5
    c. 6
    d. 7
    e. 13

16. A delivery truck traveled west for 30 miles, then south for 50 miles, then returned directly to his starting point on a diagonal. If the truck gets 8 miles per gallon of gas, how many gallons of gas will the truck use on the trip?

    a. 10
    b. 12
    c. 16
    d. 18
    e. 20

17. An octagon has seven interior angles that measure 80, 90, 105, 120, 125, 130 and 135. What is the measure of the eighth internal angle?

    a. 95
    b. 115
    c. 235
    d. 295
    e. 475

18. Tim took 96 minutes to repair the engine of a customer's car. What fraction of an 8-hour work day does this represent?

    a. 1/12
    b. 1/8
    c. 1/6
    d. 1/5
    e. 3/16

19. Pizza Hut offers six possible toppings for their personal pan pizzas: pepperoni, sausage, onion, cheese, mushrooms and peppers. If you choose four of these toppings, how many possible combinations are there?

    a. 4
    b. 15
    c. 26
    d. 24
    e. 30

20. If the population of Cedar City is 500,000 and grows by 10,000 people each year, in how many years will the population quadruple?

        a.   50
        b.   75
        c.   125
        d.   150
        e.   200

21. For the following data set, what is the mean minus the mode?
                    7, 3, 15, 6, 7, 8, 9, 12, 5, 7, 6

        a.   0.127
        b.   0.727
        c.   1.127
        d.   3.000
        e.   7.000

22. A clothing shop sells six pairs of shoes and eight pairs of socks for $995. The cost for four pairs of shoes and twelve pairs of socks is $750. How much would it cost to buy one pair of shoes?

        a. $58.12
        b. $69.75
        c. $77.50
        d. $139.50
        e. $148.50

23. If the radius of a circle is decreased by 30%, by what percent is its area decreased?

        a.   30
        b.   36
        c.   49
        d.   51
        e.   60

24. The length of Rectangle B is six times its width. If the perimeter of Rectangle B is 280 feet, what is its length?

        a.   20
        b.   40
        c.   60
        d.   80
        e.   120

25. How much larger is the surface area (in cubic feet) of a cube with an edge of 5 feet than a cube with an edge of 3 feet?

        a.   25
        b.   27
        c.   98
        d.   125
        e.   152

26. If a rectangular Rubbermaid storage unit has an area of 63 square feet, and its length is 2 feet longer than its width, what is the width of the storage unit?

    a. 1
    b. 2
    c. 6
    d. 7
    e. 9

Refer to the chart below for questions 27 & 28.

Number of Hospitals per Million Residents

Atlanta	56
Boston	94
Columbus	87
Dallas	79
Los Angeles	99
Milwaukee	78
San Diego	66

27. If the population of Boston increases from 3 million to 5 million, how many additional hospitals will be needed in the city?

    a. 182
    b. 188
    c. 282
    d. 470
    e. 488

28. If the population of Dallas is 8 million and each of its hospitals employs 180 physicians, how many total physicians work at hospitals in Dallas?

    a. 14,280
    b. 25,596
    c. 17,775
    d. 63,200
    e. 113,760

Answer Key for Quantitative Section 20

1. The two-digit positive integers that are multiples of 7 are 14, 21, 28, 35, 42, 49, 56, 63, 70, 77, 84, 91, and 98. Of these, only 77 is *also* a multiple of 11. Hence, the correct answer is **1.** Choice C is correct.

2. Jed's total cost will be $(8)(12)(\$5.00) = \$480(0.95) = \textbf{\$456.}$ Choice B is correct.

3. The first step for this type of problem is to draw a quick chart of what we know:

Truck	Distance	Rate	Time
A	30x	30	x
B	20x	20	x

Here, we can use the rate equation to determine the time at which the two Fed Ex trucks will pass each other. By definition, they are traveling the same distance, which is 300 miles. Also by definition, that distance equals the SUM of the quantities (Rate x Time) for each truck. Hence, our equation becomes:

$30x + 20x = 300$
$50x = 300.$ Thus, $x = 6.$ They will pass after **6 hours.** Choice B is correct.

4. First, we must draw a table with the information that we know.

Ingredient	% Alcohol	Amount (oz)	Total Amount of Alcohol
Liquor A	5	3,000 - x	5 (3,000 – x)
Liquor B	20	x	20x
Liquor C	15	3,000	15(3,000)

The problem asks us to calculate the amount of Liquor B that is needed to create a blend with 15% alcohol. We will let x = the oz of Liquor B needed. Therefore, the amount of Liquor A needed = 3000 – x.

Since the total alcohol in Liquor C is the sum of the amounts in Liquors A and B, we can write an equation to solve for x: Alcohol in Liquor A + Alcohol in Liquor B = Total Alcohol in Liquor C
5(3,000 – x) + 20x = 15(3,000)
15,000 – 5x + 20x = 45,000
15x = 30,000
X = **2,000 oz** of Liquor B needed. Choice C is correct.

5. The number of seconds in five hours = (60)(60)(5) = **18,000**.
The number of minutes in twelve days = (60)(24)(12) = 17,280. Choice A is correct.

6. First, let's define our variables. We will let one number = x. Therefore, the second unknown is x – 12. The sum of these two numbers is 48. Hence, our equation becomes: x + (x – 12) = 48 or 2x = 60. Therefore x = 30 and x – 12 = 18. 8.The smaller number is **18**. Choice A is correct.

7. The mean is **110.2,** or Choice C.

8. 46/98 – 23/196 = 92/196 – 23/196 = **69/196**. Choice B is correct.

9. The repeating pattern is 23896, which includes 5 digits. The 43rd[th] digit is the third digit in the string, which is **8**, or Choice D.

10. 8.75 = **35/4**. Choice E is correct.

11. 10 pounds = 160 oz. 8/160 = **1/20**. Choice A is correct.

12. If f(j) = j^2 + 0.002j, then f (0.5) = (0.5)(0.5) + (0.002)(0.5) = 0.25 + 0.001 = **0.251**. Choice B is correct.

13. 2,000 / 2,000, 000 = **1/1000**. Choice A is correct.

14. $(5y^2)^3(2y^3)^2$ = $(125y^6)(4y^6)$ = **500y^{12}**. Choice E is correct.

15. This problem is a combination of two sub-series. In the first one, each term increases by 1 (3,4,5,6); in the second, each term increases by 2 (5,7,9,11). The next number would be **7.** Choice D is correct.

16. The area the truck traveled is a right triangle with side lengths of 30 and 50. Using the Pythagorean theorem, we can use this information to determine the length of the hypotenuse:

$(30)^2$ + $(50)^2$ = x^2
900 + 2,500 = 3,400 = x^2
x = 58.31 miles.
The total distance traveled is the perimeter of that triangle, or 30 + 40 + 58.31 = 128.31 miles/ 8 mpg = **16** gallons. Choice C is correct.

17. For an octagon, the sum of the interior angles is equal to 180(8 – 2) = 1080 total degrees, so 80 + 90 + 105 + 120 + 125 + 130 + 135 + X = 1080. X = **295** degrees. Choice D is correct.

18. An 8-hour work day contains 8(60) = 480 minutes. If Tim took 96 minutes to repair the engine, then we can represent the fraction of the day he used as 96/480 = **1/5**. Choice D is correct.

19.   Use the factorial formula to solve: 6! / {4!(6! - 4!)} = 6!/{(4!)(2!)} = (6 x 5 x 4 x 3 x 2 x 1) / {(4 x 3 x 2 x 1)(2 x 1) = 6 x 5 / 2= 30/2 = **15**. Choice B is correct.

20. This problem can easily be solved using an algebraic formula. First, let's define our variables. We will let x = the # of years until the population quadruples. Mathematically, this can be expressed as:
4(500,000) = 500,000 + 10,000x
20,000,000 = 500,000 + 10,000x
15,000,000 = 10,000x
x = **150** years. Choice D is correct.

21. The mean of these numbers is 85/11 = 7.727. The mode is 7. 7.727 – 7 = **0.727**. Choice B is correct.

22. In this case, we can write one equation for the first condition and a second equation for the second condition. As always, we must first define our variables. We will let = x the cost of one pair of shoes and y = the cost of one pair of socks.

The first equation, which defines the first condition, is 6x + 8y = 995
The second equation, which defines the second condition, is 4x + 12y = 750
To solve the problem for x, we must combine the equations in a way that eliminates y.

We can do this by multiplying the first equation by 3 and the second equation by 2. When we do, we get:
18x + 24y = 2,985
8ex+ 24y = 1,500
If we subtract the second equation from the first, we get 10x = 1,485. Therefore, x = $**148.50** = the cost of one pair of shoes. Choice E is correct.

23. If the radii of the two circles have a ratio of 10:7, their areas have a ratio of 100:49. Therefore, the decrease is 51 out of 100, or 51%. Alternatively, you can try a few numbers to reach the same answer. Let's assume that a circle has a radius of 10. Its area is 100π. If we reduce the radius by 30% - to 7 – the area becomes 49π. Once again, the % reduction is **51%**. Choice D is correct.

24. The perimeter of Rectangle A is 2(Length) + 2(Width). In this case, we will let the width = X and the length = 6x. Our formula for the perimeter is therefore: 2x + 2(6x) = 280. 2x + 12x = 280. 14x = 280. x = 20 = width. 6x = **120** = length. Choice E is correct.

25. Area 1 = 5 x 5 x 5 = 125 cubic feet. Area 2 = 3 x 3 x 3 = 27 cubic feet. 125 – 27 = **98** cubic feet. Choice C is correct.

26. First, let's define our variables. We will let x = the length of the storage unit. Therefore, the width = x - 2 and the area of the storage unit (Length x Width) is x(x - 2). Our equation becomes: x(x – 2) = 63. x^2 – 2x – 63 = 0. (x – 9)(x +7) = 0. Therefore, x = 9 and -7. Since the length of the side cannot be negative, we can discard the -7 root. The length of the storage unit is 9 and the width is 9 – 2 = **7**. Choice D is correct.

27. If Boston has a population of 3 million, it will need (94)(3) = 282 hospitals. If the population increases to five million, they will need (94)(5) = 470 hospitals. The difference is 470 – 282 = **188**. Choice B is correct.

28. If Dallas has a population of 8 million, it will need (79)(8) = 632 hospitals. If each one employs 180 physicians, the total number of doctors will be (632)(180) = **113,760.** Choice E is correct.